Responsible Hospitality:

Theory and Practice

Rebecca Hawkins

and

Paulina Bohdanowicz

(G) **Goodfellow Publishers Ltd**

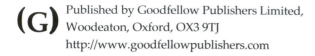 Published by Goodfellow Publishers Limited,
Woodeaton, Oxford, OX3 9TJ
http://www.goodfellowpublishers.com

British Library Cataloguing in Publication Data: a catalogue record for
this title is available from the British Library.

Library of Congress Catalog Card Number: on file.

ISBN: 978-1-906884-19-2

Design and typesetting by P.K. McBride, www.macbride.org.uk

Printed by Baker & Taylor, www.baker-taylor.com

Cover design by Cylinder, www.cylindermedia.com

For:
Simon, Jacob and Eliza
Rob.

Contents

List of figures

Foreword by Stephen Farrant

In 1992, the United Nations Conference on Environment and Development met to help governments rethink economic development and find ways to halt the destruction of irreplaceable natural resources and pollution of the planet. Hundreds of thousands of people from all walks of life were drawn into this process. They included among their number businesses from all sectors of industry.

It is no coincidence that the date of that UN meeting coincides with the formation of what was then the International Hotels Environment Initiative and is now the International Tourism Partnership (ITP). The hospitality businesses that established ITP had already recognised that they had a choice to make. They could either choose to ignore the environmental and social implications of their businesses and pursue economic development at all costs. Or they could use their collective might to find and communicate ways of doing business differently.

The early pioneers that founded ITP made their choice clear. They chose to do business differently – to do business as if people and the planet matter – in short, to do business responsibly. Over the intervening decades, hundreds of other hospitality companies have also become advocates of the responsible business message. As this text demonstrates, the collective achievements of the sector are impressive. But so much remains to be done if the sector is to reach its true potential as an industry delivering environmental and social improvements alongside economic development. In a finite world, this requires us all to find new ways of achieving growth; growth that is smart, inclusive and responsible.

This text looks at what has been achieved to date and the challenges that remain. While these challenges may seem daunting, it is clear that by working in partnership, and through strong leadership, real progress can be made. The opportunities for those leading companies who are focused on this agenda are significant – in terms of profit, people and planet.

Stephen Farrant
Director – International Tourism Partnership

Acknowledgements

The jacket of this book may make it appear that it is the result of the work of two people. This is to deny the truth. It is the culmination of more than 40 years of collective work within an industry that is, in our view, the most dynamic and exciting in the world. Over those years, a huge number of people within the industry, its trade associations and academia have given freely of their time to discuss the ideas and thoughts that are at the foundation of this book. They know who they are and we hope they approve of the results.

Thanks go to all who have reviewed the content of the text in whole or in part. They include Harold Goodwin, Geoffrey Lipman, Jan Peter Bergkvist, Xavier Font, Jason Freezer, Victor Middleton, Kate Ringham, Jane Carlton Smith, Andrew Lane, Camilla Woods, John Forte, Alexandros Paraskevas and Julian Demetriadi. We are especially indebted to J.P. Bergkvist, Victor Middleton, Geoffrey Lipman and Xavier Font whose insight helped to reshape many chapters. Geoffrey Lipman, Shaun Vorster and Terry de Lacey have also played no small part in formulating our conclusions. They have provided the light at the end of the tunnel, helping us to keep the faith that the hospitality industry can play a fundamental role in shaping the green economy and thus building a sustainable future.

Thanks are also due to Sally North and Tim Goodfellow who may have wondered on occasion whether the text was merely a figment of our collective imaginations!

Last but by no means least we could not publish without offering our heartfelt thanks to our families and friends. Not only have you loved, fed and watered us throughout the months of writing, but you have also listened, sympathised, encouraged, cajoled and occasionally harangued us into finishing.

Prologue

The publication of this text coincides with the third anniversary of the collapse of Lehman Brothers – an event that pushed the banking industry and much more besides to the edge of the financial abyss, wiping more than £50 billion off the FTSE 100 index in a single day. Three years later, western economies are still in turmoil and political and business leaders are searching for new solutions.

In their everyday reality, businesses are managing issues that even five years ago would have been the stuff of nightmares. Central to these issues is the rise in the price of oil (this increased by 110% between 2006 and 2008). Where oil prices have gone other commodities have followed. The costs of basic foods have escalated, with rice prices having increased by 217%, wheat by 136%, maize by 125%, and soybeans by 107% over the same time scale. For all businesses, the corollary of these price rises has been felt immediately and painfully in the form of an increase in costs (Kearney *et al.*, 2008).

Economic turmoil has combined with food shortages, price rises and social injustice. From Spain to Egypt and Greece to the Yemen, people have expressed their discontent with their leaders and demanded change. At the core of this desire for change is the need for greater freedom, equal access to economic development opportunities and transparency.

There are commentators who claim that the uncertain environment for business is temporary – an inevitable consequence of a cyclical economic system. Then there is a growing band of people – such as Thomas Friedman[1] – who draw parallels between the economic and impending environmental crisis. They would argue that both are characterised by (1) a huge increase in debt (in the environmental case, the debt is a drawdown of natural capital); (2) overconfidence in the ability of markets and regulatory systems to identify and mitigate the risks of this accumulating mountain of debt; and (3) incentives driving individuals and organizations to prioritize short-term gains irrespective of their long-term implications (Friedman, 2008).

For businesses, these two viewpoints pose a dilemma. If the former is true and the current turmoil is a temporary blip that is an inevitable consequence of a cyclical economic system, then the best strategy may be to implement measures that minimise exposure to increased operating costs, ride out the storm and wait for the good times to return. If it is a more fundamental symptom of a combined environmental and economic crisis, then there is a need for businesses to review their modi operandi to ensure their place in a world that is warmer, more crowded, less resource rich, less trusting of large business and less tolerant of social injustice.

---

1 Winner of three Pulitzer Prizes and internationally renowned author, reporter and columnist

Some businesses have undertaken cost minimisation procedures, battened down the hatches and are hoping to ride out the storm. There are, however, an increasing number of businesses that believe that the current situation is not merely an economic blip. These businesses generally concur that the traditional tools of policy have spectacularly failed to address the symptoms of the crisis.[2] Some (primarily global) companies believe that their own actions have, in part, caused the crisis and that through the actions they take now they can become part of the solution. Those businesses that have taken this message to heart have often embraced what has become known as responsible business practices as the vehicle for ensuring that their actions support people, promote responsible stewardship of the environment and are fair and transparent. These businesses are those that are transforming the view of the role of business by delivering social and environmental (as well as economic benefit) to society.

As a significant economic sector (and a part of the broader tourism industry which some claim to be the largest in the world), hospitality businesses have a crucial role to play in furthering the responsible business agenda. There are numerous examples of businesses from the sector that have already transformed their business practices and are reaping the rewards. There are many commentators that believe that these will be the businesses that win in the 21st century.

Earth Overshoot Day

Around the time that this book is completed, we shall be celebrating Earth Overshoot Day. Earth Overshoot Day marks the day when demand on ecological services begins to exceed the renewable supply.

Earth Overshoot Day has been creeping earlier in the year as human consumption grows. Human demand on ecological services first began to exceed nature's ability to regenerate in the 1970s. Since then, we have depleted our budget for the year earlier and earlier.

In 1980, Earth Overshoot Day was on 11 December, by 1995 it was 22 October. In 2010, it was on 21 August – some four months earlier than three decades ago.

Source: www.footprintnetwork.org/en/index.php/GFN/page/earth_overshoot_day_over_time

---

References

Friedman, T. (2008) *Hot, Flat and Crowded – Why We Need a Green Revolution and How it Can Renew America*, Farrar, Strauss and Giroux.

Kearney, A.T. Callieri, C., Hauff, J., Mahler, D. O'Keefe, J. (2008) *Rattling supply chains: – the effect of environmental trends on input costs for the fast-moving consumer goods industry*, WRI, Washington.

---

2   If you need evidence of this failure, look to the collapse of the Climate Change talks at Copenhagen, and the likely failure to meet key elements of the Millennium Development Goals.

1 | Introduction

Apparently solid financial institutions have tumbled. So what else that we currently take for granted might be prone to sudden collapse?

Schumacker Lecture, 4 October 2008 – delivered by Andrew Simms

The modern world is rife with turbulence and complexity and daunting challenges lie ahead. In the words of Jonathon Porritt (former chair of the UK Sustainable Development Commission), the world is facing a perfect storm as the forces of the financial and energy crises meet with environmental crisis, climate change, massive population increases and emerging pandemics.[1]

There is a considerable level of debate about the relative importance of each of these phenomena and – in a few cases – about the scientific basis for their existence. Most people agree, however, that effective solutions are required to secure a prosperous future for mankind.[2] These solutions will deliver radically different modes of living, consuming, doing business, interacting, distributing wealth and so on – in short, solutions that require a comprehensive revolution on a scale that has not been seen in modern history.

Some would point to the changes in policy, consumer attitudes and business practices to claim that such a revolution is already taking place. Others would point to the ongoing growth in emissions of carbon, the paltry changes consumers have made to their lifestyles; the growth in the gap between rich and poor; and the increasing influence of big business to demonstrate that – if it is a revolution – it has neither the scale nor the intensity required to safeguard the future of humankind.

In such turbulent times, there is inevitably debate and discord about the steps necessary to deliver global security. Many consider there to be a need for widespread changes throughout society to prevent a global calamity. The finger of blame for our current state is often pointed at the global corporations that have seen an astronomical growth in their wealth and cultural influence in the last thirty years or so. Over this period many have grown to have balance sheets that exceed the GDP of small states. Others see these global goliaths as holding one of the most powerful keys to securing the future of humankind.

While this latter thought may sound radical when said aloud (especially in the presence of many an environmental campaigner), it is not really such a radical or

---

1 John Beddington (UK Government's Chief Science Advisor) echoed this sentiment in 2009.

2 Many commentators claim that it is the future of the world that is at stake, but this is untrue. The aim of most modern environmentalists is not to save the world, but to secure a prosperous future of the human race on the planet.

unprecedented thought that major corporations may be able to lead the path towards more sustainable patterns of development. Visionaries such as Joseph Rowntree and the Cadbury family played a key role in improving conditions and mitigating environmental damage from their respective enterprises in the late 1800s. In modern times, economists such as Archie Carroll recognise a wide scope of responsibility, as expressed in his Pyramid of Social Responsibility Model, which comprise of economic, legal, ethical and discretionary responsibilities, which he terms 'the four faces of moral leadership' (Carroll, 1991). These are echoed by the World Business Council For Sustainable Development, which acknowledges 'we are learning that the most effective way to address many of the world's most pressing problems is to mobilize the corporate [private] sector where both companies and society can benefit' (WRI *et al.*, n.d.).

While many would applaud the sentiment behind this declaration, there are concerns that businesses are perhaps not equipped to achieve the scale of change that is necessary to avoid the 'perfect storm' described by Jonathon Porritt. Hundreds of exciting examples exist of businesses 'doing more with less' or practising 'eco-efficiency'. These businesses are typically referred to as good practice case studies. But these 'good practice' examples all too often hide a rather different reality. And that is the fact that they produce 'overwhelming resource savings [but promote] even larger growth in the production of the wrong products, produced by the wrong processes, from the wrong materials, in the wrong place, at the wrong scale and using the wrong business models' (Hawken *et al.*, 1999).

The aim of this book is to look at the evolving concepts included under the umbrella of what has become known as the responsible business movement. Specifically, the book aims to explore if the concepts of responsible business are being implemented within the hospitality sector and to assess whether the responses delivered by that sector thus far are indeed promoting the production of the wrong products, using the wrong processes, from the wrong materials, in the wrong place, at the wrong scale and using the wrong business models, or whether they have the potential to help deliver some of the solutions to global environmental and social challenges!

The focus of the text is to move the debate away from the very practical 'how to' manuals that have thus far dominated bookshelves on this topic for hospitality businesses to:

♦ Examine the theoretical context for responsible business in general and responsible hospitality in particular;

♦ Establish the core principles to which any business laying claim to responsible practices in the hospitality sector should aspire;

♦ Assess the range of actions taken by the sector to implement these principles;

♦ Build a vision of a hospitality sector that is economically successful and operates in a manner that supports people and communities, promotes responsible stewardship of the environment and is fair and transparent.[3]

The mess we're in

It is not the purpose of this book to provide a blow-by-blow analysis of the nature of the global environmental and social issues that we are facing. A detailed analysis of these issues can be found in a number of excellent texts, including the Worldwatch Institute's annual State of the World report. Those seeking information specific to global environmental issues and the hospitality sector may wish to refer to the International Tourism Partnership's *Environmental Reference Manual for Hotels – the Industry Guide to Sustainable Practice* or the publications of organisations like Food-service Footprint or Institute of Grocery Distribution (IGD) for more information.

Suffice it to say that a number of complex and interrelated environmental and social concerns are focusing the minds of policy makers. These include (in no particular order):

♦ Population growth, and particularly the potential of the planet to sustain a global population of nine billion by 2050 (Rees, 2010);

♦ Climate change, especially as regards the likelihood that carbon dioxide concentrations in the atmosphere will be double pre-industrial levels by around 2050, bringing global temperature increases of up to 7°C by the end of the 21st century (Lawton, 2010);

♦ Mass extinction of species, and particularly the fact that – of more than 50,000 edible plant species in the world – just 15 crop plants provide 90% of the world's food energy intake, with three – rice, maize and wheat – making up two-thirds of this total (United Nations Food and Agricultural Organization, 2010);

♦ Water shortages – and the focus of global conflicts around the issue of water (United Nations, 2010);

♦ Depletion of resources in general and, perhaps most widely publicised, of oil in particular. It is widely predicted – even by oil generating countries – that peak oil (the point at which global production reaches its peak before it starts to decline) will be reached in the next 40 years (ODAC, 27 May 2010) and some commentators believe that oil production has already peaked;[4]

♦ Accumulations of chemicals – and especially persistent chemicals – in the environment. Awareness of the impacts of these chemicals was first popularised by Rachel Carson in her book *Silent Spring* (published in 1962). A raft of international

---

3   Many use the phrase 'sustainable d evelopment' or 'triple bottom line' (or TBL) to embrace the achievement of these criteria.

4   It is an irony that the rush to find an alternative to fossil fuels – and development of bio fuels to this end – has been blamed by some for the increase in food prices.

regulations have followed. These have done little to reduce fear among the general public about the impacts of chemicals in the environment (Lomborg, 2001).

♦ Internationalisation of companies and issues that reduce the ability for governments to act across borders.

Text box 1: The balance sheet for ecosystem services

Nature provides the essential resources on which all industrial activity (including hospitality) depends. Many of these resources are currently being significantly degraded. The Millennium Ecosystem Assessment (MA), for example, estimates that 60% of earth's ecosystem resources are being degraded or used unsustainably, including 70% of provisioning and regulating ecosystem services. Some ecosystems have been enhanced over the last 50 years and these primarily are those associated with food production.

Balance sheet: Ecosystem services

Provisioning services		↓	Regulating services		↓
Food	crops	↑	Air quality regulation		↓
	livestock	↑	Climate regulation – global		↑
	capture fisheries	↓	Climate regulation – regional and local		↓
	aquaculture	↑	Water regulation		↓
	wild foods	↓	Water purification and waste treatment		↓
Fiber	timber	+/-	Disease regulation		+/-
	cotton, silk	+/-	Pest regulation		+/-
	wood fuel	↓	Natural hazard regulation		↓
Genetic resources		↓	Cultural services		↓
Biochemicals, medicine		↓	Spiritual and religious values		↓
Water	freshwater	↓	Aesthetic values		↓
			Recreation and ecotourism		↓

↑ globally enhanced
↓ globally degraded

The MA evaluated the global status of provisioning, regulating and cultural services. An upwards arrow indicates that the condition of the service globally has been enhanced and a downwards arrow that it has been degraded in the recent past.

According to WWF, the 'ecological footprint' from humanity has increased to 125% of global carrying capacity and could rise to 170% by 2040. The scale of pressure from such resource use in natural eco-systems is clearly unsustainable in the long term and raises concerns for future generations.

Source: World Business Council for Sustainable Development (2008)

These issues are often presented as if they are newly emerging. Sadly, this is not the case. Policy makers at national and international level have been focusing on seeking effective solutions to many of these issues for decades. What is newly emerging is a realisation that the tools of government that have traditionally been used to tackle issues such as transnational air pollution are not effective when it comes to the complex and interrelated problems explored above. High-profile policy failures in recent years include:

♦ The Millennium Development Goals, promising among other things education (especially for girls) were heralded as one of the solutions to **poverty and population growth**. It is now acknowledged even by the organisation responsible for overseeing the implementation of these goals, the United Nations, that the Millennium Development Goals are unlikely to met in their entirety (BBC, 20 September 2010);

♦ The Copenhagen Summit with its ambitions to broker an agreement on emissions of greenhouse gases and **climate change**. The Copenhagen process is now widely viewed as a failure. The subsequent meeting in Cancun in Mexico hosted in 2010, while hailed as a success, also failed to set binding targets for carbon emissions post 2012 (when the targets specified in the Kyoto Agreement come to an end);

♦ Intervention by national agencies to reduce the **decline in biodiversity** has been largely ineffective and the rate of species decline has continued since the ratification of the Convention on Biological Diversity in 1993;

♦ In the Middle East, where **water** is considered a 'strategic' resource, tensions between countries in the region over it remain high. There it has become a major political issue, and the various peace agreements that have been proposed or signed in recent years all include water. This has led to claims from various sources – attributed (but unsubstantiated) to such individuals as Boutros Boutros Ghali and the late King Hussein of Jordan – that 'the next war in the Middle East will be over water'. This rhetoric has captured the public imagination and caused much consternation in the intelligence communities of various countries, who worry whether water – or other scarce resources – may be a future flashpoint for international conflict (UNEP, 2010);

♦ There are no global agreements on **resources**, and the likelihood that any will be brokered as resource values soar is slim. Resource-rich states (including some with questionable regimes such as Sudan) have become increasingly the focus of attention of some governments (including the Chinese) bringing accusations from some commentators of a form of colonialism (*Financial Times*, 23 December 2010).

The failure to achieve policy solutions to these issues is exacerbated by the fact that they are often packaged as 'environmental issues'. In the popular media, those seeking resolution to them are portrayed as 'campaigners' who are on a collision course with those seeking to promote economic growth and remove barriers to global trade. Thus, in the words of Jeffrey Frankel,[5] 'national efforts to reduce emissions of greenhouse gases instil among environmentalists fears of leakage and among businesspeople fears of lost competitiveness' (Frankel, 2008).

---

5   James W. Harpel Professor of Capital Formation and Growth at the Harvard Kennedy School at Harvard University.

Society's capacity to respond to complex issues

> *I don't think we're yet evolved to the point where we're clever enough to handle as complex a situation as climate change.*
>
> James Lovelock,[6] *The Guardian*, Monday, 29 March 2010

The complexity of the issues that require resolution combined with the apparent conflict between those seeking to resolve them and those seeking to promote economic growth makes one thing clear: that the traditional tools available to policy makers will not deliver the changes in behaviour (of companies, individuals and society as a whole) required to resolve the wide ranging issues described above. It is this failure of policy makers that has stimulated the search for new solutions.

The search for new solutions

Pessimists would argue that the failure of the traditional instruments of policy to address global environmental and social issues will result in a catastrophe for humankind. But this is not an inevitable conclusion.

It is very likely that the world of the future will be more crowded, warmer, have fewer mineral resources and so on, but this does not necessarily mean that a catastrophe will follow. There is no scientific proof that the world cannot sustain nine billion people, but there is a considerable body of evidence that it cannot sustain nine billion people living the lifestyles currently enjoyed by many in the Western world.[7]

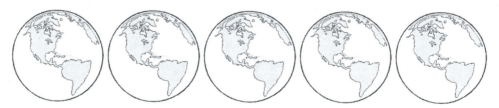

Figure 1: We would need five of these to sustain a global population living at US standards

Whether or not the planet can sustain those nine billion people will depend upon the decisions that are made now about how individuals and businesses respond to a warming planet, the steps they take to limit that warming, the way resources are shared and managed, food is produced, poverty is addressed and so on.

---

6   James Lovelock is the author of *Gaia – A New Theory of Life on Earth*, a book published in 1975 that has had a significant influence within the environmental movement.

7   There is evidence that standards of living in the western world are starting to decline – more as a response to economic crisis than a transition to a more sustainable society. The growth in economic wealth and the middle classes in the emerging economies of China, Russia, India and Brazil will, however, pose the same sustainable development challenges.

The role of business in society?

Corporations are social institutions. If they don't serve society, they have no business existing.

Henry Mintzberg, management expert

Politicians are no longer sufficiently powerful or empowered (and some would say, trusted) to make those decisions. The traditional tools of policy and diplomacy (that operate on the basis of bargaining environmental concessions for individual state benefits) cannot deliver the changes required and do not have the potential to reach across international boundaries in pursuit of environmental ends. To make the transition towards a more sustainable future, action is instead required by a wide range of different organisations – individuals, communities, scientists, businesses of all sizes and so on. It is this type of thinking (along with considerable persuasion from the third sector) that has stimulated the business community to move beyond their normal comfort zone of doing business as usual into the less comfortable arena of seeking to be seen to be doing business responsibly. As a result, in the words of Henry Mintzberg (above), the role of the global corporation has begun to embark on something of a revolution in recent years.

Global business – a part of the solution?

In the light of the recent high profile collapses of some of the more august financial institutions in western society it may seem foolhardy to put the word 'responsible' and 'business' in the same sentence. But what can at best be described as ill-judged and, at worst, immoral trading practices by a few global companies does not mean that businesses cannot either be responsible or play a role in addressing the global economic, social and environmental issues described above.

It is a fact that the expectations that society places upon modern global businesses have never been greater. And hot on the heels of the start of one of the greatest recessions in Western economies in living memory, those expectations have spectacularly failed to be met. In America at least, trust in global businesses is only just recovering from an all-time low (Edelman, 2010). What is the basis for that rebirth of trust? Partly it is a growing trend among US corporations to listen to and engage their stakeholders, treat their employees well, and play a role in solving major societal challenges (ibid). In short, it is the adoption and implementation of business practices that are, in some ways at least, responsible.

It would be naïve to suggest that the changing expectations of businesses grew out of the recession alone or that they permeate through all businesses and at all levels. They have had a much longer gestation period and have been stimulated by a diverse range of pressures. Some businesses have wholeheartedly embraced their newfound responsibilities where others have shirked them (see, for example, the opinion of Michael O'Leary, Chief Executive of RyanAir that 'We would welcome a good, deep, bloody recession in this country for 12 to 18 months ... It would help see off the environmental nonsense' (Crace, 2009). For those businesses that have responded, it is clear that changing market demand, the actions of pressure groups and the need to build trust among consumers have been a key stimulus for action along with the need to gain resource efficiencies and a desire to protect the environment and society. These desires have been shaped, in part at least, by the power of the new media to undermine all important brand values and stimulate global action.

The value of reputation

We reckon that 25–30% of anyone's stock price is related to their reputation – how admired or not admired they are.

Christopher Satterthwaite, Chief Executive of Chime Communications

It takes 20 years to build a reputation and five minutes to ruin it. If you think about that, you'll do things differently.

Warren Edward Buffet

Whatever the impetus, the pressure brought to bear on major corporations has been remarkably successful. Almost all of the top companies in the FTSE, Dow Jones and Nikkei stock exchanges have some form of a commitment to Responsible Business practices. These companies range from financial institutions to oil corporations and chemical to food manufacturers and their policies demonstrate their 'keenness' to be seen to contribute not only towards economic wealth, but also towards the well-being of the societies and environments in which they operate. One could speculate that these policies demonstrate that business has finally embraced its moral responsibilities. However, it is not that clear cut. Morality aside it is evident that a failure to uphold responsible business values (and to get caught in the act) can make or break a brand. Thus for many, the conversion to responsible business has its roots firmly planted in conventional market economics. The question is whether or not this latter fact matters.

The upshot of developments over the last two decades or so is the fact that for global corporations from the Western World, a responsible business policy is now almost as much a component of routine procedures as the annual report and statement of accounts. There remain, of course, many who are cynical about the potential for businesses – whose raison d'être is to generate a profit for their shareholders – to operate in a truly responsible way. These commentators would point to responsible business policies as little more than 'puffery'. Many of these commentators (including the pressure group CorporateWatch) play a valuable role by acting as global policemen – blowing the whistle on corporations found to be bending the rules.

Indeed, a good dose of cynicism is important when reviewing many responsible business claims. The truth and rhetoric do not always match. It is now true, however that many of the organisations that have adopted responsible business programmes recognise that they have got to be seen to be a part of the solution to the global challenges. Many third sector organisations also recognise this fact and willingly join forces with credible businesses because they recognise their potential to deliver the necessary change. WWF, for example are working with UK retailer Marks & Spencer, telecoms giant BT with Childline and global accommodation provider Accor with reforestation partner SAS Sahel.

Why the hospitality sector?

The hospitality sector is the largest subset of the tourism industry and the latter is considered – by some (most notably the World Travel & Tourism Council) – to be the largest industry in the world. The tourism and hospitality sectors are also often identified as having the potential to protect the environment and support local economies and to play a leading role in the transition towards more sustainable forms of development. According to the World Travel & Tourism Council, Earth Council and UN World Tourism Organisation in their interpretation of Agenda 21 (1996), the tourism industry (and hospitality businesses) has the potential to:

♦ Create economic value for resources whose conservation would otherwise be seen as having no financial value;

♦ Provide the incentive and means for environmental enhancement in areas such as city centres and old industrial sites;

♦ Establish essential infrastructure such as water treatment plant for residents as well as visitors;

♦ Research and develop environmentally sound technologies and techniques;

♦ Use communication opportunities with customers and host communities to pass on the messages and practices of sustainable development;

♦ Provide an environmentally sound growth alternative for developing countries and island states;

♦ Lead other industries into the adoption of business practices that contribute towards sustainable development.

The sector has until recently been seen as 'clean', in comparison to the more traditional targets of environmental groups such as mining and chemical manufacture. It is this clean image – combined with the geographically dispersed nature of the industry and the dominance of small enterprises that fall below the regulatory radar – that has made it a latecomer to the responsible business debate. There are some commentators (including WWF) who believe that this position is shortly to change and that in future years organisations involved in the production, manufacture and service of food will be viewed by third sector organisations with the suspicion that is currently reserved for the oil extraction industry. The reason is the significant ecological footprint associated with food (see Figure 2).

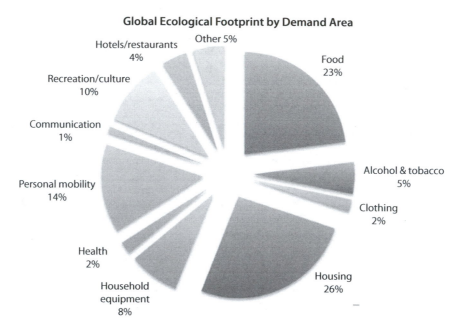

Global Ecological Footprint by Demand Area

Other 5%

Hotels/restaurants 4%

Recreation/culture 10%

Communication 1%

Personal mobility 14%

Health 2%

Household equipment 8%

Food 23%

Alcohol & tobacco 5%

Clothing 2%

Housing 26%

Figure 2: Food accounts for almost one quarter of the ecological footprint

Note: the controversial issue of agri-chemical accumulation and genetically modified organisms (GMOs) is a key issue in the food supply chain but does not fall within the scope of this diagram.

Source: Kleanthous (2010).

In the last decade most of the largest global hospitality businesses have become converts to the responsible business movement (in their business literature if not in practice). This conversion has occurred for multiple reasons (these are explored in detail in Chapter 4), not least the fact that the hospitality sector depends upon clean environments, vibrant communities and stable societies for survival. Given the number of businesses that have brought into the responsible business concept, it is perhaps a little surprising that there is no clear definition of the term for 'hospitality businesses' (or 'business' in general come to that). Instead, the field is full of jargon (see Figure 3).

Despite (or perhaps because of) the lack of clarity, most global hospitality businesses have escaped thus far with their reputation vis-à-vis environmental and social impacts largely untarnished. There are a few notable exceptions. McDonald's and Starbucks, for example, have both been caught in the act of being (or being seen to be) irresponsible but both now have impressive responsible business programmes. Even these brands have escaped the vitriol that third sector organisations reserve for some global players who fail to meet their own lofty responsible business aspirations. This is despite the fact that much of what has been achieved by hospitality businesses on the responsible business agenda has been delivered within what can broadly be described as a 'business as usual' framework. That means that it has been delivered using the normal structures of business management, with tried and tested technologies and – in most cases – with an anticipation that any environmental investments provide a reasonable return within a fairly short timescale (usually five years or less).

A lot of buzz words

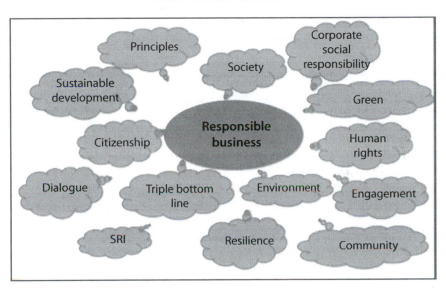

Figure 3: The responsible business lingo
Source: adapted from Bergkvist (2006)

Can prosperity be decoupled from growth?

> *Every society clings to a myth by which it lives. Ours is the myth of economic growth. For the last five decades the pursuit of growth has been the single most important policy goal across the world. The global economy is almost five times the size it was half a century ago. If it continues to grow at the same rate the economy will be 80 times that size by the year 2100.*
>
> *Tim Jackson, (2009)*

The debate within the hospitality sector to date has been conducted with little reference to the wider responsible business movement. Admittedly, the views of some of the leading thinkers in the responsible business movement, such as Tim Jackson (see above), provide challenging reading for any chief executive charged with achieving business growth. The composition of the sector – with a very high proportion of small businesses – also means that many businesses lack understanding of the concept.

This is hardly a surprising fact. The focus of the responsible business debate in the hospitality sector to date has been neither visionary nor strategic. Moreover:

♦ With a few notable exceptions, the associations that represent the sector have demonstrated a lack of leadership in this field;

♦ Most of the advice and guidance that is available for executives and students of the sector has focused on the implementation of cost-saving environmental management programmes and the potential for local purchasing processes to deliver environmental benefit;

♦ Most of the best practice that is available for the sector focuses on the issues of energy, waste or water management – or on occasion – corporate philanthropy;

♦ Almost all of the certification schemes that reward progress in the sector focus primarily on the topics of energy, waste and water management.

As more and more hospitality businesses set out on their responsible business journey, the time is perhaps right to review what 'responsible business' means for the sector, to review the priorities and to see what can be learned from leading companies in other sectors to identify possible new directions. This is timely as the Rio process (the Earth Summit) that placed the actions of businesses so firmly at the core of the sustainable development agenda passes its twentieth anniversary.

Those reading this text should be aware that a number of textbooks are available on the topic of environmental or 'sustainable' management in the hospitality sector. Most of these are 'how to' manuals, helping readers to understand how hospitality businesses implement responsible practices and listing examples of good practice. Many are excellent guides to implementing eco-efficiency programmes. Readers who are unfamiliar with the 'nuts and bolts' of environmental management should perhaps refer to one of these texts alongside this book. Particularly useful are the resources of the International Tourism Partnership (and especially the magazine *Green Hotelier* and the reference manual *Environmental Management for Hotels – the Industry Guide to Sustainable Operations*), VisitEngland's website www.better-tourism.org and the resources offered by specialist organisations like the Caribbean Alliance for Sustainable Tourism and Foodservice Footprint. For business leaders in the hotel sector, Jan Peter Bergkvist's text *Sustainability in Practice – a Fast Guide for Business Leaders* (available from order@sleepwell.nu) is particularly helpful.

A word on words!

A whole new lexicon has emerged around what was once known as environmental management and is now more frequently referred to as 'corporate responsibility', 'sustainable business' or 'responsible business'. We choose to use the latter term within this text, but many businesses use these terms entirely interchangeably. Figure 3 aims to provide a guide to the uninitiated into the range of terms used within the debate. A lack of clarity of terms is one of the frustrations of working in this field. Almost all businesses that use the term 'responsible business' will understand different things from it. One of the purposes of this text is to seek to establish a working definition of the term that can be applied within the hospitality sector.

We have chosen to use the term 'responsible business' because this is the term that is in most common parlance among those businesses that are transforming their business model to become a part of the solution to the range of economic, social and environmental issues described in the chapter. It is a term that is increasingly being adopted by hospitality businesses. It is also the term that has the broadest range of issues within its scope and this in itself makes application of all elements of the responsible business concept challenging.

Defining hospitality

Much of the focus of what has been written to date about responsible business for the hospitality sector has focused either on the broader tourism industry or on one subset of the sector – hotel businesses. While an important activity, it is essential to bear in mind that the standard industrial classification for hospitality is much broader than hotels alone. It includes within its scope the activities of:

♦ Hotels and other accommodation

♦ Holiday centres and villages

♦ Youth hostels

♦ Other holiday and short-stay accommodation

♦ Camping grounds, recreational vehicle parks and trailer parks

♦ Other accommodation

♦ Licensed restaurants

♦ Unlicensed restaurants and cafes

♦ Take-away food shops and mobile food stands

♦ Event catering activities

♦ Other food service activities

♦ Licensed clubs

♦ Public houses and bars.

Figure 4 illustrates how the hospitality sector fits into the broader travel and tourism industry. Within the scope of hospitality, but excluded from this diagram are the operations of catering businesses within schools, hospitals, prisons and other public sector venues and within business and industry (known collectively as the cost sector).

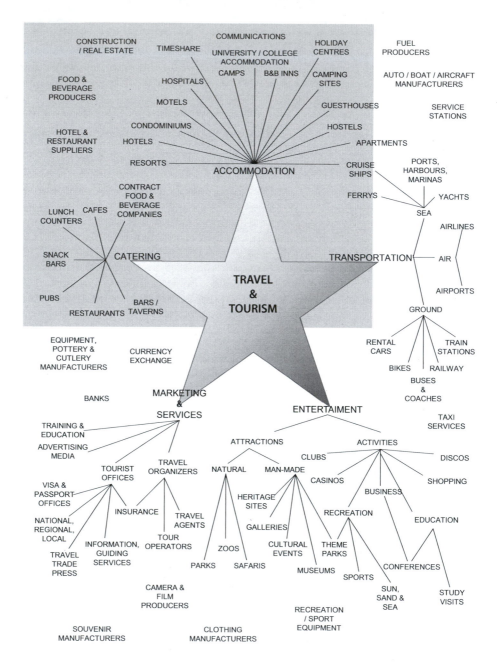

Figure 4: Where tourism and hospitality meet
Source: Bohdanowicz (2003)

One could be forgiven for considering hotels to be dominant within the sector. This is not the case. Accommodation businesses are a large component of the sector, but when looking across other indicators of size (such as the number of operating units, turnover and number of employees), hotel units become less significant to the performance of the sector as a whole.

This book seeks to embrace within its scope the range of hospitality businesses. This includes the global hotel industry, comprising 301,400 hotel properties with over 13 million rooms – focusing on the global corporations to which circa 20% of global hotels are affiliated (WTTC. IFTO, IH&RA, 2004). It also includes:

♦ The global contract catering or food service businesses that provide meals and increasingly facilities management services for school children, prisoners, hospitals, business and industry among others. They include among their number the French catering giant Sodexo, the American-owned Aramark and UK-based Compass Group. Global figures for the size of the sector have not been found, but according to Horizons, the largest 19 contract catering businesses in Europe had a combined turnover of Euro 21.4 billion in 2007. Source: Bachman, P (14/04/2009), 'Top 100 Foodservice Operators in Europe', Horizons FS Limited, London.

♦ Pubs, inns and bars from the global organisations like Mitchells and Butlers with thousands of units to small independent pubs and bars worldwide providing food and beverage services (of which Caterlyst record 60,000 in the UK alone). Source: Caterlyst database (www.caterlyst.com).

♦ The quick-service restaurants from the global giants of Starbucks and McDonald's to the smaller chains of three or four cafes and the individual units (from burger vans to kebab shops and beach-front ice cream or drink stalls); of which Caterlyst record 56,000 in the UK alone). Source: Caterlyst database (www.caterlyst.com).

♦ The restaurant sector from the major global brands such as Tragus with multiple high street brands to the smaller individual units that make up the bulk of all restaurants (of which Caterlyst record 43,000 in the UK). Source: Caterlyst database (www.caterlyst.com).

A note on data

For each of the principles included within parts 2 to 5 of this text, tables are provided to illustrate the number of global hospitality businesses that are already responding to the principle in whole or in part. This data is drawn largely from the environmental and social reports published by corporate hospitality businesses operating in the UK. Where companies do not include this data within their environmental or social reports or do not provide a formal corporate environmental or responsible business report, the data has been gleaned through their websites or we have personal knowledge of a company's actions, this information is also used. A list of the company reports and other sources consulted is included in Appendix 1.

Readers should be aware that these tables are indicative only. There are three factors that prevent them from being in any way statistically representative of progress within the sector as a whole:

♦ Not all large international hospitality businesses produce a corporate environmental or responsible business report. Even very large companies such as Gondola Leisure frequently do not provide publicly available reports. Those companies that do not report into the public domain may be making more progress than is evident from public documentation (and wary of accusations of greenwash) and thus the data provided across all hospitality businesses may under-represent the actual level of activity;

♦ Those companies that do report frequently only report for a part of the business (most commonly the wholly owned and managed part of the operation). Thus for those businesses in which a large proportion of units are operated on a franchise or lease basis, the corporate environmental report may only reflect progress in a tiny proportion of the total business and an overly optimistic picture of progress can occur from analysis based on these reports;

♦ The quality within and scope of reports is variable. Some companies (for example, Rezidor, Inter-Continental Hotel group, Sodexo and Compass) report against international criteria such as the Global Reporting Initiative. Others report against other indexes (for example Business in the Community) or derive their reports against the issues that matter to their stakeholders.

The scope of this book

This book has been developed to focus on the large international businesses that have become growing rapidly in size in recent years. These businesses make up a minority of all hospitality businesses (for example, around 14% of hotels in the UK are owned by a corporate brand) but a disproportionately large share of the market in terms of the number of units operated. In recent years, it has been these large international businesses that have promoted their responsible business credentials most vigorously, publicised their responsible business achievements and supported the development of organisations that help other businesses achieve their responsible business aims. There are, of course, many thousands of small independently owned and operated hospitality businesses that actively implement responsible business practices. These have been the focus of many academic papers and other textbooks and while some are included within this text for illustrative purposes most are excluded from its scope. The principles of responsible tourism are, however, as relevant to small as large business.

Structure of this book

This book is divided into five parts and 15 chapters as follows:

Part 1 focuses on the theory of responsible business. It describes the reasons that businesses adopt responsible business programmes, the codes of conduct that have steered the development of these programmes and identifies the four core themes that emerge from these codes of conduct as the fundamental foundations of responsible business practice. It then defines the underlying principles against which any hospitality business laying claim to responsible operations will be able demonstrate progress.

Parts 2, 3 and 4 examine each of the key themes of environmental protection, people and communities and fairness and transparency in turn. Within each section:

+ The underlying principles of responsible hospitality are explored
+ The approaches to implementing the principle examined
+ Progress within the sector described
+ Indicators from which a business can assess whether it is meeting the principle are presented
+ The tools available to help hospitality businesses implement the principle are explored.

Part 5 provides an assessment of the progress of the sector in implementing the principles as a whole and provides some thoughts for the future.

Each chapter within the text has been developed so that it can be read as a mini essay in its own right. Inevitably there is some overlap between chapters. Readers will gain more from reading the text as a whole, but this approach has been taken to help those with specific responsibilities with companies (environmental management, supply chain management, human resources and so on) identify the chapters that will have relevance to their role.

References

Bergkvist, J.P. (2006) 'Ecolonomy – sustainability in the hospitality business at Scandic and Hilton International', keynote speech at BEST-en Think Tank VI, 'Corporate Social Responsibility for a Sustainable Future', University of Girona, Spain, 16 June.

Bohdanowicz, P. (2003) 'A study of environmental impacts, environmental awareness and pro-ecological inititatives in the hotel industry', Stockholm: Royal Institute of Technology.

Carson, Rachel (1962) *Silent Spring*, Houghton Mifflin.

Carroll, A (1991) 'The Pyramid of Corporate Social Responsibility: Toward the Moral Management of Organizational Stakeholders', *Business Horizons*, July/Aug.

Crace, J. (2009) 'Michael O'Leary in his own words', *The Guardian*, 4 June. http://www.guardian.co.uk/business/2009/jun/04/michael-oleary-ryanair-airline-industry

Edelman 2010 – Trust Barometer, www.edelman.com/trust

Frankel, J (2008) *Global Environmental Policy and Global Trade Policy*. Harvard Project in International Climate Agreements, Belfer Centre for Science and International Affairs, Harvard Kennedy School. October 2008

Hawken, P., Lovins, A.B. and Lovins, L.H. (1999) *Natural Capitalism – The Next Industrial Revolution*, London: Earthscan Publications.

Jackson, T. (2009) *Prosperity without Growth*, London: Sustainable Development Commission.

Kleanthous, A. (2010) 'Eating Earth', presentation to the Food and Drink Innovation Network, available at www.fdin.org.uk/seminars/previous-seminars-and-documentation/

Lawton, J. (2010) *Royal Commission on Environmental Pollution – Adapting Institutions to Climate Change: 28th Annual Report*, London: Stationery Office.

Lomborg, B. (2001) *The Skeptical Environmentalist – Measuring the Real State of the World*, Cambridge: Cambridge University Press.

ODAC (27 May 2010) http://www.odac-info.org/peak-oil-primer

Rees, M. (2010) 'Surviving the century', broadcast on BBC Radio 4, Saturday, 12 June 2010.

Rutes, W., Penner, R. and Adams, L. (2001) *Hotel Design, Planning, and Development*. Oxford: Architectural Press.

UNEP (2010) 'Water and war', http://www.unep.org/ourplanet/imgversn/154/lonergan.html, accessed 9 June 2010.

United Nations Food and Agricultural Organization (2010) Staple foods – what people eat', www.fao.org/docrep/u8480e/u8480e07.htm

World Business Council for Sustainable Development (2008) *Sustainable Consumption Facts and Trends – from a Business Perspective*, Geneva: WBCSD.

World Travel & Tourism Council, Earth Council and UN World Tourism Organization (1996) *Agenda 21 for the Travel & Tourism Industry – Towards Environmentally Sustainable Development*, Brussels: WTTC.

2 | The reasons for doing good

The dogmas of the last 30 years have been discredited. The unwavering pursuit of economic growth – embodied in the overwhelming focus on Gross Domestic Product (GDP) – has left over a billion people in dire poverty, and has not notably improved the well-being of those who were already rich, nor even provided us with economic stability. Instead it has brought us straight to the cliff edge of rapidly diminishing natural resources and unpredictable climate change. No wonder that people are desperately seeking an alternative vision to guide our societies.

(Abdallah *et al.*, 2009)

This chapter opens with the heralding of a silent revolution. A revolution in which business leaders in most major global companies have come to acknowledge (in their business literature if not their operational practices) that business, economic prosperity, society and the quality of the environment are interdependent. With this realisation has come an acceptance, albeit modest, that the role of business has changed. In short, businesses have come to recognise that (alongside others), they need to play a role in addressing the issues associated with increasing population, resource consumption and so on

It would be fantastic – not to mention fantastical – to state that this change has resulted from a moral conversion within the business community. The early advertisements from some would certainly lead us to believe that this is the case. The reality, however, is rather more pragmatic as explored below.

The evolution of the responsible business concept

The concept of the caring corporation is, of course, not new. The responsible business movement has its roots in the early businesses (many of them run by people with strong religious beliefs) that built villages for their employees to live in, established schools for the children of their employees and so on. In today's context, it probably has its roots in the 1950s and emerged in a more coherent framework in the 1970s. Key points in the evolution of the concept are demonstrated in Figure 5.

1970	Milton Friedman's commentary on business
1972	United Nations Conference on Human Environment held in Stockholm
1973	Convention on International Trade in Endangered Species (CITES)
	OPEC oil crisis
	Businesses implement energy saving measures
1976	Shell includes responsible business in General Business Principles
1977	Global Sullivan Principles launched
	The International Labour Organization (ILO) Tripartite Declaration of Principles concerning Multinational Enterprises and Social Policy
1980	Business in the Community formed
1987	Publication of Brundtland Report
1989	Launch of Valdez (now Ceres) principles
	Launch of ICC Code of conduct (updated 2010)
	Publication of early environmental reports
1990	Montreal Protocol for the Protection of the Ozone Layer ratified
1992	United Nations Conference on Environment and Development – business invited
	World Travel & Tourism Council launches Environmental Research Centre
	International Hotels Environment Initiative formed
1994	Convention on Biological Diversity ratified
1996	Agenda 21 for Travel & Tourism published
1996	ISO 14001 introduced
1997	United Nations Convention to Combat Desertification ratified
	Global Reporting Initiative launched
1999	Global Compact launched
2001	UNWTO Global Code of Ethics published
2001	Enron collapses
2002	World Summit on Sustainable Development, Johannesburg
2003	Launch of Benchmarks for Global Corporate Responsibility
2004	Kyoto Protocol ratified
2005	Aarhaus Convention on public right of access to environmental information ratified
	Launch of UN Principles for Responsible Investment
2006	First meeting of World Economic Forum
2008	Lehman Brothers files for bankruptcy
2009	COP 15
2012	Rio + 20 event

Awareness of envirnmental/sustainable development issues →

Figure 5: The evolution of the responsible business concept

In the early years, most businesses that engaged in responsible practices couched their initiatives in the language of environmental protection, but it was more than a happy coincidence that they also provided significant savings on the bottom line. A notable band of businesses also engaged in philanthropic gestures. Businesses engaged in these gestures generally targeted causes that attracted public opinion and they soon realised that 'doing good' could, in some cases, add brand value (see the examples of cause related marketing below).

The leading businesses of this caring image in the 1980s and 1990s were ironically global organisations from business sectors that had historically been associated with the most significant environmental impacts. They include:

♦ Dow Chemicals, which even in the 1980s was reported as working its way towards a goal of zero toxic emissions, but had been previously associated with the production of Agent Orange and napalm;

♦ Shell, which produced its first environmental report in 1997, after suffering from the public relations fiasco around its decision to break up the Brent Spar oil storage buoy in 1995;

♦ Rio Tinto, which reported in 2002 for the first time against the Global Reporting Initiative indicators and the additional Mining and Metal Sector Supplement indicators. Critics of the company claim that this report was made despite ongoing questions about its human rights record.

Later adopters of the principles of responsible business were the global businesses that had traditionally associated themselves with having lower environmental impacts, including many service sector businesses. Many of the global brands in the hospitality sector did not start the process of seeking to actively ameliorate negative environmental impacts until the early 1990s and the focus on broader societal impacts and environmental reporting came much later (see Chapter 4).

The case for responsible business

The following reasons are commonly quoted as the rationale for the adoption of responsible business practices.

Who cares wins

One only has to look at the troubles of oil giant BP off the Louisiana coast to understand the way in which associations with environmental catastrophe can undermine the share value of a company.[8] BP is not the first global giant to experience turbulence as a result of perceived or real environmental or social failings. Union Carbide (now a subsidiary of Dow Chemicals), Nike, Exxon, Unilever, Primark, McDonald's,

---

8   BP's stock price fell by 11% in the first week of the Deep Water Horizon oil leak crisis (The Independent, 30 April 2010). Share prices have subsequently stabilised but profits have been depressed in part by on-going issues surrounding the leak.

Gap, Shell among others have all at some point fallen victim on the altar of social conscience or environmental degradation. These failures, while often short-lived, have demonstrated with great clarity to multinational corporations one fact – and that is that brand and share value and social or environmental practice are intricately linked.

To these multinational companies, the value of the brand is fundamental.[9] A point aptly demonstrated by Naomi Klein in *No Logo*, 'successful corporations must primarily produce brands, as opposed to products' (Klein, 2001). The difficulty for companies is that the success of brand value lies in the establishment of emotional ties with customers. And the essence of these ties lies not just in the product itself, but in the way customers feel about a company.

Evidence of poor social or environmental practice can undermine customer confidence – especially in the developed world where the trend is for customers to positively favour products and brands that have an active association with doing social or environmental good.

Indeed those businesses that have adopted environmental and social practices often find that they deliver economic return in unexpected ways. For example, as early as 1998, drinks giant Diageo reported that in the previous four years, 22 cause-related marketing[10] projects helped to raise £600,000 for causes while increasing sales of tracked brands by 37% (Kemp, 2001).

Burgeoning markets

Consumer choice in developed marketplaces has been a potent driver of the new morality within businesses. Mature markets challenge products to find key points of differentiation. The 'ethics' of a brand or a product can provide this for many consumers.

It is the emergence of distinct market segments like Generation G that has led to an explosion of new brands with an 'ethical' slant: brands which use their organic, fair trade or community trading status as selling points (in the case of hospitality, see the explosion of hotel or restaurant business laying claim to be eco-lodges). An increasing number of businesses make the most of their corporate social responsibility programmes, and shout loudly about their measurable environmental footprints or about how well they comply with highly technical environmental standards. Time and again we hear of how goods are produced using sustainable methods. The growth of the eco-chic or eco-conscious consumer has brought about the age of eco-design.

---

9   This is especially the case for multinational hospitality businesses and especially those that provide franchise or management contract arrangements to third-party property owners.

10 Cause-related marketing involves a partnership between a for-profit and not-for-profit organisation for mutual benefit. Examples of cause-related marketing would include a soft drinks company promoting its product as a part of a drink-driving campaign and donating a proportion of the profits to the not-for-profit partner.

Text box 2: Consumer demand for products that do good

Mintel manages a Global New Products Database (GNPD) which has tracked market trends for more than 13,000 new sustainable food and drink products since 2005. Data collated indicates that consumers are keen to buy products that do good, even when they don't understand all of the claims on the label:

- 84% of consumers say they regularly buy green or sustainable food and drink
- Some consumers who buy such products are unaware of what the claims mean.
- Sustainable product claims such as solar/wind energy usage or Fairtrade have yet to enter the mainstream consumer consciousness;
- 34% say they've never heard of the Fairtrade claim.

Contrary to popular opinion, consumers do not always buy products that do good because of the product claims about lower environmental or social impacts. For 45% of sustainable food and drink users, their purchasing decisions for responsible products is based on a belief in superior quality while for 43% the decision is taken because they're concerned about environmental/human welfare and 42% say they're concerned with food safety (www.globalcstorefocus.com).

LOHAS (Lifestyles of Health and Sustainability) tracks trends in the market segment focused on health and fitness, the environment, personal development, sustainable living, and social justice. It estimates that this market is worth $290 billion in the US marketplace. The consumers attracted to this market represent a sizeable group in this country. Approximately 13–19% of the adults in the USA are currently considered LOHAS consumers. This is based on surveys of the US adult population estimated at 215 million.

Trendwatching define the group of consumers that are driven by ethics as Generation Generosity (or Generation G). According to their definition, Generation G are consumers who are disgusted with greed and its current dire consequences for the economy. The growth of Generation G coincides with the ongoing (and pre-recession) emergence of an online-fuelled culture of individuals who share, give, engage, create and collaborate in large numbers.

According to Trendwatching, businesses should follow this societal/behavioural shift, however much it may oppose their decades-old devotion to me, myself and I. 'The growth of Generation G is likely to spur on the trend for responsible business in the economies of India and China where 78% of Indian, 77% of Chinese and 80% of Brazilian consumers prefer brands that support good causes, compared to 62% of global consumers' (http://trendwatching.com/briefing/#rak).

Of course statistics such as those noted above demonstrate how consumers say they make purchasing decisions (their aspirations) rather than recording the actual purchasing decisions they make. Trend data over time demonstrates an on-going interest in ethical or environmental issues. Actual sales data for ethical products would, however, point to the fact that the aspiration to purchase ethical or environmental products and services is not always converted into practice.

The results? The overall ethical market in the UK was worth £43.2 billion in 2009 compared to £36.5 billion two years earlier. The growth was despite a 2% fall in over-all household expenditure over the same period. However, ethical spend remained a small proportion of the total annual consumer spend of some £700 billion. It is of interest that expenditure on ethical food and drink increased more than many other consumer products (by 27% to reach £6.5 billion). Ethical food and drink sales, now represent 8% of all food and drink sales. Fairtrade food grew by 64% to reach £749 million, while sales of animal welfare Freedom Food certified products tripled in two years to reach £122 million, but organic food sales fell (http://www.goodwithmoney. co.uk/ethical-consumerism-report-2010, accessed 27 May 2011). Similar trends are evident in other developed countries. Market analysts predict a continuing growth in demand for ethical and sustainable products despite the recession, although the exact scale of this is difficult to define. Data for hospitality in particular is not available. Although it is for a specific segment of the tourism market – responsible tourism – and it points to a rising trend, albeit from a very small base (Cooperative Bank, 2010).

Capital gains

It is a fortunate coincidence that initiatives that seek to reduce emissions of gases implicated in climate change, reduce the consumption of water, limit the produc-tion of waste and so on also reduce operating costs for businesses. One of the most potent drivers of the responsible business movement, is the pursuit of these savings. And the rewards even in the early days of these programmes were significant. For example:

♦ Over the five years from 1993–98, Unilever sought to increase environmental effi-ciency within manufacturing processes with anticipated savings of £100 million;

♦ Dow Chemicals – one of the early adopters of the responsible business phi-losophy – invested US$1 billion in a 'ValuePark' initiative which sought to locate units in close proximity and facilitate the waste from one outlet being used as the feedstock for the second. Anticipated returns on investment of 30–40% were predicted;

♦ Intercontinental Hotels and Resorts reported a reduction in energy consumption of 27% over the period 1988–95;

♦ Scandic calculate actual cost savings on energy and water between 1996 and 2006 to be in the region of €18 million;

♦ Hilton Hotels in Continental Europe reported a 15% reduction in energy consumption per square metre of the hotel area and an 8% reduction in water consumption over a three year period which resulted in avoided costs equal to US$16 million.

Source of data: Kemp, 2001; Hawkins, 1996; Bohdanowicz, Zientara, Novotna, 2011.

There are, of course, a few businesses that have expanded their cost base in order to operate according to sustainable principles. Scandic, for example, has chosen to purchase food that can meet organic standards and to create the 97% recyclable room, Whitbread have constructed a low-energy hotel in Tamworth, UK, catering giant Sodexo have chosen to ensure that 100% of their sea food is certified as sustainable by the Marine Stewardship Council or produced according to Best Aquaculture Practices by 2015 and McDonald's has switched to UK-sourced beef in British restaurants. But these remain the exception rather than the rule.

The strong arm of the law

The second half of the 20th century saw a remarkable growth in environmental regulation across the globe. This was introduced initially as a response to the immediate health hazards associated with high levels of pollution (such as smog incidents in London) or specific pollution incidents (such as the Union Carbide disaster in Bhopal, the Love Canal incident at Niagara Falls). It has subsequently developed to embrace a much wider range of issues, including the protection of human rights. Regulation has also changed its emphasis. Rather than seeking to act as global policeman (catching out those who abuse the environment or society) it seeks to prevent pollution incidents (this is known in the jargon as the 'precautionary principle'). Often prevention of pollution is achieved through fiscal measures such as the proposed schemes in the EU, Australia and some US states to make businesses buy permits to allow them to emit CO_2 into the atmosphere.[11] Thus, theoretically at least, regulators heighten the costs of pollution providing a cost advantage to those businesses that invest in prevention technologies.

It is broadly accepted by most businesses as well as other stakeholders that a base of good quality regulation is fundamental to environmental and social protection. It shields the vast majority of responsible businesses (as well as society in general) from the small percentage that would otherwise wilfully pollute or exploit.

Once this baseline of regulation is achieved, many businesses would prefer to take voluntary or self-regulatory initiatives to deliver further improvements. In fact this principle is enshrined in Agenda 21 as one of the guiding principles for business action. There are now some examples of business effectively working in advance of regulation. These include, for example, decisions within the UK to phase out the sale of incandescent light bulbs by the end of 2011 in advance of regulation banning their use.

Industry has been keen to demonstrate to governments that it can operate according to responsible principles and that regulation is not a necessary precursor of good practice. The enthusiasm among many large companies to adopt the mantle of responsibility has been broadly embraced by the international community and a

---

11 In the case of the EU, this is under the EU Emission Trading Scheme targeting large industrial producers of carbon dioxide (or equivalents).

number of 'best practice' guides now exist to demonstrate the ways in which self-regulation (or voluntary initiatives) can be an effective means of achieving environmental and social goals, sometimes in the place of regulation.

A caveat must, however, be added to the way in which the success of these programmes is heralded. And that is that all voluntary initiatives are not created equal and voluntary initiatives if poorly defined or inappropriately implemented are as prone to failure as regulation with the same defects. Even those businesses with apparently comprehensive self-regulatory procedures can fail to deliver on the responsible business commitments (see Text box 3). Nevertheless, over the last two decades, business has shown a very clear preference for voluntary action in advance of – or instead of – regulation. The evidence of improvements delivered through voluntary initiatives combined with the shortcomings of regulation to tackle current environmental and social issues, mean that many in the third sector and governmental community support this trend.

Text box 3: Businesses that have fallen foul of self-regulatory initiatives

Businesses that apparently have high profile commitments to responsible business practices have experienced some very high profile failures. These include:

- Primark – despite belonging to the Ethical Trading Initiative, the company was described by the Institute of Development Studies as failing to stop the exploitation of workers who produce the bulk of products sold in UK shops (*The Independent*, 16 October 2006);

- Starbucks – which was found to be using water inefficiently in the UK despite its own company commitments to environmental responsibility

- BP with its strong focus on renewable energy and commitments to environmental improvements and membership of organisations such as Business in the Community with its failure to stop the oil leak off the Louisiana coast.

Resilient businesses

According to Bloomberg (2002), the average lifespan of an international corporation is 40 years and it has been proven that those businesses that survive in the long term are those with a firm eye on the future. The environmental challenges (especially, in the short term, the threat of depletion of oil resources) are such that most businesses have come to accept that they must adapt (and to retain the support of their consumer base in so doing) to survive.

At a more pragmatic level, businesses are only too well aware that demand for resources is outstripping supply and that the world of the future is likely to be warmer and more populated. The balance sheets of many have been damaged by the unexpected – see for example, the impacts of the oil price rises in 2007–08. Most have learned the lesson – dependence on a dwindling stock of resources makes the future of their businesses little more than hostages to fortune.

Minds have thus been focused on the need to adapt and evolve as a core tenet for remaining in business. Thus for many, the conversion to responsible business relates not only to the urge to do better business now but to ensure that company continues to do business into the future. As a result, an increasing number of businesses now link responsible business and risk management processes.

Staff required

It is not only customers that are integrating an ethical or moral dimension to their decision-making – employees are also increasingly insisting that their employers adopt ethical business practices. A recent survey from Price Waterhouse Coopers found that 88% of 4721 graduates interviewed around the world who entered the workforce after 1 July 2000 seek employers with social responsibility values that reflect their own. Moreover, 86% say they would consider leaving an employer whose social responsibility practices no longer reflected their own values. And these values were not just held dear by respondents from the developed world. They were consistently high with respondents from Argentina and Brazil among others (PWC, 2009). It seems that businesses will need to compete for good staff not just on the pay and reward package they can offer, but also on the extent to which they can meet prospective new employees' social and environmental values.

Businesses that do good

These reasons are compelling and have motivated a significant number of companies to reorient their businesses strategies (and in some cases their brands) wholly around responsible business issues. Interestingly, the responsible orientation of some products has made them particularly attractive to other corporates seeking to benefit from their 'clean' image. From the Body Shop (now owned by L'Oréal) to Green and Blacks (now a part of the Cadbury family of companies which is itself part of Kraft Foods), Innocent Drinks (now part-owned by Coca Cola), Rachel's Organic (a subsidiary of American conglomerate Dean Foods) to Pret-a-Manger (until recently a third owned by McDonald's), business have found that ethics sell!

Given the apparent benefits of responsible business, it is perhaps surprising that more businesses have not publicised their commitment to it. There are a number of reasons for this, not least the complexities of implementing responsible business strategies throughout large and complex organisations. This is especially the case in the hospitality sector, where many units branded by large multi national companies are not owned or operated by the company that provides the brand but by a franchisee or other agent. Chapter 4 provides more information on these issues.

The danger for many businesses that have genuinely embraced responsible business principles is the very crowded nature of this marketplace and the inability of most consumers to differentiate those businesses that are genuinely 'good' from those that adopt the mantle of responsibility without implementing its full principles'. It is this definition of what makes a business responsible that we will focus on in the next chapter.

References

Abdallah, S., Thompson, S., Mechealson, J., Marks, N. and Steuer, N. (2009) *The Happy Planet Index*. London: New Economics Foundation.

Bloomberg Business Week (2002) 'The living company: habits for survival in a turbulent business environment', www.businessweek.com/chapter/degeus.htm.

Bohdanowicz P., Zientara P., Novotna E. (2011), International hotel chains and environmental protection: An analysis of Hilton's *we care!* Programme (Europe, 2006-2008), *Journal of Sustainable Tourism*, **19**(7) 797-816.

Cooperative Bank (2010) *Ethical Consumer Report*, Cooperative Bank.

Hawkins, R (1996) Environmental reviewing for the hotel sector: the experience of Inter-Continental Hotels and Resort, *UNEP Industry and Environment*, **19**(2).

Kemp (2001) *To whose profit – building a business case for sustainability*, WWF Surrey.

Klein, N (2000) *No Logo*, London : Flamingo Press.

PWC (2009) *Managing Tomorrow's People: Millennials at Work: Perspectives from a New Generation*, London: PWC.

Sodexo (2011) Sodexo Commits to 100% Certified Sustainable Seafood by 2015, www.sodexousa.com/usen/newsroom/press/press11/sustainableseafood.asp

Mintel (2010) Consumers crave sustainable products, www.globalcstorefocus.com/cgi-bin/newsletter.pl?edition=201011&this_page=14

World Business Council for Sustainable Development (2008) *Sustainable Consumption: Facts and Trends*, WBCSD, Switzerland

3 | Defining good – the principles of responsible business

> *Fundamentally transforming the foundations of the economy is the biggest contribution we can make towards building a sustainable future. The current economic crisis may be painful, but it will be nothing compared with the crises we will face if we continue to grow in a way that threatens the life-support systems on which we rely.*
>
> Jonathon Porritt, Chair, Sustainable Development Commission, announcing *Prosperity Without Growth* report (March 2008)

One of the greatest challenges for those businesses claiming that they operate according to the principles of responsible business is defining what this complex and multidisciplinary term actually means for their operation. Poor definition of the term within company literature and a lack of transparent reporting of progress has left some of those laying claim to 'responsible business practices' open to accusations of 'greenwash'. Multiple definitions of the term responsible business exist with significant differences between them. There are also a wide range of other commonly used terms that have more or less the same meaning. As a result, some businesses (including a number of hospitality businesses) that are engaged in little more than energy management, lay claim to operating in a responsible manner alongside others that are engaged in a much wider range of programmes.

Greenwash

Greenwash is a term that is commonly used to describe a business that lays claims to environmental practices or responsible business programmes that either do not materially address its key impacts or that it cannot substantiate in fact.

Genuinely responsible business practices extend way beyond resource efficiency and embrace a wide scope of issues, including: reducing the environmental impacts of the business; making a positive contribution to the local and global community; treating employees, suppliers and others engaged with the business fairly; applying the principles of fairness and ethics in marketing and sales activities and applying good standards of corporate governance throughout the operation. We will explore these issues further below.

Defining responsible business

Most definitions of 'good' business have their roots in the definition of sustainable development produced by the World Commission on Environment and Development in 1987 (commonly called the Brundtland Report). Multiple terms are commonly used to describe business practices that contribute towards environmental protection and social enhancement as well as economic development. These include the relatively recent use of the term responsible business and the slightly earlier term corporate social responsibility. As the text below demonstrates, there are multiple definitions of these terms (many thousands if Google is to be believed).

> *The basic idea of CSR is that business and society are interwoven, rather than distinct entities.*

(Moir, 2001)

> *The commitment of businesses to contribute to sustainable economic development – working with employees, their families, the local community and society at large to improve the quality of life, in ways that are good for business and good for development.*

(World Business Council for Sustainable Development, 2007)

> *A concept whereby companies integrate social and environmental concerns in the business operations and in their interactions with stakeholders on a voluntary basis.*

(Commission of the European Communities, 2001)

These definitions are rather too broad to be of help to the average business, and do little to elucidate those issues in which the business should engage.

The principles of responsible business

The desire by businesses to engage in responsible practices has driven the development of a number of guidelines and principles. In combination, these tease out the steps that businesses can take to support a fair and functioning society, engage in enhancing environmental quality and protect human dignity. Most responsible business executives will be able to name at least a handful of these agreements, of which the ICC Business in Society guidelines are perhaps the best known and the CERES principles the most far-reaching. Many businesses use the principles enshrined in these documents as the foundations for the responsible business initiatives within their organisations:

♦ **Global Sullivan Principles of Social Responsibility** (1977). A set of general principles about the legitimate role of business in society. The principles specifically encourage companies to support economic, social and political justice wherever they do business.

♦ **The International Labour Organization (ILO) Tripartite Declaration of Principles concerning Multinational Enterprises and Social Policy** (1977). Principles laid down in this universal instrument offer guidelines to MNEs, governments, and employers' and workers' organizations in such areas as employment, training, conditions of work and life, and industrial relations. Its provisions are reinforced by certain international labour conventions and recommendations which the social partners are urged to bear in mind and apply, to the greatest extent possible.

♦ **CERES Principles** (1989 and subsequently updated) Drawn from the Valdez principles,[12] these wide-ranging criteria affirm a belief that corporations have a responsibility for the environment, and must conduct all aspects of their business as responsible stewards of the environment by operating in a manner that protects the Earth, guards a fair and functioning society and protects human dignity. The principles aim to guide both investors and businesses.

♦ **ICC Business Charter for Sustainable Development** (1989 – subsequently updated) and subsequent **Business in Society** – a voluntary commitment by business to manage its activities responsibly. These are perhaps the best-known principles that lay out 16 key activities in which businesses should engage.

♦ **Agenda 21** (1992) Declaration by the United Nations of the responsibilities of all in society (including business and industry) to contribute towards the achievement of more sustainable forms of development.

♦ **Caux Round Table Principles for Business** (1994). These state that the world business community should play an important role in improving economic and social conditions.

♦ **United Nations Global Reporting Initiative** (1997). A process to help companies understand the mechanisms that they should use when seeking to report on progress against environmental and social criteria. The Initiatives provides a number of sector-specific guides and these have covered tour operators and the food processing industry.

♦ **The ILO Declaration on Fundamental Principles and Rights at Work** (1998). An expression of commitment by governments, employers' and workers' organizations to uphold basic human values.

♦ **United Nations Global Compact (1999)**. Brings companies together with UN agencies, labour and civil society to support universal environmental and social principles that include many of the actions that are now embraced within the responsible business agenda.

♦ **European Parliament resolution on 'EU standards for European enterprises operating in developing countries: towards a European code of conduct' (1999)**. A code of conduct governing the ways in which European companies should operate when working in developing countries. The principles cross many responsible business themes.

---

12 Principles developed in the wake of the Exxon Valdez oil disaster in Alaska to motivate all business in the protection of the environment. The principles were developed by the Coalition for Environmentally Social Economics (CERES). CERES was a coalition of 14 environmental groups and the Social Investment Forum (an organisation of 325 bankers with an interest in pursuing more environmentally and socially responsible forms of development).

- **The Guidelines for Multinational Enterprises** annexed to the Declaration on International Investment and Multinational Enterprises of the Organisation for Economic Cooperation and Development (2000 and subsequently updated). Guidelines that aim to encourage corporate responsibility and accountability among multinational enterprises. These guidelines have much in common with the Global Reporting Initiative, but they have been approved by governments (although they do not have the force of regulation);

- **The Johannesburg Declaration on Sustainable Development** (2002). Reaffirmation of the principles of sustainable development, emphasising the importance of equity and multilateral cooperation as essential tools.

- **United Nations Principles of Responsible Investment** (2005). A series of principles devised by the investment community. They reflect the view that environmental, social and corporate governance (ESG) issues can affect the performance of investment portfolios and therefore must be given appropriate consideration by investors if they are to fulfil their fiduciary (or equivalent) duty. The Principles provide a voluntary framework for all investors with the aim of aligning investment objectives with those of society at large.

- **Benchmarks for Global Corporate Responsibility** (2008). A comprehensive set of social and environmental criteria and business performance indicators. Offers over 100 principles, 129 criteria and 118 benchmarks to assist companies who are genuine about responsible corporate behaviour.

There are also some hospitality and tourism specific codes (such as the UNWTO Global Code of Ethics, the Cape Town Declaration on Responsible Tourism, the Global Sustainable Tourism Criteria and these are discussed in Chapter 4).

The power of voluntary initiatives

'… voluntary initiatives have been said to present a number of advantages as a form of regulation. Voluntary initiatives may provide a means of regulating the activities of companies operating globally (Campbell, 2006), allowing for the regulation of local and global environmental impacts in the absence of effective national or international laws. Far from being 'toothless' and 'unimportant', Braithwaite and Drahos (2000) argue that voluntary initiatives play a significant role in the globalisation of standards and the mobilisation of business towards improved performance. The potential of voluntary initiatives for transboundary application may also fill a gap for companies that operate across a number of jurisdictions and seek consistent international standards'.

(Gleckman, 2004)

These international codes of conduct were initially concerned with either environmental or social impacts. As the 21st century has unfolded they have expanded their scope to embrace the combined environmental, social and economic impacts of businesses and to include the issues of corporate governance and responsible investment. The organisations engaged in the development of these codes have also changed. Initially, the codes were issued by business for business. As time has gone on and inter-governmental organisations have recognised the power of voluntary initiatives, they have increasingly been issued with the support of the UN and other 'agents of government'. In some instances they have been presented as a precursor to tougher regulation. Many have subsequently also become underpinned by regulation in some countries. The international nature of many of these codes makes them potentially more powerful than regulation.

Three fundamental themes underpin all of the codes of conduct in one way or another (and are central to many of the mainstream business guidelines such as the Global Compact and are also essential underpinnings to the concepts of sustainability and triple bottom line). These are the central tenet for responsible business programmes. They reflect the following values:

♦ Responsible stewardship of the environment

♦ Respect for people and 'communities'

♦ Fairness and transparency.

There is of course a fourth principle that is excluded and that is the fundamental and important role that businesses play in generating economic benefits. However, this is the raison d'être of businesses and it is anticipated within these themes that businesses will continue to generate a profit and that by applying the themes and principles they will ensure that that profit is used in part at least to perpetuate 'good'.

The authors have analysed the principles contained within the international codes of conduct to refine ten core principles of responsible hospitality. They are:

The Ten Principles of Responsible Hospitality

Promote responsible stewardship of the environment

1 Avoid wasteful use of resources and protect, and, where possible, improve, the environment

2 Prepare for the (un)expected

3 Develop products that are responsible and can be operated responsibly

Respect people and communities

4 Take full account of the views of people and communities

5 Embed responsible business practices throughout the supply chain

6 Engage employees and customers in actions that support environmental, economic and social wellbeing

7   Contribute to the development of public policy that promotes environmental, social and economic wellbeing

Fairness and transparency

8   Define responsible business values and communicate good practice

9   Build trust through transparency

and

10 Take responsible business to the heart of the company.

In an ideal world, these principles would be mutually exclusive. In reality, they inevitably contain some duplication and overlaps. On occasion they also require trade-offs to be made.

The Ten Principles explored

The scope of the Ten Principles of Responsible Business is expansive. It extends way beyond the direct operations of the business to embrace supply chain practices, new investment decisions and customer behaviour. Below, we provide a very brief summary of what is embraced within each principle (they are the subject of Parts 2 to 5). Many of these principles form the subject of multiple text books in their own right and, where we can, we include references to more detailed reading.

Promote responsible stewardship of the environment

Principle 1 – Avoid wasteful use of resources and protect, and, where possible, improve the environment.

This principle is the most widely accepted and acted upon. In a world of growing population and dwindling resource base, most businesses would accept that the environment should be at least protected. In the light of escalating resource costs combined with the current fashion for austerity, few businesses decline the potential to make the efficiency savings that are implicit in this principle.

Resource scarcity on the horizon?

> *The era of 'abundance' is over. The future will see our natural resources, from oil to food, having some level of restriction placed on them.*
>
>   *Andy Bond, CEO, Asda (May 2009, www.philharding.net)*

While most businesses would concur with this principle, few implement it in its entirety. Willingness to avoid wasteful use of resources, especially through eco-efficiency measures is high. Environmental protection and improvement when implemented at a cost to the business is less universally popular.

There are multiple texts and journals dedicated to the relationship between businesses and the environment. Those with a practical slant may find the 'how to' documents produced by organisations from the Journal of Cleaner Production to the World Business Council for Sustainable Development and the International Tourism Partnership of great value.

Principle 2 – Prepare for the (un)expected

Change is inherent to any business and change management is an art at which most managers are well practiced. Those organisations that prepare now for the predicted changes in global climate, food security and other environmental and social issues are likely to be those that thrive in the long term.

This principle recognises that businesses cannot prepare for the range of environmental and challenges in isolation. To do so, they must become embedded into the communities in which they operate. Resilience is a key to adaptation and survival.

As this chapter demonstrates, hospitality businesses are increasingly involved in the development of risk and emergency preparedness plans. Many, however, have got their heads firmly stuck in the sand over issues such as the need to adapt to the likely implications of climate change.

For more information on this topic, we would suggest that you read the International Food Policy Research Institute's document *Food Security and Climate Change – Challenges to 2050 and Beyond* or the United Nations Environment Programme document *Climate Change and Tourism – Responding to Global Challenges*.

Principle 3 – Develop products that are responsible and can be operated responsibly

Most businesses would claim to seek to make a positive contribution to the environment, economic and social fabric of society. There is an increasing body of evidence to demonstrate that customers are seeking out businesses that do just this. However, it is important to differentiate between those businesses that have been designed (or reengineered) with a positive contribution at their very core and those that seek to embrace these elements as an add-on extra. It is the former examples that embrace the spirit of the principle.

To date – critics of new products in the sector have reserved their ire for specific companies (global multinationals) or product types (e.g. fast food restaurants, integrated resorts). The chapter contends that this focus is misplaced. What is required is a clear assessment of the extent to which any business developing new products or services does good or causes harm.

The need to develop new products that can flourish in a resource-depleted world

> *Today we find ourselves faced with the imminent end of the era of cheap oil, the prospect (beyond the recent bubble) of steadily rising commodity prices, the degradation of forests, lakes and soils, conflicts over land use, water quality, fishing rights and the momentous challenge of stabilising concentrations of carbon in the global atmosphere... In these circumstances, a return to business as usual is not an option. Prosperity for the few founded on ecological destruction and persistent social injustice is no foundation for a civilised society.*

> *(Jackson, 2008)*

It is clear that, outside of the designated 'eco' or 'green' market, few hospitality businesses review new products or services to ensure that they meet their responsible business claims or can fulfil their potential to do good. As a, result new buildings continue to be constructed in areas where the construction compromises the quality of the environment aesthetically or because there are insufficient water or other resources to support it and so on. New food service offers are all too often developed without the principles of good nutritional value, animal welfare or waste minimisation at their core.

For more information on this principle, we would suggest that you read the International Tourism Partnership's *Sustainable Hotel: Siting, Design and Construction Manual* or the guidance available from organisations such as CIRIA, LEED, BRE or the *Journal of Sustainable Product Design*.

Respect people and communities

Principle 4 – Take full account of the views of people and communities

This principle recognises that business does not operate in isolation from society. Moreover, it recognises that those individuals and organisations in society that are affected (negatively or positively) by the activities of a company increasingly expect to be engaged in dialogue about its activities. Collectively called stakeholders,[13] they are distinct from shareholders (i.e. those with a direct stake in the business), who were until relatively recently seen as the major and potentially only individuals with a legitimate interest in the future of the business.

The concept of stakeholders has been widely applied within business organisations as a core part of their responsible business programme (including hospitality

---

13   There are various definitions of a stakeholder. The most commonly used is Freeman's 'any group or individual who can affect or is affected' by an organisation's activities (Freeman, 1984). Some people believe that this is too broad a definition. Beauchamp and Bowie (2001) consider that there is also a narrow definition of stakeholders (i.e. those individuals/groups who are vital to the survival and success of the organisation).

businesses such as global catering company Sodexo) and is now also commonly applied to regional, national and global issues (see for example, Clulow, 2005; Getz and Timur, 2005; Markwick, 2005).

Businesses seeking to take full account of the views of stakeholders typically face four challenges (adapted from (Waligo):

1 defining who the stakeholders of any given organisation are;

2 identifying what stakeholders want;

3 perhaps the most vexing for companies, understanding how stakeholders get what they want (Mitchell, 1997); and

4 identifying how to effectively engage with stakeholders.

While it sounds simple in theory, the mechanisms for engaging with stakeholders are not always well developed and typically different groups of stakeholders will respond to different mechanisms. In the case of hospitality business, some stakeholders, such as suppliers, have been easily engaged. Others such as customers have been more difficult to engage (especially in super luxury properties where responsible business practices are not put to the fore for fear of alienating specific client groups). Some leading hospitality companies have, however, become aware that there is a need to engage with a wider range of stakeholders, including those who are critical of the business model. As a result some surprising partnerships have emerged in recent years.

We would recommend that you visit organisations such as the Stakeholder Forum for a Sustainable Future (http://www.stakeholderforum.org/sf/) to learn more about this issue.

Principle 5 – Embed responsible business practices throughout the supply chain

It is well known that the most significant impacts of many businesses (including hospitality businesses) come not from their direct operations, but from their supply chain. Those companies that lay claim to responsible business practices must, therefore, find fair and just mechanisms to engage the myriad of supply organisations in addressing their own social and environmental impacts. In practice, most businesses interpret this principle as requiring them to either select products that meet responsible business criteria (such as fairly traded beverages) and/or ask all suppliers to meet minimum responsible business criteria as a condition of doing business. Those organisations that embrace its full meaning, however, go further to embed within supplier relationships the principles of fairness, transparency and partnership.

Many large hospitality businesses have begun to recognise that responsible business policies must extend through the supply chain. With the notable exception of some of the contract caterers and major QSR companies, however, there is more awareness than action. This is despite the fact that effective supply chain management can deliver cost savings on a par with those that are gleaned from resource efficiency. A greater awareness among the public about supply chain impacts will without doubt make this a bandwagon that more will join over time.

For more information on this principle, we would suggest that you read *Green Hotelier*, the Scandic Supplier Declaration and information from organisations such as the World Business Council for Sustainable Development, Business in the Community and CSR Europe.

Principle 6 - Engage employees and customers in actions that support environmental, economic and social wellbeing

Behaviour change lies at the core of resolving the range of issues described in Chapter 1 (SDC, 2006). Effective behaviour change can only be achieved through initiatives that win the hearts and minds of consumers, employees and others. Most successful businesses already have the creativity and flair to change the behaviour of consumers and employees – whether engaging them in decisions to swap product preferences or to consume more of a specific product. The trick is to find ways in which this creativity can be applied to help consumers and employees to make sustainable lifestyle choices.

Some businesses have effectively engaged with consumers on this principle, but many businesses have not seized the opportunity. A small number have abused customer trust by making at best, opaque and at worst, misleading claims. In some cases, consumers, employees and non-governmental organisations have become frustrated with the inertia (and occasionally duplicity) of businesses in this regard. They have used their capacity to motivate the masses through networks like Facebook and AVAAZ to force change upon major businesses, including hospitality businesses.

Customer Demand for Responsible Products

> We're increasingly seeing that our prospects and customers want to be dealing with a company that is trustworthy, reliable, ethical and honest … it helps if that reputation is rooted in a company's history and culture. … Honesty leads to trust which is at the root of good business relationships.

> Keith Sharp, Marketing Director, Tata Consultancy Services (in Mullins, 2010)

There is now a great deal of theory on how to influence behaviour to favour choices that are socially just, environmentally benign and respect human dignity. The market research data indicates that consumers have a willingness to act to select environmentally friendly choices. However, progress in delivering actual behaviour change takes time. To date, hospitality businesses have been reluctant to directly influence customer behaviour (outside the business to business market and a few easy-win issues such as stocking fair trade products), but have achieved much through technology and other indirect mechanisms. They have been more proactive when it comes to working with their direct employees to change behaviour. A yawning gap, however, exists when it comes to ensuring that these behaviours are embedded into the educational establishments that are preparing the employees of the future.

For more information on this principle, we would suggest that you read the Sustainable Development Commissions report *I Will if you Will*, NESTA's publication on *Selling Sustainability* and the campaigns of organisations such as AVAAZ.org.

Principle 7 – Contribute to the development of public policy that promotes environmental, social and economic wellbeing

Chapter 1 demonstrates that the tools of policy have been ineffective when used alone to tackle the diverse range of environmental and social pressures. With their multinational scope, businesses are often more powerful than government agencies. It is becoming evident that policies made without input from business are unlikely to deliver the benefits desired. Responsible businesses, thus, are increasingly being invited to the policy table to hone initiatives and government targets. In some instances, they have abused this power. Less publicised are the occasions on which businesses proactively influence public policy to deliver positive environmental or social outcomes. Examples include initiatives to introduce voluntary taxation systems to ensure that communities are remunerated for use of resources (see for example, the initiatives by Pepsi-Co and Puma).

Some hospitality businesses are now operating well in advance of regulation. On occasion the associations that represent hospitality businesses have been an essential conduit, helping policy makers to formulate a policy framework within which responsible business can flourish. All too often, however, they have lobbied against any reforms that deliver environmental or social good. While it is essential that these organisations focus on supporting business profitability, there is also a need for more visionary approaches to maintain the leadership role of the sector as one that can lead the transition towards a more sustainable economy that supports economic, environmental and social improvements.

For more information on this principle, we would suggest that you review websites of some of the inter-governmental organisations (such as the United Nations Environment Programme) and the organisations that lobby for a supportive responsible business framework such as the International Tourism Partnership.

Operate fairly and transparently

Principle 8 – Define responsible business values and communicate good practice

Few would argue with the essence of this principle. It implies the need for businesses to define what responsible business means for them, to ensure that this definition is communicated to all managers, to employ the tools and techniques to ensure that all units are able to meet their responsible business commitments and communicate good practice.

This principle has been heartily embraced by most sectors, including hospitality, in spirit at least. There are, however, some difficulties when interpreting it, not least in defining business values and communicating genuinely good practice across the range of responsible business issues. To date, the blinkered definitions of responsible business and the tendency for some award schemes to reward mediocre progress on individual environmental issues has hindered real progress.

For more information on this principle, we would suggest that you view the many award schemes that have emerged to recognise good practice in the sector. These include the Virgin Holidays Responsible Tourism Awards, the Footprint Awards and national schemes, such as the sustainability category of the Cateys in the UK.

Principle 9 – Build trust through transparency

This is perhaps the most complex of all of the principles and one that is particularly hotly debated. It is through greater transparency that businesses are able to access the benefits of enhanced customer trust and greater brand value (two of the assets frequently associated with responsible business programmes). As the 21st century progresses there can be little doubt that secrets will be ever harder to keep. Those with a political aversion to the business model of the global corporation (there are many) have made them a specific target for actively seeking out news of unethical practices. Businesses that have ignored the warning signs and laid claims to responsible business practices that cannot be substantiated in every detail have in many instances seen the value of their balance sheets drop (albeit only temporarily), investor confidence waiver, customers abandon the brand and observed their names in the media for all the wrong reasons. These warning signs have made many a chief executive wary of making information about the responsible business operation available to anyone. But those with an eye on the future see an increase in transparency especially around the issues of reporting on responsible business practice, the treatment of suppliers[14] and employees as a key trend.

---

14 Companies in food retail have adopted considerable criticism for their lack of transparency about their dealing with suppliers. See http://www.tescopoly.org/ for a demonstration.

> ## Text box 4: The Internet, an unstoppable force
>
> As at 2011, nearly 2 billion people have access to the Internet (www.internetworldstats.com/stats.htm) – that is almost 1 in 3 of us. With 420 million users, the number of people with access to the Internet in China alone is almost as large as within the whole of Europe. Internet usage is booming in developing countries as populations eschew fixed telephone lines for hand-held devices that provide greater functionality – including easy and cheap access to Internet and SMS texting services. Social networks – accessed via these devices – have huge influence. Facebook alone has more than 750 million active users – making it the largest single 'population' outside India and China (www.worldatlas.com). These hand-held devices provide a vital weapon for any organisation seeking to discredit the actions of one or a group of companies. Through them, the discontent can organise activists and demonstrations in real time and can easily outflank and out manoeuvre even the most sophisticated corporate PR machine that takes days rather than hours to react. It is the power of the Internet – and the willingness of groups such as Corporatewatch, Greenpeace and AVAAZ to use it – combined with the investment of so many companies in brand-value that makes transparency so vital for the modern organisation.

The increased fashion for scrutiny of responsible business claims will – without a shadow of a doubt – mean that businesses that ignore the warning signs and lay claim to practices that they do not preach, will be exposed. In this chapter, we examine the extent to which hospitality businesses have engaged with growing demands for transparency through the reports and exhortations they make.

Those with a fascination for transparency and its relationship to responsible business are recommended to read Tapscott and Tiscoll's book *The Naked Corporation*, the website of the Global Reporting Initiative (www.globalreporting.org/Home) or that of think tank Sustainability (www.sustainability.com).

Principle 10 – Take responsible business to the heart of the company

Organisations that are keen to benefit from enhanced customer trust and improved brand value often claim that responsible business in their DNA. If it is, then sadly, it is usually buried in a tiny element of the nucleotides! Those businesses that have really embraced responsible business in its true sense have made it a core part of the mission, vision and products of the entity, rather than an 'add on' component. The difference between an organisation that has responsible business principles at its core and one that has a responsible business (CSR, ethical or whatever else they choose to call it) as an add-on department is considerable.

In the former, the responsible business values and principles drive the entire ethos of the organisation. New products that are unsustainable or unethical will not even get off the drawing board. All staff will be engaged in the responsible business programme. Any supplies purchased will be vetted to ensure that they meet the businesses criteria. Responsible business priorities will be embedded into brand value and mission statements and targets. Regulatory compliance will be guaranteed and customers will convert to the product because it is ethical, reliable, probably perceived as of better quality and trustworthy.

In the latter, responsible business issues are often designated to one or more individuals who are charged with tracking and reporting on corporate performance indicators, ensuring compliance with regulations and implementing eco-efficiency procedures. For companies with this type of responsible business initiative, new product development opportunities will often be developed with little reference to responsible business criteria and may – on occasion – emerge into the marketplace at the cost of the company's reputation. Oil companies have particularly been victims of this trend. BP, for example, has attracted criticism from CorporateWatch among others about the apparent mismatch between brand positioning and responsible business credentials (Fauset, 2006).

The essence of this principle is accepted by only a tiny proportion of global businesses. For many of these, the responsible business journey has been transformative. Among them are a handful of hospitality businesses (most small and independent) although a few global players may also lay claim to being placed in this category.

For more information on this principle, we would suggest that you read Jeffrey Hollender's book *The Responsibility Revolution: How The Next Generation Of Businesses Will Win,* or JP Bergkvist's *Sustainability in Practice.*

Degrees of responsibility?

Many businesses – including hospitality businesses – are likely to be implementing some of these principles, but few will be implementing all in their entirety. This is no surprise. Responsible business is a journey and for many organisations it is one that has only just started. Within this journey, there are key milestones that take a business from doing little or nothing to operating responsibly. The milestones have been described by Hollins (n.d.) and are discussed below:

♦ **Businesses that have yet to introduce any initiatives to reduce their impact on society and the environment**. In many instances these businesses will deny or be unaware of the reasons they should become more responsible or of the type of initiatives they should implement. Many will have poor procedures in other parts of the business. Many will (probably inadvertently) fall foul of the law even if they do not get caught.

In truth, most businesses probably fall into this category and they will, in all likelihood, not be implementing any of the Principles of Responsible Business.

♦ **Businesses that do responsible things.** These businesses usually comply with national laws and seek to operate with a minimum of harm to the environment and society. These are the businesses that implement eco-efficiency practices and may also have a small number of corporate philanthropy programmes.

- **Businesses that operate responsibly.** These businesses usually have a number of initiatives that address environmental and social impacts. These programmes will seek not only to ameliorate harm, but crucially, to deliver good. For these companies responsible business initiatives will extend beyond the immediate boundaries of the organisation to address supply chain impacts and customer engagement. These businesses usually have a 'department' for CSR or responsible business issues. Typically this 'department' will have limited influence on the core activities of the business.

- **Businesses that do responsible things responsibly.** This category includes only that tiny proportion of businesses that have really taken responsible business to their core. It is these businesses that are striving to become a part of the solution to the global environmental and economic issues discussed in the Introduction. For these businesses, responsible business considerations are at the heart of the company, they influence investment and product decisions and all other aspects of the operation. Responsible business priorities permeate all operating units (through, for example, integration into brand standards) and are implemented with the same rigour as health and safety, risk management and other business procedures. Other authors have called the businesses in this category 'transformational' and this is a term that we also use in this text. It is these businesses that are reviewing their products and processes in the light of the range of global challenges. In essence, they are taking steps to ensure that they are producing the right products, using the right processes, from the right materials, in the right place, at the right scale and using the right business models.

Businesses in this category will be implementing principles 1–10 from the above list. In the words of Mihaly Csikszentmihalyi,[15] the businesses that fall into this category rarely view themselves as 'profit-making machines whose only reason for existing is to satisfy escalating expectation for immediate gain'. They view their purpose as 'entailing responsibility for the welfare of the wider [global and local] community', whilst operating profitable and successful enterprises.

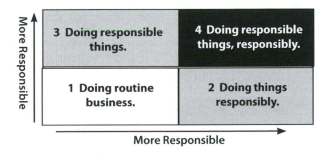

Figure 6: Doing good – business attitudes towards responsibility. Adapted from Hollins (n.d.)

---

15 Former Head of the Department of Psychology at the University of Chicago, widely acknowledged for his work in the fields of happiness and creativity.

Some may question whether the journey towards responsible business practices is in the interests of businesses, consumers and products. A recent survey by Edelman, however, found that consumers are increasingly expecting the companies that they use to have embraced all of the ten principles of Responsible Business. 'A full eighty percent [of Americans] feel that corporations are in a uniquely powerful position to make a positive impact on good causes. Nearly two-thirds (62 percent) feel that it is no longer enough for corporations to simply give money away to good causes, they need to integrate them into their day-to-day business' (Edelman, 2010). Other opinion formers would appear to agree. Trendwatching, for example, found that '86% of global consumers believe that business needs to place at least equal weight on society's interests as on business' interests'.

Consumers distrust company claims

While the volume of green products available to US consumers increased by 73% between 2009 and 2010, only 5% of products were not found to include some 'green-washing' claims.

(Terrachoice, October 2010)

For those businesses that use eco-efficiency, philanthropy or cause-related marketing to demonstrate their social conscience, the writing is on the wall. Good business means the integration of responsible business principles into the company, rather than using philanthropy to salve corporate souls. And the public are becoming increasingly canny and untrusting of pretenders.

The next chapter will focus specifically on the hospitality sector and examine the reasons that it is embracing the responsible business message. Subsequent chapters will review the sector's progress in implementing each of the 10 principles of responsible business.

References

Beauchamp, T. L. and Bowie, N.E. (2001) *Ethical Theory and Business*, Prentice Hall

Brundtland Commission (1987) *Our Common Future*, Oxford University Press

Clulow (2005) 'Future dilemmas for marketers: can stakeholder analysis add value?', in *European Journal of Marketing*, **39**(9-10), 978-997

Fauset, C. (2006) 'What's wrong with corporate social responsibility', CorporateWatch

Freeman, R. E. (1984) *Strategic Management: A Stakeholder Approach*, HarperCollins

Getz and Timur (2005) *Stakeholder involvement in sustainable tourism: balancing the voices*. In W.F. Theobald (Eds.) *Global Tourism*, 3rd edition (pp 230-247), London: Elsevier.

Gleckman (2004) 'Balancing TNCs, the States, and the International System in Global Environmental Governance: A Critical Perspective', in N. Kanie and P.M. Haas (eds), *Emerging Forces in Environmental Governance*, Tokyo/New York: United Nations University Press, pp. 203-15.

Hollands, R. (2008) *An Audit Framework for Corporate Social Responsibility* A presentation made to CATS, University of Warwick, available from www.cipfa.org.uk

Jackson, T. (2008) *Prosperity Without Growth*, Sustainable Development Commission.

Markwick (2005) in Sonia Dickinson-Delaporte, Michael Beverland, Adam Lindgreen, (2010) 'Building corporate reputation with stakeholders: Exploring the role of message ambiguity for social marketers', *European Journal of Marketing*, **44** (11/12), 1856 - 1870

Moir, L. (2001) 'What do we mean by corporate social responsibility?', *Corporate Governance*, **1**(2)

Mullins, L.J. (2010) *Management and Organisational Behaviour*. 9th edn, FT Prentice Hall

SDC (Sustainable Development Commission) (2006) *I Will if You Will*, London: SDC.

Terrachoice (2010) *The Sins of Greenwashing – Home and Family Edition*. http://www.sinsofgreenwashing.org.

Tapscott, D. and Tiscoll, D. (2003) *The Naked Corporation*, Free Press

World Business Council for Sustainable Development, 2007, *The Business Case for Sustainable Development*, WBCSD, Geneva

4 | Good in the context of hospitality

Hotels, airlines, tour operators and others are engaging in a variety of activities that would have been unheard of ten years ago. As travellers seek out more unique experiences, pioneering companies are trailblazing new practices for the entire industry. The glimmers of the future of tourism are evident in this work.

Michael Seltzer, Director, Business Enterprises for Sustainable Tourism, quoted in *Corporate Social Leadership in Travel & Tourism* (WTTC, 2002)

The hospitality sector was a relative latecomer to the concept of responsible business. Nevertheless a number of hospitality businesses, including many global corporations, now claim to operate according to its principles (see Text box 5). Most of these businesses have at the very least engaged executives with dedicated roles to implement responsible business programmes. Some have gone further and host training programmes to engage employees in the implementation of responsible business strategies, have reviewed their supplier registers to ensure that their supply chain practices match their own responsible business criteria, and/or have developed 'eco' brands with clear environmental and/or social associations. A handful claim that responsible business is embedded into the core of their business (or their corporate DNA) and one or two would claim to have integrated a responsible business dimension into all business decisions.

What has been achieved by some hospitality companies is impressive. It would, however, be misleading to claim that all hospitality businesses that claim to be operating responsibly are doing so, or even that the corporate companies that have adopted responsible business practices (usually with highly motivated and passionate responsible business managers) are able to implement them to a consistent standard throughout all units. There are undoubtedly some real champions of responsible business, many of which are referenced in the chapters that follow. Even those businesses that are champions often realise that the responsible business journey is a long one and that it is difficult to take every business unit in all locations along on that journey.

When one takes a look at practices worldwide it is likely that the vast majority of hospitality businesses have done little to respond to the full breadth of issues embraced by the responsible business agenda. In fact, many of those that claim to be operating responsibly have done little more than implement a handful of eco-efficiency practices, most of which provide pay-back periods of less than five years. While eco-efficiency initiatives are important, one has to question whether they represent the sea change in practices that is required to address the range of social, environmental and economic issues that are referenced in the Introduction.

Text box 5: Responsible business in the hospitality sector

The Rezidor approach

'Our ambition is to be a good company to work for, stay with and invest in. This means that we take our commitment to being a responsible business seriously: taking responsibility for the Health & Safety of guests and employees, respecting social and ethical issues in the company and the community and minimizing our environmental footprint.'

The IHG approach

'Corporate Responsibility is integral to the way we conduct our business and sits at the heart of our strategy. As well as helping us to create value for IHG and build competitive advantage, acting responsibly plays a key role in our efforts to manage costs and drive revenue more effectively.'

Scandic's vision

'We want to be a source of inspiration for conscious people and we want to help to make a better world. We can provide the inspiration by making guests aware of simple, sustainable solutions that they can put into practice at work and at home. We believe that people are going to become increasingly conscious of the choices they make – and we want those conscious people to opt for Scandic because we are a good choice in every way – economically, socially and environmentally. They know what we stand for and share our values.

Omtanke (care and consideration for others) has been an important value for Scandic. Omtanke in how we relate to others and in how we relate to the world around us.'

The Baxter Storey approach

'After keeping you healthy we also like to keep the planet healthy too. We have a huge respect for the produce we work with and are committed to driving forward new and innovative environmental schemes that will help protect those resources.

We are currently the only company in our sector to have invested in a dedicated specialist responsible for developing environmental management schemes – for our business and those of our clients. '

The Pret-a-Manger strategy

'We don't believe in long-winded 'eco' policies that simply don't ring true. This is our Sustainability Strategy; it explains what we actually do at Pret rather than just what we'd like to. We looked at each part of Pret that affects the environment and drew up a list of our priorities and, more importantly, what we're doing about them. '

Within accommodation establishments at least, the importance of protecting the environment and community assets of destinations has long since been accepted (see, for example, early works by Krippendorf, Butler and Young). This acceptance came alongside a realisation that accommodation businesses (in leisure tourism destinations at least) are dependent on the quality of the environment, culture and communities in which they are located for their success. Within the food service sector, the impetus has been rather more recent and has its origins in the issues of food price rises, food security and health. Figure 7 provides an illustration of the context for responsible hospitality from the 1970s (when business first began introducing energy efficiency programmes) to the present day.

1970	Oil crisis – energy efficiency in businesses
	Manila Declaration on World Tourism (1980)
1987	Brundtland Report coins the term 'sustainable development'
1989	Publication of energy-efficiency guidance for managers by Trusthouse Forte Hotels
1989	Publication of *IHG Environmental Reference Manual*
1993	Formation of World Travel & Tourism Council's Environment Research Centre
1992	Reporting criteria for tour operators issues by UN GRI
1992	Rio UNCED
1992	IH&RA host environmental meeting in Stockholm
1993	Formation of IHEI
1994	UN Food Security initiative launched
1995	Lanzarote Charter for Sustainable Tourism
1996	Publication first environmental report by hotel business
1996	Agenda 21 for Travel & Tourism
1996	First certification scheme to recognise environmental good practice by accommodation businesses launched (Green Globe)
1999	Criteria for Nordic Swan label for accommodation developed
2001	Publication of *Canadian Pacific Hotels and Resorts Green Partnership Guide*
2001	Compass Environmental Handbook Published
2002	Cape Town Declaration on Responsible Tourism
2003	Djerba Declaration on Climate Change and Tourism launched
2003	Criteria for EU Flower label for tourist accommodation established
2007	Davos Declaration on Tourism and Climate Change
2008	Kerala Declaration
2009	Global sustainable tourism criteria published

Increase in environmental awareness

Figure 7: The emergence of responsible hospitality

For most hospitality businesses, the rationale for implementing responsible business programmes does not emerge from a moral conversion or broad based awareness of the initiatives in Figure 7. It is rather more pragmatic and rooted in the fundamentals of conventional business practices. Readers will note that there is a great deal of overlap between the reasons that hospitality businesses adopt responsible business initiatives explored below and those presented for business in general in Chapter 2.

Reasons for responsibility

Efficiency gains

One could be led to believe that the vogue for efficiency savings within hospitality businesses is a recent phenomenon inspired by the credit crunch. It is far from recent. It does, however, have its roots in an earlier economic crisis – that brought on by the OPEC oil crisis of the 1970s. As is the case for many other sectors, it was the drive for eco-efficiency that attracted many hospitality businesses to adopt environmental practices and programmes. In the late 1970s, for example, Trusthouse Forte hotels[16] had recognised the potential to deliver cost savings through energy management and issued its first energy management manual in partnership with the then UK Energy Efficiency Office. This was updated in 1989 with its Energy Monitoring and Targeting for Hotel Groups that clearly stated 'Any restaurateur or hotelier who ignores energy management may as well burn bank notes' (Forte, 1989).

Text box 6: Efficiency savings

- Inter-Continental Hotels & Resorts introduced its comprehensive energy management programme reporting a reduction in energy consumption of 27% over the period 1988–95 (Webster, 1999);

- Compass Group introduced its energy management programme in 2001 and in 2009, went further to introduce improved logistics models that could save up to 1,360,000 road miles each year (Compass Group plc, 2009);

- Hilton introduced its 'we care!' initiative in Continental Europe in 2006, providing evidence of US$16.5 million in three years (Bohdanowicz et al., 2011)

- Taj introduced the Eco Taj concept in 1998 with a wide range of savings reported for individual hotels.

Energy costs were the impetus for action because of their scale. In many hotel premises at least, energy costs are one of the highest elements of operational expenditure. For many businesses energy prices have risen sharply in recent years. In the UK, for example energy price rises of 7.2% have been experienced and further rises are expected. What started with energy has now expanded to include the issues of water, waste, logistics and supply chain management. Within all of these issues, businesses have discovered the potential for savings.

---

16 This later became Forte Hotels before being merged into a larger entity and then re-established some time later (with a different suite of properties) under the Forte brand.

Market appeal

It has become the mantra of many a responsible business executive in the sector that responsible business programmes are a precursor to gaining market share (see Text box 7). Within the business-to-business market there is incontrovertible evidence that responsible business (or environmental) programmes are a precursor to gaining contracts. When it comes to the leisure market, the picture is rather more difficult to interpret. When asked in market research surveys, there is ample evidence that consumers prefer to choose hospitality providers with good environmental and/or social credentials.[17] There has also been a significant growth in demand for responsible travel experiences (see Principle 6). There are, however, few studies that are able to explicitly demonstrate how these aspirations translate into action for the consumers of mainstream leisure hospitality products.[18] There has, however, been a long-term trend of growth in the value of specific hospitality and tourism choices that are responsible (see Cooperative Bank, 2010 for up-to-date data).

Text box 7: Responsible business requirements that must be met to secure contracts from PwC

As the UK's largest professional services firm we know PwC has significant buying power and that also brings responsibility too. We work hard to incorporate not only economic but social and environmental considerations into the purchasing decisions we make. In the current economic climate cost is important, but we will not compromise our sustainability objectives in our selection of goods or services.

Roger Reeves, Partner with responsibility for infrastructure and procurement,
PricewaterhouseCoopers

Source: www.ukmediacentre.pwc.com

Within the corporate hospitality sector it is certainly true that large corporate companies such as PWC (see Text box 8), Shell and the Cooperative Bank among others are asking the businesses that provide their hospitality services about their environmental (if not broader responsible business) credentials.

---

17 See for example the data contained in Harold Goodwin's *Taking Responsibility for Tourism*, pp. 58–64 and surveys commissioned by organisations such as the Sustainable Restaurant Association.

18 When making purchasing decisions most customers have primary criteria that must be satisfied. Once more than one business can satisfy these primary criteria, then secondary criteria come into play in the final purchase decision. Primary criteria will vary from customer to customer. They are typically purchase price, quality and location. For those committed to ethical issues or concerned about food provenance these issues may also be included within the list of primary criteria. Secondary criteria can then differentiate between two apparently similar products in the marketplace. For the majority of mainstream consumers, it is likely that ethical or environmental criteria come into play at this secondary purchasing decision stage if at all. Work by some authors, e.g. Miller et al. (2007) concluded that 'on the whole, participants did not think about the environment when making leisure and tourism choices'.

Furthermore, for those businesses such as global banking corporations or retail outlets that invite hospitality business to provide a catering function within their business premises,[19] the requirement that hospitality contractors have responsible business practices in place (or carbon management as a minimum) is becoming a core condition of contract. The motivation for this development is far from altruistic. It is in fact an extension the eco-efficiency measures already practised by many of these corporate giants. There is a clear realisation among those businesses that contract in hospitality services that effective energy, water and waste management programmes can significantly reduce the costs of hosting the catering facility. More corporate businesses that contract in hospitality services are also making the link between – for example – the integration of fair trade beverage products – and the values that staff and visitors associate with their own brand (see Text box 8).

Text box 8: Customer demand driving sustainability credentials – what hospitality businesses say

Caterers unable to demonstrate a clear sustainability policy will not make it past the first stage.

(Phil Roker, Vacherin)

Potential clients are very keen on seeing prospective catering partners having sustainability high on their priority list, which is only good news for business success.

(Caroline Fry, Charlton House)

If we just comply with what expectations are, we will be fine but won't have any competitive advantage … if we go that extra mile, people notice and that gives us an advantage.

(David James, Bartlett Mitchell)

Source: British Hospitality Association (2010)

Responsible business practices are also becoming a precursor to winning contracts for those organisations that operate in some areas of the public sector in some countries. In the UK, for example, the Government introduced a Public Sector Food Procurement Initiative (PSFPI) that requires organisations serving food within specific settings (e.g. school and hospital) to reflect certain sustainability credentials (especially vis-à-vis food sourcing). Hotels within the UK also, in theory at least, have to provide evidence of carbon emission reductions to secure Government contracts.

Keeping on the right side of the law

As is the case for the responsible business movement in general, the need to keep on the right side of the law has been a particular factor pushing hospitality businesses

---

19 One of the largest segments of the global hospitality market is providing catering services within a broader business or industry unit. This is known in the jargon as Business and Industry catering. The demands for demonstrable evidence of responsible business practices are particularly well developed in this marketplace.

to adopt responsible practices. The move by regulators away from systems that seek to catch and penalise polluters and towards regulations that tax the use of resources has already caught some hospitality businesses out. In the UK, PWC estimate that in the worst-case scenario, one such scheme – the CRC Energy Efficiency Scheme that applies to the UK – could increase energy costs in the sector by 20% by 2015 (PWC, 2009) and the costs of waste disposal over the period 2009 and 2014 could double (albeit from a small base).

Within Europe, the USA and Australia, emission trading schemes for carbon have all been proposed. And while some are floundering under the cloud of recession it seems likely that the trend to tax polluters at source is one that will not blow over. Hospitality business have found from experience that it is much more cost-effective to act in advance of regulation rather than react to it.

Community spirits

Businesses in the hospitality sector have become increasingly aware that their licence to operate can be revoked by resistant communities. Businesses in the QSR sector and some hotel companies have, on occasion, been unable to gain the planning permissions they desire because of perceptions (true or otherwise) about their business model. In other countries, communities are able to boycott developments with which they disagree or gain media footage that can deter customers.

In response, companies such as Sandals have developed extensive programmes to work with communities and also ensure that a high proportion of employees are drawn from the local community (see Text box 9).

Text box 9: Sandals initiatives in the community

Sandals Resorts International launched its philanthropic arm, The Sandals Foundation on 18 March 2009. This foundation was launched in order to bring the three decades of charity work that the company had been doing throughout the region under one umbrella.

One of the most significant achievements is the Sandals partnership with Great Shape Inc., which has expanded beyond the Thousand Smiles Program to include training and other programmes. The Thousand Smiles Program ensures that around 15,000 Jamaicans each year get access to affordable dentist treatments.

Source: www.gsjamaica.org, accessed 8 August 2011

As is so often the case, it is the businesses that have experienced the greatest community resistance that often have the most evident responsible business programmes. McDonald's, for example, has introduced a wide range of environmental and community initiatives within a comprehensive responsible business programme that is rated in many of the sustainability indexes. These include the green branded restaurants outlets in France that utilise only energy from renewable sources. Other

QSR businesses such as Max Hamburgers have also responded to negative perceptions about fast food meals by providing a transparent declaration of the carbon dioxide emissions associated with different burgers, thus promoting vegetarian choices.

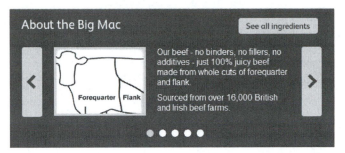

Figure 8: McDonald's keep responsible sourcing at the forefront of customers' minds

Building resilient businesses

The energy price rises of 2007/08 changed the way in which many hospitality businesses viewed their responsible business initiatives. Initially, many businesses had placed 'environmental issues' under the sole remit of technical or operational managers. The energy price rises have combined with an increased threat of taxation and climate change to encourage some business to also focus risk management strategies on these issues. For these businesses, the watchword is resilience. And for a sector where – in Europe at least – 60% of hotel capacity lies in the coastal zone with variable flood risks (www.deduce.eu/IFS/IFS14.pdf) – there is an urgent need to build this resilience.

Motivated staff required

Hospitality competes in a global marketplace for employees. The industry is dogged with very high levels of staff turnover (turnover rates of more than 100% are not uncommon for some posts in some countries) and is acutely aware of the costs associated with a failure to retain staff. A very small number of enlightened companies have realised that good responsible business programmes can both increase the appeal of their business to motivated and skilled staff and can help improve retention of existing staff. If the findings of the PWC research into Generation Y hold true (see Chapter 2) this factor is likely to become more influential globally.

IFC Policy and Performance Standards on Social & Environmental Sustainability and Policy on Disclosure of Information

New, Better and Expanded Standards

The Performance Standards are a major step forward in strengthening all aspects of IFC's social and environmental policies:

▶ **New standards.**

Integrated Assessment and Management Systems: a new standard integrates social and environmental assessments and requires use of management systems to ensure effective performance in these areas throughout a project's life

Labor Rights: a new standard addresses all four core ILO labor standards (forced labor, child labor, nondiscrimination, and freedom of association and collective bargaining) and requires a comprehensive approach to labor and working conditions.

Community Health and Safety: a new standard requires firms to consider a project's effects on health and safety in the surrounding community beyond the project itself.

Pollution Prevention and Abatement: a new standard requires clients to prevent or minimize pollution and its impact on the environment and quantify a project's greenhouse gas emissions.

▶ **Expanded social review.** Integrated social and environmental assessment means that the performance standards now encompass all vulnerable groups and related social issues, while continuing to put special attention on the complexity of involuntary resettlement, Indigenous Peoples and cultural heritage. It also includes:

Human Rights. IFC now references human rights and incorporates key concerns including adequate housing, security of tenure, and voluntary princples on security into its performance standards.

▶ **Increased community engagement.** IFC requires early and informed community participation in developing a project and ongoing community engagement throughout a project's life cycle. Related new requirements:

Broad community support. IFC must be satisfied that this is in place before it supports large projects with significant impacts.

A grievance mechanism must be established by the community to address any community concerns.

▶ **New comprehensive approach to biodiversity.** IFC is expanding its focus beyond preservation of natural habitats to a broader view of protection and conservation of biodiversity.

Habitat destruction and *invasive alien species* are recognized as the major threats to biodiversity, and the standard specifies how to address them in natural and modified habitats.

Sustainable management of all renewable natural resources is required, to be demonstrated by *independent certification* in sectors such as forestry.

Policy Highlights

The Sustainability Policy & Performance Standards and Disclosure Policy support and reflect IFC's commitment to sustainability. They introduce:

▶ **New, better, and broader standards** that strengthen IFC policies to protect people and the environment, engage communities, and achieve high-impact development.

▶ **A new, outcomes-based approach** that moves from a system of rules to a system of principles with clear requirements for client performance and project outcomes.

▶ **Greater transparency** through more disclosure of information to the public.

▶ **Clarity, by better defining roles** and responsibilities in a clear, concise and comprehensive way for IFC and its private sector clients, thus increasing accountability.

For more information, visit the Environment & Social website: http://www.ifc.org/EnvSocStandards

IFC
International
Finance
Corporation
World Bank Group

Figure 9: Social and environmental criteria integrated into IFC Investment Decisions

Source: www.ifc.org/ifcext/sustainability.nsf/AttachmentsByTitle/pr_PolicyReviewFactSheet/$FILE/FactSheet.pdf

Employee attitudes to the environment

> *… if an employee genuinely cares about the environment and pays attention to green issues (believing, for instance, that the problem of climate change, as a man-made phenomenon, needs to be effectively tackled), he will be more likely to identify himself with – and, accordingly, to be more committed to – a company that explicitly makes broadly-understood ecofriendliness an integral part of its corporate philosophy. That is why such a company will not only be well-positioned to retain and motivate 'green-sensitive' employees, but, critically, to attract and recruit such individuals. And, indeed, more and more university graduates do not want to work for companies that, in their eyes, do not care for the environment (being, for example, big greenhouse gas emitters) and/or fail to do enough to promote environmental sustainability. It follows that, while recruiting, an organization that embraces CSR-inspired environmentalism – being thereby perceived as an attractive employer – might have an edge over other (less green) companies.*

> *(Bohdanowicz and Zientara, 2008)*

Canny investors

Like most global businesses, the hospitality sector is largely dependent on external investors for its prosperity. This is especially the case as leasehold modes of ownership have grown. Powerful investors have introduced some interesting challenges for the responsible business model. On the one hand, there are a hard core of investors that pursue development at any cost. While on the other, there are investors – including the International Finance Corporation (the investment arm of the World Bank) that has invested around US$2 billion in hotel projects since its establishment in 1956 – that impose sustainability criteria on new investment decisions (see Figure 9).

Hospitality businesses – playing a vital role in reducing global environmental impacts

It is predicted that the hospitality sector will double in size by the year 2025 (www.tourismpartnership.org/Publications/SDCGuidelines.html). This is because there is a strong link between the market for hospitality services and the relative affluence of the population and the number of 'middle-class' consumers. Goldman Sachs expects the number of middle class consumers to triple by 2030 (see Figure 10). Specific areas that are likely to experience growth are China where there are expected to be 220 million middle-income consumer households by 2025 (approximately four times as many as there were in 2004).

Hospitality businesses generally view this trend as good news – driving the growth in demand. As competition for land and resources intensifies, however, it will be more important than ever that hospitality businesses are able to operate responsibly to deliver benefits to the local and global community. To fail to do so would be to risk the image of the industry as one that has powerful potential to 'do good'. If this image is compromised communities and government agencies in some areas may revoke its licence to operate freely, pushing prices up and restricting development. Those who doubt the severity of backlash against businesses that are perceived to 'do bad' would do well to view the difficulties and costs oil companies experience in some countries when seeking development permits.[20]

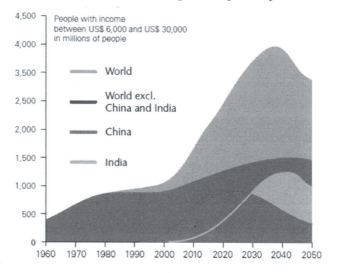

Figure 10: Growth depends on the burgeoning middle class
Source: World Business Council for Sustainable Development (2008: 8) quoting Goldman Sachs (2008).

Many authors have documented the potential for hospitality businesses to do good (see for example, International Tourism Partnership, International Finance Corporation). These organisations demonstrate how the activities of the sector provide positive benefits for local communities, stimulate the market for fair trade products, provide an incentive for environmental protection, provide local development opportunities, stimulate markets for agricultural products, in some instances provide power and fresh water to communities and so on.[21] Equally powerful examples exist of instances in which hospitality businesses have acted as agents of negative change, damaging natural environments, depleting water resources, exploiting farmers, encouraging unsustainable farming methods, employing poor animal welfare standards or 'exporting' profit to head office locations, etc. These are documented by organisations such as Tourism Concern (www.tourismconcern.org.uk) or more radically in the case of very large companies, social networks such as AVAAZ and

---

20 Perhaps it is timely at this juncture to remind readers that some organisations – including WWF – believe that the food industry will soon be viewed in the same light as the oil industry (see Kleanthous, 2010).

21 To view some of these examples, we would recommend that you visit websites such as the BEST network (http://www.besteducationnetwork.org/) or consult publications such as Green Hotelier, Cost Sector Caterer and Foodservice Footprint.

Corporatewatch (www.corporatewatch.org.uk). Figure 11 demonstrates the main inputs and impacts associated with hospitality businesses.

Regardless of whether large or small, privately owned or part of a global organisation, all hospitality businesses have the potential to be significant agents of change (positive and negative) within the local and global environment. The crucial ingredient that makes a hospitality business a positive agent of change is not – as many critics would claim – the type of business. It is its management ethos.

For example, a hospitality outlet (whether a hotel, café, restaurant or bar) owned by an international company may be welcomed by local people because of its potential to:

♦ Provide a marketplace for local food producers

♦ Provide much needed employment opportunities to keep young people within the community

♦ Provide educational outreach programmes to help local people develop careers within the hospitality sector

♦ Offer recreational/leisure opportunities to local people at affordable or no cost

♦ Provide new business opportunities for local entrepreneurs seeking to establish cafes, restaurants or retail outlets alongside the new development

♦ Provide an economic incentive for the local council to invest in the development of a renewable energy plant, rail and other infrastructure to the area and so on.

That same hospitality business, however, may be despised because it:

♦ Takes land away from local people and causes house prices in the area to rise

♦ Provides menial jobs for local people with few opportunities for career enhancement

♦ Buys up local agricultural products, increasing prices for local people

♦ Exacerbates wildlife depletion by providing a market for – for example – local fish thus encouraging blast or cyanide fishing methods

♦ Uses scarce water resources that would otherwise be available to local people

♦ Brings congestion into the area

♦ Brings people with values that sharply contrast with existing residents (or other customers).

In both instances, the new development will have environmental and social impacts. The management ethos in the former, however, ensures that the issues of social justice, human dignity and environmental protection are employed, where in the latter these issues are ignored. Those businesses that have taken responsible business principles to their core, as a general rule, will be the positive agents of change.

The scale of hospitality impacts

There is broad-based agreement about the range of impacts associated with hospitality businesses (see Figure 11). At a global level, however, it is difficult to provide an assessment of the magnitude of those impacts.

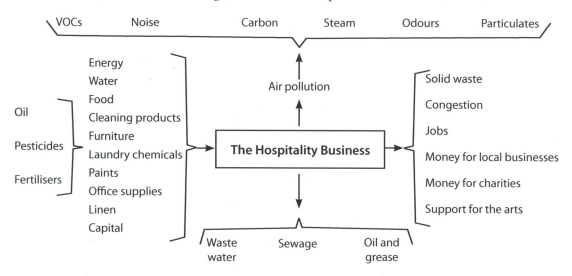

Figure 11: The main inputs and impacts of hospitality businesses

The data that is available points to a growing level of impact across a range of issues:

- Carbon emissions of the travel and tourism sector equate to around 5% of total global emissions (Chiesa and Gautam, 2009). Around 2% of this is directly related to aviation. The remaining 3% is allocated to all other tourism-related activities of which hospitality is likely to be the most substantial component. The level of emissions from the sector, therefore, is in all likelihood on a par with small European countries like Italy and the United Kingdom. Moreover, accommodation carbon emissions are forecast to grow at 3.2% per year, reaching 728 million tons by 2035 (Chiesa and Gautam, 2009); an estimated increase of 156% by 2035.

- Water is the most important resource for hospitality businesses. Within hotels at least, tourists visiting developing countries can consume up to ten times more water on a daily basis than local inhabitants (Genot *et al.*, 2001). The volume of water consumed within hospitality businesses globally varies significantly. In the UK, the hospitality sector is estimated to consume around 2% of water consumed via the public water supply (Envirowise, 2009). Global figures are not available. Given that most fresh water is discharged as waste water (around 95% in establishments that do not have a treatment plant that recirculates cleaned water for a second purpose), the sector also makes a significant contribution to waste water. Contamination by food and grease can make waste water from the sector particularly costly to treat – and is a significant health hazard in countries where the public infrastructure for waste water treatment is inefficient.

♦ It is not possible to provide a global estimate of the volume or weight of waste originating from hospitality businesses. In the UK, it is estimated that the profit sector alone disposes of around 3.4 million tonnes of waste per annum, of which just under half is currently recycled and the rest sent to landfill (WRAP, 2011). Disposing of wastes to landfill represents a waste of resources[22] and these wastes are a significant producer of methane – one of the most potent gases implicated in climate change. Waste is often considered as less important than programmes to reduce energy or water consumption. This is probably because waste is perceived of as cheap to dispose of (in some countries it can be free) and waste disposal and especially formal recycling options are very limited in some countries. However the real costs of waste lie not in the disposal costs alone but in the whole life costs (these include, for example, freezing, thawing and cooking foods that are later disposed of). According to Envirowise (now part of WRAP), when these costs are added in, waste can account for as much as 4% of turnover (http://envirowise. wrap.org.uk/uk/Business-benefits-from-reducing-waste.html);

♦ It is also not possible to provide an estimate of the range of chemicals that result from the sector's direct and indirect activities. However, hospitality businesses with grounds use a wide range of chemicals to maintain them, hygiene standards require chemical cleaning of kitchen facilities and foods that are produced using intensive farming methods will inevitably have had some chemical input over their lifespan.

Hospitality businesses also have an impact on a range of other global environmental issues, but these are largely unquantifiable. For example, they are significant consumers of refrigerant gasses (implicated in the depletion of the ozone layer), consume large volumes of global agricultural products, utilise large numbers of hazardous materials and so on. Data about the social impacts is of hospitality businesses is especially poor (see, for example, Houdré, 2008; Levy and Duverger, 2010) and the full implications of, for example, supply chain decisions for small farming communities remain elusive.

A word on statistics

Statistics about the hospitality sector in general are very poor. Many businesses operating within the sector are small or very small (most hospitality businesses globally are classified as small and medium enterprises[23] and a large proportion of these are

---

22 In some countries waste disposal sites are 'mined' to reclaim the raw materials they contain.

23 Definitions of SMEs vary by country. However, companies with fewer than 50 employees are generally defined as 'small', and those with fewer than 250 as 'medium'.

micro enterprises[24]). Many of the very small business will not be operating within the formal economy and are, thus, not recorded in official statistics.[25] This fact, in combination with the large number of businesses in this sector that are transient, results in a wide range of estimates of the total number of operating units within hospitality. This situation is compounded by relatively high failure rates in the sector. This means that global estimates of the number of businesses cannot be relied on over time. For example, in the UK one study uncovered the fact that two out of every three restaurants close within two years of opening (BBC, 2004) and another reported failure rates of 15% among restaurants, compared to 5% for other sectors (BBC, 2009). Pub failure rates among free houses in the UK is running at around one in every 3.5 compared to one in 13 tied businesses and one in 26 managed houses (Morning Advertiser, 2009).

The lack of good quality data about the number of hospitality units, makes the compilation of data about the scale of their impact across the responsible business agenda (or even the range of pressing environmental issues) rather difficult to come by. The estimates within this book should, therefore, be seen as just that, estimates.

Impediments to progress

Like any sector, there are those in hospitality businesses that claim that the principles of responsible businesses are not only more important to this sector but are also harder to enact. Those who make this latter claim often quote the following reasons as core impediments to progress (readers will become familiar with these as they work their way through the following chapters):

* **The dispersed nature of the industry**. Even the global giants such as McDonald's and Starbucks operate through thousands of small individual units scattered across the globe. In many cases, the units from which the industry operates are neither owned nor managed by the corporate head office. They are instead owned by individuals who operate them as their own small business (under franchise arrangements for example) or by external landlords (including on many occasions investment banks or other financial institutions). Communicating and getting the 'buy-in' to responsible business programmes by such a wide range of units across such a variety of cultures is a particular challenge for the sector.

* **The fact that the industry rarely owns and operates its own buildings**. The growth of the lease, management contract and franchise style of operation throughout the sector (and especially among the major corporates) means that

---

24 A micro enterprise has less than 10 employees and is characterised by much smaller businesses often comprised of sole traders operating, for example a roadside cafe.

25 For example, many bed and breakfast establishments operate as lifestyle choices, are seasonal, are not registered with a regional tourist board, are not members of any professional or trade associations and are not registered for local taxes. For obvious reasons the precise number of these businesses cannot be quantified (they are in the invisible economy).

hospitality businesses rarely are able to dictate the location, scale or energy efficient requirements of the building into which they operate let alone the nature of technologies available to reduce environmental impacts.

♦ **The relatively small number of employees in each unit** and the lack of exposure to potentially hazardous working environments. While the sector is a considerable global employer, employees are widely dispersed in thousands of small units. Most units employ only a handful of individuals and so fall under the radar for many of the third sector organisations that seek to name those global companies that fail to implement good standards of employment. Training such a large workforce in such a wide range of environments is both challenging and expensive. High levels of staff turnover compound this issue and provide significant difficulties for any organisation wishing to standardise practices in such an ill-defined area as that of responsible business.

♦ **Its limited resource consumption per unit.** While the cumulative resource consumption of the sector may be significant, the resource consumption patterns from individual units are generally small. The benefits of good resource management to small units are sometimes questioned in relation to the level of training input required to deliver results.

♦ **The sector does not usually deprive local communities of access to resources** (and on occasion can make resources such as sewerage treatment capacity available to local communities), is not a consumer of heavy chemicals or other products that have a high resource input or storage risk. As such, there is little point in embracing responsible business principles.

♦ **The sector services the local community as well as customers from further afield**. It brings its customers to its sites and, therefore, has an interest in being seen to be considerate and non-polluting. It also has been seen in some circles as an agent for over-coming cultural prejudices.

♦ **The franchise model of operation provides local people with opportunities to become entrepreneurs**. Thus the local community are often not excluded from ownership in this sector by high technical skill requirements of a lack of access to capital that so plagues other sectors.

♦ **The industry has a relatively low skill requirement and employs local people** to support its operations, even outside of the franchise businesses. To some extent, it also relies of local supply chains for fresh produce and so on, thus stimulating local economic growth. It is these factors that has made it so favoured by development agencies and urban regeneration projects.

♦ **The relative lack of clear demand from consumers for 'responsible' experiences provides little incentive** for the sector as a whole (despite the claims made in market research reports).

Does responsible hospitality mean 'good' hospitality?

In 2011, most major global corporate hospitality businesses have made a commitment of implementing at least some responsible business practices. However, the evidence from other sectors demonstrates that a commitment to a few responsible business initiatives (for example a philanthropic giving or carbon management programme) does not result in businesses playing a transformative role in society. Enron, for example, was a strong advocate of for environmental and social responsibility of businesses. However, few commentators would suggest that it acted responsibly! The crucial question is whether the initiatives taken by the leaders in the sector are sufficient to retain its reputation as a relatively low impact sector with considerable potential to 'do good'.

The following parts of this book aim to examine the extent to which responsible business policies and programmes have penetrated the business models of hospitality businesses, to review how this compares to the practices of transformative businesses and to give an overview of the adequacy of the tools that have been developed to help businesses implement responsible business programmes.

References

BBC (2004), Why cooking for a living is no picnic, news.bbc.co.uk/1/hi/business/4002659.stm

BBC (2009), Cash and Curry, http://news.bbc.co.uk/1/hi/business/7934918.stm

Bohdanowicz P., Zientara P., Novotna E. (2011), International hotel chains and environmental protection: An analysis of Hilton's *we care!* Programme (Europe, 2006-2008), *Journal of Sustainable Tourism*, **19**(7) 797-816.

Bohdanowicz, P. and Zientara, P. (2008) 'Corporate social responsibility in hospitality: issues and implications. a case study of Scandic', *Scandinavian Journal of Hospitality and Tourism*, **8** (4), 271–293.

British Hospitality Association (2010) *Food Service and Management Survey*, London: BHA.

Chiesa, T. and Gautam, A. (2009) *Travel and Tourism Climate Change Report: Working Towards a Low Carbon Travel and Tourism Sector*, World Economic Forum, available from http://www. booz.com/media/file/TT_Climate_Change_Report_Copenhagen_2009.pdf

Compass Group (2009) *Compass Group Corporate Responsibility Report*, Compass.

Cooperative Bank (2010) *Ethical Consumer Report*, Cooperative Bank, available from http://www.goodwithmoney.co.uk/ethicalconsumerismreport/

Envirowise (2009) www.envirowise.wrap.org.uk

Forte, J. (1989) *Energy Monitoring and Targeting for Hotel Groups*, London: Forte Hotels.

Genot, H, Pogson, N., François, P. and Carbone, G. (2001) *Sowing the seeds of change*, Paris: UNEP, available from http://www.unep.fr/shared/publications/pdf/2991-HospitalityIndustry.pdf

Goldman Sachs (2008), as reported in Financial Times, *"Boom time for the global bourgeoisie"*, July 15.

Goodwin, H. (2010) *Taking Responsibility for Tourism*, Oxford: Goodfellow Publishers

Hawkins, R. (2010) *The Hospitality Sector in Focus – A stakeholder Review*, report developed for the Waste and Resources Action Plan.

Houdré, H. (2008) 'Sustainable Hospitality©: sustainable development in the hotel industry', *Cornell Hospitality Industry Perspectives*, August, pp. 4–22.

ITP (2008) *Sustainable Hotel: Siting, Design and Constuction Guidelines*, London: ITP.

Kleanthous, A (2010) Eating Earth, a presentation made to the Food and Drink Innovation Network, (www.fdin.org.uk/seminars/previous-seminars-and-documentation/).

Levy, S. E. and Duverger, P. (2010) 'Consumer perceptions of sustainability in the lodging industry: examination of sustainable tourism criteria', International CHRIE Conference-Refereed Track, paper 31, available at http://scholarworks.umass.edu/refereed/CHRIE_2010/Friday/31

Miller, G., Rathouse, K., Scarles, C., Holmes, K. and Tribe, J. (2007). *Public understanding of sustainable leisure and tourism: A report to the Department for Environment, Food and Rural Affairs*. University of Surrey. Defra, London

Morning Advertiser (200), 'Failure rate highest among freehouses', www.thepublican.com/story.asp?storycode=64567

PWC (2009) 'PwC brings top suppliers together to collaborate on sustainability agenda', www.ukmediacentre.pwc.com/content/detail.aspx?releaseid=3060&newsareaid=2

PWC (2009) *Environmental Value at Risk in the Hospitality and Leisure Sector – The CRC Energy Efficiency Scheme and Landfill Tax* www.pwc.co.uk/pdf/evar_for_hospitality_and_leisure.pdf

Webster (1999) *Environmental Management in the Hospitality Industry – A guide for students and managers,* Butterworth Heinemann, Oxford.

World Business Council for Sustainable Development (2008) *Sustainable Consumption – Facts and Trends from a Business Perspective*, Geneva: WBCSD.

World Travel & Tourism Council, Earth Council and UN World Tourism Organisation (1996) *Agenda 21 for the Travel & Tourism Industry – Towards Environmentally Sustainable Development*, WTTC, Brussels.

World Travel & Tourism Council, Earth Council (2002), *Corporate Social Leadership in Travel & Tourism*, WTTC, Brussels.

WRAP (2011) *The Composition of Waste Disposed of by the UK Hospitality Industry,* Waste and Resources Action Programme, Banbury.

Part 2: The Environment

The issues that are the topic of Part 2 are familiar to most hospitality businesses. In many cases, these were the issues that put responsible business on the agenda for corporate hospitality businesses and they are most frequently the topic of corporate responsible business reports.

The principle of avoiding wasteful use of resources and protecting the environment is by far the most widely accepted of all of the principles of responsible hospitality included within the whole of this text. There is abundant information to demonstrate progress on this issue. The other principles included within this section (preparing for the unexpected and developing new products and services that make a positive contribution to environment and society) are also widely accepted as significant, but for many companies they have been more difficult to progress.

Principle 1: Avoid wasteful use of resources and protect and, where possible, improve the environment

In the past, a great deal of progress in environmentally-sensitive hotel management has been made by people who had a personal passion for the environment or saw new ways to reduce costs. Those achievements were real and important, blazing a trail for others to follow. Yet the imperative of finding new and better ways to reduce environmental impacts and above all, minimising climate change, requires a step change in all our thinking.

H.R.H. Prince Charles (International Tourism Partnership, 2008)

The concept of ensuring that emissions from companies do not adversely affect human health and/or the environment is far from new or revolutionary. It is the basis upon which many of the early anti-pollution laws in countries as far apart as Australia, America and the UK were founded. What has changed is the perception of companies towards these issues. Where once they were addressed in a bid to avoid the wrath of the regulator, they are now perceived by many international companies as providing the opportunity to reduce operating costs and protect against long-term increases in the price of resources. The hospitality sector has not been slow to recognise these synergies.

Indeed, this principle is interpreted by most hospitality businesses as a diktat to make prudent use of resources and to ensure that those assets on which hospitality businesses depend are preserved for future generations to enjoy (for those businesses that are part of the tourism experience, these include, the heritage, culture and physical environments of the destinations in which they are based). It is a principle that is accepted by almost all global hospitality businesses and against which impressive progress has been made. It was action on environmental issues that spawned the responsible hospitality debate and that firmly linked responsible business practices with enhanced profitability (a link that some commentators have subsequently come to regret). It is this principle that remains the core (and in some notable cases the only) tenet of responsible business programmes in hospitality settings.

The enthusiasm with which many hospitality businesses have embraced this issue sometimes belies the inevitable tension between the need to reduce environmental impacts/resource consumption and that to:

- Facilitate business growth (by expanding the portfolio – perhaps to include hospitality facilities that have been designed by external developers with little consideration for environmental or social impacts);

- Maximise profitability for shareholders (and especially short-term return on investment. This is a particular tension when installing technologies that have long payback periods into properties that are not owned by the business);

♦ Enhance the standard of facilities (by, for example, adding spa facilities, or providing greater capacity for choice of hot meals in restaurant outlets thus increasing resource consumption per customer served);

♦ Improve comfort levels (for example, by installing relatively energy intensive air conditioning into existing facilities).

Text box 10: Resource consumption and operating costs

There is a direct relationship between resource consumption and operating costs for nearly all hospitality businesses. In those settings where the hospitality business bears the full burden of resource costs, the drive to deliver energy, water and waste efficiencies is clearly entwined with profitability. Canny corporations have linked resource savings to performance bonuses for general managers – often with impressive results. For example:

■ Marriott reduced energy consumption by just under 13% between 2007 and 2009 with significant environmental and cost benefits (Marriott, 2010);

■ The environmental initiatives in the area of energy and water conservation and waste reduction at Scandic are estimated to have allowed savings of almost €19 million in 1997–2007 (Bohdanowicz, and Zientara, 2008,);

■ 1300 Hilton Worldwide properties recording their performance in the LightStay system conserved enough energy to power 5700 homes for a year, saved enough water to fill more than 650 Olympic-size pools and reduced carbon output equivalent to taking 34,865 cars off the road. These reductions translated into dollars saved for hotel owners, with estimated savings of more than $29 million in utility costs in 2009 (Hotel Online, 2010);

■ QSR operator McDonald's has installed energy management systems into many of its restaurants, saving around 10% of energy consumption per outlet. They have also eliminated 300 million pounds of product packaging by redesigning and reducing materials in the 1990s with significant cost and environmental benefits (www.aboutmcdonalds.com/mcd/csr/about/environmental_responsibility.html);

■ Pub chain Mitchells and Butlers reduced energy costs by 5% by rolling low energy lighting out throughout the business (*Daily Telegraph*, 21 March 2011).

In the many food service settings where business provide a catering or accommodation function within a broader business (for example, a canteen within premises owned and operated by a hospital, or a café within a retail outlet), the relationship between resource consumption and cost is indirect for energy and water use and waste production at least. Usually the costs of consumption of these resources in such settings are borne by the organisation operating the whole site. There is some evidence – within the business and industry market at least – that some clients are now seeking to pass the resource costs for the provision of hospitality services onto their hospitality provider. A few trail-blazing companies are trying to ensure clients take these steps as a core condition for hospitality businesses to function. But these cases are the exception rather than the rule. Within settings where resource consumption is not monitored and costs are not borne by the hospitality provider, there is a less obvious incentive to deliver resource efficiencies.

Many corporate hospitality businesses have had to balance these tensions, seeking to deliver resource savings whilst increasing service standards. This is not always an easy issue to negotiate in boardrooms. Shareholder return and service quality remain the primary concern for most hospitality businesses and responsible business decisions that are perceived as having potential to damage these concerns are often viewed with suspicion. This means that the focus of most environmental management initiatives within the sector has remained on the issues of energy, waste and water management over the last decade and most businesses have targeted staff initiatives to switch off equipment when not in use or installed low cost technologies to perform more-or-less the same function.

With the exception of some of the very large companies and especially the major food service businesses, the indirect impacts of activities (e.g. those associated with the construction of the building that houses the hospitality operation, those that arise through the supply chain or those that arise from customers reaching hospitality destinations) are much less frequently addressed. Nevertheless these are important impacts. In some businesses they almost certainly make a greater contribution towards global environmental change than the direct impacts associated with the operation of the business. These issues are the topics of Principles 3, 5 and 6 respectively.

Protecting the environment and making wise use of resources – what the responsible business guidelines say

This is one of the few aspects of the responsible business agenda that is governed by a myriad of national and international regulations. It is these regulations that dictate the disposal route for specific items of waste, the level of emissions of gases, etc. that is permissible within certain zones and so on. Where they are implemented, these regulations have made a significant contribution towards environmental protection and most hospitality businesses make every effort to ensure that their practices and processes comply. Within the international corporations, the mechanisms of compliance are often contained within detailed management manuals and the like.

The adoption of taxation by some governments as a mechanism to encourage businesses to make wise use of resources has added additional impetus to resource reduction strategies and focused corporate minds.

It was the issue of environmental protection and resource consumption that stimulated many of the responsible business guidelines. Indeed in the late 1980s and early 1990s most of these principles included the word 'environment' in their title and had very limited scope beyond environmental issues.

Perhaps because of the range of regulations on this issue, most of the guidelines have now moved away from focusing on environmental impacts specifically. The CERES Roadmap for Sustainable Development is among the more rigorous and it focuses on a challenging range of issues, including greenhouse gas emissions, water management and zero waste strategies. Other guidelines are less prescriptive, proposing that businesses need to set up effective systems to minimise environmental impacts and maximise efficient use of resources. As a rule the processes specified broadly match those in the Deming Cycle that lies at the base of most environmental management systems (see Appendix 2). Given the link between good environmental management and enhanced profitability, few businesses could fail to agree with the logic that is expressed in the exhortations of most of the codes of conduct.

Identifying environmental impacts

There is little debate about the range of environmental impacts associated with hospitality businesses, although the scale of these impacts is much debated (as we saw in Chapter 4). The pattern of resource consumption and environmental impacts from most hospitality businesses are more dispersed than for other industrial sectors and it is for this reason that the impacts of the sector have largely escaped the attention of pressure groups.

Three issues have dominated the environmental activities of most hospitality businesses. These are:

♦ The carbon challenge (energy consumption and carbon emissions) and to a lesser extent the depletion of oil resources

♦ The wet stuff (water consumption, pollution and waste water treatment)

♦ The throw-away culture (waste minimisation and management – including hazardous materials).

The dominant focus on the issues of energy, waste and water management is not something that is unique to hospitality businesses. A number of businesses in other sectors (many with award-winning responsible business initiatives of their own) also have a tendency to focus on them. It is important to bear in mind, however, that responsible business initiatives which aim to reduce environmental impacts only when they save the business money are often viewed with scepticism by voluntary organisations and consumers. As Hetan Shah and Martin McIvor (2007: 33) argue 'Today's capitalist system, with its focus on maximising shareholder value, has a tendency to bias economic policy away from these wider concepts and towards narrower measures of economic efficiency. Not only is this tendency destructive of the good society, it is also inefficient in the wider economic sense'. It also fails to offer the brand differentiation that most businesses anticipate from their responsible business strategy.

When reviewing reports about resource consumption from hospitality businesses, it is easy to form the opinion that total resource consumption from the sector is in decline. This is, however not the case. Some businesses have produced impressive resource savings through the introduction of comprehensive management programmes. Nevertheless, the overall resource consumption of the sector has increased.

This is especially the case for hotels. Over the last decade electricity consumption in many hotels has grown in the range of 25–30%. This increase in consumption can be attributed to the increased number of facilities, more demanding standards of accommodation (TV-sets, mini-bars, and air conditioning units in all rooms), as well as development of the operating equipment (electric heating and cooking, cold rooms, lifts and escalators, accounting, computing and control equipment). It is estimated that the demand from commercial buildings of which hotels are a part may further increase with total delivered commercial energy use among non-OECD nations growing by 2.7% per year from 2007 to 2035 (US Energy Information Administration, 2010). In some countries, this growth will be substantially higher. In China, for example, it is expected to reach 7.1% (McKinsey, 2007).

The fundamentals: reducing environmental impacts and resource consumption in the hospitality sector

The level of commitment hospitality businesses make to addressing these three issues varies significantly. Some global organisations are only just beginning to develop management strategies, whilst others now have mature programmes with complex and stretching targets. Theoretically at least, these targets apply across all business outlets owned, operated, franchised, leased and/or managed by the business.

Most corporate head offices, however, have little power to actively engage all business units in meeting their responsible business ambitions. Head office units of large international companies can set targets, provide incentives to managers and staff to achieve those targets, provide staff training materials and make cost-effective use of carefully selected technologies to support implementation of targets. A manager who is cynical about issues such as the need for energy efficiency or reducing water consumption, however, will usually fail to implement management strategies and often the business unit that s/he manages will not meet the ambitions of the company on environmental issues. When that manager is a part of a franchise unit or other entity that is associated with, but not directly owned or managed by head office, there is limited scope to impose sanctions that deliver the required changes in performance.

Add to this fact the growing trend within the sector over the last decade or so to favour leaseback[1] and franchise modes of operation (as opposed to direct ownership) and it becomes clear that the potential for large international hospitality businesses to directly influence resource consumption across their respective estates is declining. In the light of the reluctance by land lords to invest in technologies, hospitality businesses are becoming increasingly reliant on a motivated and committed pool of managers and staff to deliver on their responsible business commitments (and as we report in Principle 6, these staff are often not provided with responsible business input into their formal training courses).

Text box 11: Fairy Godmother technologies

A phrase stolen from a colleague Shaun Vorster* – although used here in a slightly different context to that originally intended. There are already in the marketplace, technologies that are the answer to every hospitality managers wishes. They reduce resource consumption and operating costs whilst also maintaining levels of service quality and meeting core health and safety and risk management criteria and improving corporate reputations. Some such as building management systems, low-energy lighting and flow restrictors for taps and showers can be installed into existing properties, others are best installed during a new build or refurbishment. Admittedly many of the technologies that really fulfil all of our desires (and especially those that provide alternative forms of energy) have longer payback periods than their conventional cousins, but they are a part of the answer to allow the sector to continue to grow and deliver economic benefits whilst reducing its carbon, water and waste footprint (if not its social one). The range of such technologies will increase hugely over the coming decades and those hospitality businesses that invest are likely to recoup multiple rewards.

* Shaun Vorster is the Special Advisor to the Minister of Tourism in South Africa. He is without a doubt one of the most passionate and effective advocates of climate change adaptation within the sector and a great believer in the potential of tourism to play a major role in the green economy.

In essence, environmental management initiatives in the area of energy, waste and water management (and responsible business ambitions) will only be achieved when they are embedded into brand standards and given equal significance to quality and service issues. The structural changes in the sector combine with the current economic situation to make this unlikely in the short term.

---

1   These arrangements have become popular with some of the major branded hotels in recent years (for example Accor and Inter-Continental Hotel Group) and are now permeating other parts of the sector. The arrangement means that major hospitality businesses lease properties from one or (more commonly) a group of external investors or manage properties that are constructed by external investors. In some instances, these properties may have previously been owned by their portfolio.

The carbon challenge

The potential implications of climate change combined with concerns about the longevity of oil supplies and the increase in energy prices that is affecting many economies, has made this issue a strategic priority for many businesses. Public and investor interest in carbon emissions – and the increasing propensity to develop 'blacklists' of organisations that fail to report on emissions – is also a key driver of this agenda (see Text box 12).

Text box 12: The significance of carbon disclosure

The Carbon Disclosure Project is one of the most significant initiatives in the field. Through it, at March 2011, a little over 3000 organisations globally measure and disclose their greenhouse gas emissions and climate change strategies. The results are used by – among others – more than 534 institutional investors, with combined assets under management of more than $64,000 billion. Few companies disclosing their carbon emissions through the index, are from the hospitality sector (for example, TUI Travel plc are currently engaged and Scandic were included in early phases of the project but are excluded from its modern iteration because they are not listed on the stock exchange)*.

Some organisations (including the magazine *Corporate Responsibility*) have now started to try to engage more businesses in the carbon agenda by establishing a 'black list' of companies that do not have procedures in place for carbon disclosure (see http://www.thecro.com/content/bad-business-crs-black-list to view a sample of this approach).

Other agencies are also getting in on the act. In 2011, for example, the UK-based Environmental Investment Organisation ranked the 100 largest companies in the UK for their greenhouse gas emissions and levels of transparency. As at 2011, this ranking includes Whitbread (ranked 25th), IHG (66th) and Compass Group (87th). Follow this link to view the full report: www.eio.org.uk/pdf/Carbon_Ranking_Report_2011.pdf. With an eye to the importance of environmental credentials to brand value, regulators are following suit. The CRC Energy Efficiency Scheme in the UK, for example, will establish a league table listing performance of all organisations that are obligated to report on performance.

* This should be kept in context. Only listed companies can become members of the Carbon Disclosure Project and so only a tiny proportion of all hospitality businesses qualify under the criteria.

Most businesses develop a range of strategies to tackle the issue of carbon. Within the hospitality sector, these fall under two broad headings:

♦ Strategies to reduce carbon emissions by implementing measures to use energy efficiently within business as usual procedures

♦ Strategies to adapt to a low carbon future.

Some businesses have adopted a third strategy and sought to become carbon neutral. Among these have been Dell (which claimed in August 2008 to have achieved carbon neutrality some months in advance of its own targets), Ryman (the stationer), Meridian Energy and interestingly enough some airlines. Most organisations have, however, found that this is a vexed path to follow. Despite the emergence of a recent British Standard and a huge array of guidance on the issue (including that from DECC that can be found at http://www.carbonretirement.com/content/how-does-deccs-carbon-neutral-guidance-affect-you), aiming for carbon neutrality can be complex. Given the level of debate around issues like carbon offsetting, the way in which carbon neutrality is achieved can mean that this route is not necessarily the best path to achieve good PR credentials. Businesses that have laid claim to carbon neutrality have implemented a number of strategies from generating 100% of the energy they consume using renewable technologies (a considerable challenge for many hospitality businesses) to purchasing carbon offsets to the equivalent value of their emissions. It is businesses that have pursued the latter path that have found themselves particularly laid open to criticism and there is significant debate both about the usefulness of carbon offsetting as a means for halting climate change *and* about the relative cost of each offset (see, for example, the joint statement by Friends of the Earth, Greenpeace and WWF on this issue www.wwf.org.uk/filelibrary/pdf/august06.pdf*).*

Companies that implement measures to reduce carbon by using energy efficiently

Businesses world wide have embraced the potential to reduce carbon emissions (and energy costs) by improving efficiency and hospitality businesses are no exception. Energy costs in hospitality businesses can be significant – accounting for between 4 and 10% of revenue depending on the operating model (RGA Consulting, 2007). Figure 12 provides an illustration of where energy is used in a restaurant in America. A number of organisations also provide benchmarks for specific types of hospitality businesses. These include ITP, the Carbon Trust and US Environmental Protection Agency.

Carbon offset

The term 'carbon offset' refers to compensating for the release of one tonne of CO_2e (carbon dioxide equivalent) in one area of the business by avoiding the release of, or removing from the atmosphere the same amount of CO_2e somewhere else. Carbon offsets can be generated by a number of activities such as energy efficiency (e.g.installing energy saving technologies in housing developments), renewable energy (e.g. wind farms) and sink (e.g. forestry) projects.

(WWF and Friends of the Earth Joint Statement).

Most hospitality businesses that have yet to tackle the issue of carbon reduction have found that they can reduce energy consumption by up to 20% for little or no investment (www.carbontrust.co.uk, 2011). Hilton, for example, have found that staff training initiatives alone in some hotels can deliver immediate energy savings in the region of 6% (Bohdanowicz *et al.*, 2011).

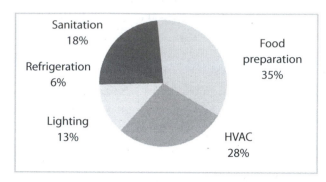

Figure 12: Average energy consumption in a full service restaurant, USA.
Note: Energy costs measured in British Thermal Units. One BTU = 0.293 watt hours
Source : www.energystar.gov/ia/business/small_business/restaurants_guide.pdf

> Many hospitality businesses take a relatively ad hoc approach to carbon and energy management. Those that implement a more strategic approach, however, generally achieve better results. Table 1 describes the steps that are included in the energy management plans used by hospitality businesses to deliver carbon savings and maps these against the typical actions in a structured energy management plan.

Table 1: Steps in a strategic approach to carbon/energy management

Phase	Steps in a structured energy management plan	Typical actions taken by hospitality businesses
1	Undertake energy audit	Review patterns of energy consumption throughout the business.
2	Compare performance with industry benchmarks	Identify the potential for savings – if possible by sub area
3	Take expert advice	If necessary, take in expert views to identify savings opportunities and assess different technologies
4	Establish realistic goals	Set goals that are achievable but challenging
5	Communicate commitment	Involve all staff and motivate them to support achievement of the goals
6	Allocate responsibility	Make someone responsible
7	Ensure participation	Encourage all employees to participate. They know routines and practices the best and have the greatest opportunity to deliver savings
8	Monitor consumption and target specific reductions	Record changes in consumption and review targets for specific activities regularly
9	Provide training	Train staff to ensure they are able to meet targets in specific areas'
10	Establish standard operating procedures and install low cost technologies	Look at start up and shut down and routine procedures to ensure energy efficiency consideration are embraced
11	Review supply contracts	Engage suppliers in matching consumption and demand to secure tariff reductions.

Source: Adapted from ITP (2008) and Carbon Trust (2011).

Most of the major global hospitality businesses have taken a systematic approach to reducing their energy consumption. Many businesses are using these processes to deliver on stretching targets. For example, InterContinental Hotel Group intends to cut its CO_2 emissions by 25% by 2017, Marriott International by 20% and Hilton Worldwide by 20% in 2009–14. Scandic aims to operate on a carbon-neutral basis by 2025, Fairmont Hotels & Resorts aspires to reduce GHG emissions to 20% below 2006 levels by 2013, and Wyndham intends to offset a portion of its carbon footprint, equal to 68 tons of CO_2 via a partnership with Native Energy.[2]

Figure 13 demonstrates how many of the major hospitality businesses have made a public commitment to reducing carbon emissions.

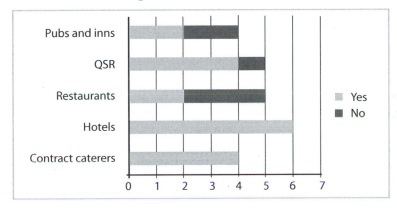

Figure 13: Number of leading hospitality businesses with a commitment to reducing carbon emissions on website or in published 'responsible business' report.

Notes: Includes only companies that specify carbon reduction as opposed to energy efficiency.

Data compiled from published data on websites or in corporate reports from 24 large hospitality businesses (see Appendix 1 for a list of companies included).

Some companies have interests that cut across sectors – for example some businesses that are primarily pub operators (and are included in the pub category) also operate a small number of hotels.

It would be pertinent at this point to compare carbon performance from different business types. Differences in methodologies for calculating carbon emissions render comparisons between carbon data from different businesses fraught with difficulty. This is, however, an issue that is likely to reduce for hoteliers at least. A new initiative by the International Tourism Partnership (ITP) and the World Travel & Tourism Council (WTTC) seeks to unite hotel industry efforts to calculate and communicate carbon impact by agreeing on a standardised methodology and metrics informed by the GHG Protocol standards. The Carbon Measurement Working Group is being driven by hospitality members within ITP and WTTC includes leading international hotel companies such as Fairmont Hotels & Resorts, Hilton Worldwide, Hyatt Hotels & Resorts, InterContinental Hotels Group, Marriott International Inc., MGM Resorts International, Mövenpick Hotels & Resorts, Red Carnation Hotel Collection,

---

2　All data sourced from individual company websites, accessed 1 August 2011

Starwood Hotels & Resorts Worldwide, Inc., Premier Inn – Whitbread Group and Wyndham Worldwide.

Comparable data apart, carbon reduction initiatives have been helped by a number of technologies and these are becoming increasingly common in both large and smaller hospitality businesses (see Text box 13). In many businesses they have delivered impressive results and many offer pay back periods of months rather than years.

Text box 13: Carbon reduction initiatives

- Installation of LED or other forms of energy efficient for lighting – can reduce electricity consumption by circa 10%*
- Installation of devices to switch lights/equipment off in vacant spaces (including guest rooms in the case of hotels). These include photocells on lights, motion detectors on hot water taps and so on.
- Investment in energy efficient boilers (can deliver fuel energy savings of up to 70% in accommodation properties).
- Installation of individual temperature controls for different zones – can deliver energy cost savings of 8% for every degree of heating reduction.
- Installation of double or secondary glazing in temperature climates and shading in warm climates.
- Installation of flow restriction devices for hot water (such as aerators for taps and low flow shower heads).
- Installation of curtains or doors on display fridges/chillers.
- Installation of energy efficient refrigeration systems.
- For large companies, the installation of integrated building management systems that monitor energy consumption throughout a property and switch off specific pieces of equipment or whole areas of the building at specific times.
- Installation of sub-meters to allow for effective recording of energy consumption in parts of the business (energy savings of 2–3% achievable if acted upon).
- Installation of cooking technologies, such as induction ovens, that reduce air conditioning and direct cooking related energy consumption.

Note: All savings estimates are in a UK context. Savings estimates cannot be summed to identify total saving potential.

The development of benchmarks for energy consumption (a minefield in its own right) has helped businesses to assess the good from the poor performers. A number of organisations, including the Building Research Establishment (and latterly Carbon Trust) in the UK, the International Tourism Partnership, Energy Star in the USA and the EU-funded Hotel Energy Solutions among others, have sought to produce energy consumption benchmarks or automated tools that provide tailored benchmark reports.

Benchmarks are most useful when used within a single business unit over time as a part of a consistent programme of monitoring consumption and targeting reductions (see Figure 14).

KEY: Let = room let

[**change hotel name on h/c]

Current Month			^MAY	Year To Date		
ACTUAL	BUDGET	LAST YEAR	Novotel YORK	ACTUAL	BUDGET	LAST YEAR
3,242	3,650	3,011	RMS SOLD	14,880	15,766	14,420
5,876	6,224	5,189	SLEEPERS	26,560	29,349	25,605
			ELECTRICITY			
87,989	3,650	78,895	TOTAL KWH	426,278	0	389,199
£3,684	£3,974	£3,325	TOTAL £	£17,845	£16,351	£16,398
710	-	636	KWH/RM Built	688	-	628
27.14	0.00	26.20	KWH/Let	28.65	0.00	26.99
£1.14	£1.09	£1.10	£/Let	£1.20	£1.04	£1.14
			Gas			
85,678	0	85,266	TOTAL KWH	547,404	0	587,993
£989	£1,010	£984	TOTAL £	£6,320	£4,157	£6,788
891	-	688	KWH/RM BUILT	883	-	948
26.43	0.00	28.32	KWH/LET	36.79	0.00	40.78
£0.31	£0.28	£0.33	£/LET	£0.42	£0.26	£0.47
			WATER			
1,292	0	1,040	Total M3	6,082	0	5,071
£1,596	£2,192	£1,510	Total £	£7,468	£8,758	£6,459
0.40	0.00	0.35	M3/LET	0.41	0.00	0.35
0.22	0.00	0.20	M3/SLEEPER	0.23	0.00	0.20
£0.49	£0.60	£0.50	£/LET	£0.50	£0.56	£0.45
£1.90	£1.97	£1.93	TOTAL £/LET	£2.13	£1.86	£2.06

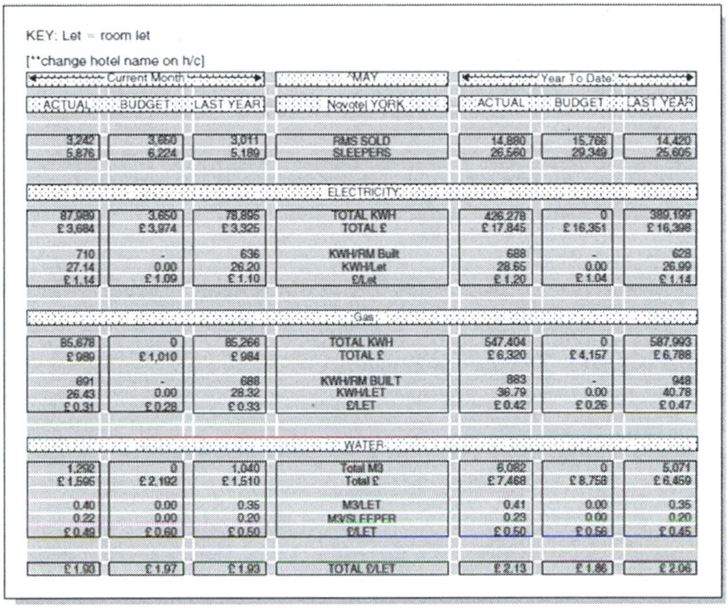

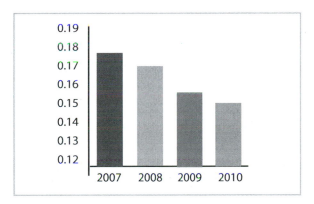

Figure 14: Using energy monitoring data to manage consumption within Accor (UK and Ireland) hotels
Source: Hawkins (2006)

Figure 15: Carbon emission reductions at apetito

Some businesses have produced their own benchmarks of energy consumption and use their monitoring activities to drive a programme of continual improvement (see Figure 15) demonstrating year-on-year reductions in carbon emissions although different calculation methods mean that the data from different companies cannot be compared. Businesses that use this approach include:

- **Whitbread** (the organisation that manages the Premier Inn and Costa Coffee brands alongside a number of restaurant brands of which Beefeater is perhaps the best known) has made a commitment to reduce its carbon emissions by 26% by 2020. This commitment comes on the back of a carbon saving of 4% over the period 2008–10. It will be achieved through a process of measuring consumption and targeting savings year-on-year (Whitbread CSR Report, 2010).

♦ **apetito** reduced CO_2 per tonne of product by 11% over each of the last two successive years (Apetito CSR Report, 2011);

♦ **IHG**, that collates data through its Green Engage initiative and that calculates that its carbon footprint is 59 kg per guest night sold (http://www.ihgplc.com)

♦ **Yum!** has achieved total annualized savings of 60,000 metric tons of CO_2, about 18% above the goal of 51,000 metric tons. The savings – equivalent to 10,700 cars being taken off the road or eliminating the energy use of 4400 households – benefited shareholders as well, saving $17 million in energy costs (Yum! Corporate Responsibility Report, 2008);

♦ Following on from their involvement in the early stages of the carbon disclosure project, Scandic have continued with our own carbon disclosure plan aiming for zero emissons in 2025. In 2011, the company will achieve its interim target of a 50% reduction in carbon emissions. The zero emission target includes energy for heating and cooling, electricity, kitchen energy and business travel within its scope.

Strategies to adapt to a low carbon future

Energy efficiency has been the dominant (and for most hospitality businesses) only element of carbon management programmes. A few businesses have strayed into the area of electric cars and other initiatives as a part of a programme to promote their green credentials and demonstrate their commitment to low carbon living. Given the scale of the challenge, however, these initiatives are often seen as little more than frippery and, while they can generate PR benefits, if delivered alongside a failure to recognise the main impacts of the business can be damaging to corporate reputations (see Text box 14).

As Principle 2 demonstrates, the landscape for carbon adaptation is littered with test projects within corporate businesses such as the installation of solar panels but with little commitment to broader adaptation measures. Smaller businesses such as the Scarlet Hotel in Cornwall and Sånga Säby Kurs & Konferens Centre in Sweden are far ahead of the corporate players in this regard. The latter, for example, has been fully powered by renewables since 1996 (Martinac et al., 2001). Admittedly, grafting an ambition to adapt to a low carbon future onto a conventional business model (especially when operating into a business unit that is owned by an external owner) is no easy feat. But for those businesses that are genuinely committed to responsible operations it is an essential pre-requisite of the seriousness with which the senior management team take the issue.

> ### Text box 14: Failure to recognise major impact when doing good can damage reputations
>
> Last week, Disney put out a new corporate sustainability report declaring its intention to reduce water use, cut waste, protect nature, head for zero-carbon emissions at its offices and parks and try to buy green electricity in future.
>
> Some eye-catching features include the train at Disneyland in California, which now runs on biodiesel made with used cooking oil from the resort's restaurants.
>
> In case anyone thought this do-goodery would damage the bottom line, CEO Robert Iger promised that the wider purpose was to 'make our brands and products more attractive, strengthen our bonds with consumers, make the company a more desirable place to work, and build goodwill in the communities we operate. All of this contributes to shareholder value.'
>
> I am not cynical about such motives. Climate change will only be solved when corporations like Disney see that cutting emissions is good for the bottom line. My problem is that Disney's business model is unchanged. It remains tied to global promotion of trips to its resorts – just about the most environmentally damaging leisure activity you can imagine.
>
> *Source:* www.guardian.co.uk/environment/2009/mar/19/disney-greenwash-fred-pearce

In other industrial sectors, businesses leaders have demanded harsher climate targets. The Chief Executive of Nestlé, for example, is one of a number of signatories from major companies that are calling for harsher EU carbon targets. In making the case for such targets, the Chief Executive of Nestlé stated that:

> By moving to a higher target, the EU will have a direct impact on the carbon price through to 2020 and deliver the economic signals that companies need if they are to continue investing billions of Euros in low carbon products, services, technologies and infrastructure. European leadership will also help rebuild the international momentum towards an ambitious, robust and equitable global deal on climate change.
>
> /www.decc.gov.uk/en/content/cms/news/eu_cc_article/eu_cc_article.aspx

Some businesses have now started the process of establishing stretching targets in the area of carbon management. Often these targets embrace not only direct emissions of carbon from the business, but also emissions throughout the supply chain. It is this small cohort of businesses that are really looking beyond cost-saving energy efficiency and towards the business models of the future. They include among their number, one or two hospitality businesses (for example, Scandic, which aims to operate on a net zero carbon basis by 2025) and also include major industrial players such as:

♦ **Continental Clothing** with their mission to create 'an entire industry in low carbon corporate wear, work wear, promotional wear and leisure wear, built upon fundamental principles of sustainable production and socially positive supply chain management. Our mission now is to turn our customers, our competitors' customers, from all industry sectors, onto the products and services that we offer now and will continue to develop in the future.' (www.continentalclothing.com)

+ **Unilever** have set three big goals for achievement over the decade to 2020:

    + Halve the environmental footprint of our products

    + Help more than 1 billion people take action to improve their health and well-being

    + Source 100% of our agricultural raw materials sustainably (source: www.unilever.co.uk)

+ **GSK** which aims for its company and value chain operations to be carbon neutral by 2050 with interim targets to reduce the companies global footprint by 10% by 2015 and 25% by 2020. Savings associated with the reduction of 84,000 tonnes of CO_2e emissions reduction to date are an estimated £3.8 million across 200 sites in 65 countries (www.carbon trust.co.uk)

+ **Marks and Spencer** with its plan A programme that aims to:

    + make the UK and Irish operations carbon neutral by 2012

    + ensure that none of the packaging or clothing from the company needs to be disposed of to landfill

    + move all whole fresh turkey, duck and geese to free range and have already introduced clothing ranges made from organic linen and cotton (source: www.corporate.marksandspencer.com).

The imperative for action on carbon emissions

The imperative to invest in low carbon technologies is more than just moral. In Europe, some 60–70% of hotel development (www.deduce.eu/IFS/IFS14.pdf) is in the coastal zone. Where there are hotels, there will also be the plethora or restaurants, cafes and other paraphernalia that accompany leisure tourism developments. If predictions of sea level rise are met, a high proportion of this will be at risk of more frequent flooding incidents, placing severe pressure on investors and operators.

In the Caribbean, the situation is even more severe as demonstrated in the work of Murray Simpson for the United Nations Environment Programme and others.

When comparing the progress of most major players in the hospitality sector to the very ambitious and stretching targets of other sectors, it is clear that there is still some distance to travel. It is of course the structure of the industry that makes this issue so challenging, but technological developments in recent years make the establishment of stretching targets for a low carbon future seem more feasible. Many of these technologies have now been extensively tested by the sector. These include solar hot water and space heating, photovoltaics, biomass boilers and ground source heating as well as passive solar techniques, venturi air conditioning systems and a host of other technologies. The impenetrable barriers to seeing these technologies fully employed by the sector relate to the long period between installation and return on the investment, the fact that technologies cannot be universally applied but need to be selected according to geographic and climatic considerations, the fact that most need to be supported by mechanical backup from conventional fossil fuel based systems and – fundamentally – the fact that they need to be installed into properties that are neither owned or managed by the businesses that operate them and often that lack secure long-term tenure over contracts.

Few investors are prepared to bear the additional cost burden that these technologies imply without an obvious incentive and hospitality businesses with relatively short lease arrangement (15 years or less) are unlikely to recoup the value of investing in these technologies themselves. Many engineers and architects have insufficient knowledge about alternative technologies and fear the implications of installing them. Insurance companies are able to exert some pressure (through higher premiums in areas of known flood risk). Until there is a genuine market based advantage for businesses to adapt these technologies (and rising oil prices combined with emissions trading schemes are beginning to provide that incentive) or a necessity for investors to ensure that carbon adaptation is as important as energy efficiency, it is unlikely that many hospitality businesses will be able to give this issue the consideration it deserves.

The wet stuff

The issue of water is often seen as secondary to those of energy and carbon management. But for many regions of world, the issues associated with water supply (and the costs of providing water to facilities) exceed those associated with energy. This is especially the case in small island states that are heavily dependent on tourism – many of these locations have had to adopt strategies to effectively 'manufacture' or import water supplies. Moreover, waste water is one of the deadliest pollutants in the world and poses a threat to human health and the environment, especially in those countries that lack effective waste water treatment infrastructure.

When dealing with the issue of reducing water consumption, hospitality businesses tend to adopt strategies that have the following core elements:

1 Reducing water wastage

2 Introducing plant and/or technologies to generate fresh water and/or treat waste water.

Reducing wastage of water and ensuring effective water treatment

The processes to reduce water consumption are now well tried and tested and many deliver significant cost savings within a very short timescale. Many require little more than good staff training to deliver results (see Text box 15).

Text box 15: Water savings through staff training

Ramada Jarvis asked staff to reduce the number of times toilets were flushed during routine cleaning procedures. As a result, the company reduced the volume of flushing in its 3651 toilets saving £28,656 per year (source Green Tourism Business Scheme)

Apetito have reduced their water consumption by 28% between 2007 and 2010. Key to the achievements have been staff training initiatives.

There are significant similarities between the processes applied to reducing water consumption and reducing energy consumption (and strategies taken to reduce water consumption will often also deliver energy savings because they eliminate the need to pump, heat and/or treat it). As is the case for energy, many companies adopt an ad hoc approach to water management, but those that take a strategic approach achieve better results (according to UK NGO Envirowise – now a part of WRAP – water reductions of 20% or more can be easily achieved in many hospitality businesses). As is the case for energy and carbon, a number of benchmarking tools have been produced for water management (see Figure 16 for an example).

Restaurant benchmarks

The benchmarks developed for water use for non-Asian style kitchens are below.

(litres of water per food cover)[*]
Good <35
Fair 35 – 45
Poor >45

[*]Use based on total kitchen use divided by the number of covers or restaurant customers

Figure 16: Water consumption benchmarks developed by SydneyWater for restaurants. This study also produced benchmarks for other hospitality business types.
Source: www.sydneywater.com.au/water4life/InYourBusiness/Howtosavewater/HotelsandClubs.cfm

The steps in a good water management programme are the same as those that are applied for energy management (see Table 1)

As is the case for energy management, a number of tried and tested technologies are available to help hospitality businesses reduce water consumption and the most commonly utilised are presented in Text box 16.

Text box 16: Commonly used water management techniques/ technologies

- Towel cards, asking customers to reduce water use by, for example, reusing towels or switching taps off in bathroom areas
- Reporting and repairing leaks
- Toilet dams or WCs with low flush options/waterless urinals
- Flow regulators for taps
- Low-flow shower-heads
- Percussion (Push taps)
- Motion detectors that switch taps off automatically
- Water-efficient dishwashing or laundry machines
- Technologies that limit operating hours for grounds watering
- Thawing frozen food in the air rather than under running water
- Reusing opened bottles of mineral water for plants
- Washing on full loads only – and at reduced temperatures where possible
- Recycling water in fountains and decorative features.

As is the case for energy, the ease with which water consumption can be measured has led to a drive to deliver savings through benchmarking and a number of companies have now actively benchmark performance year-on-year across all business units.

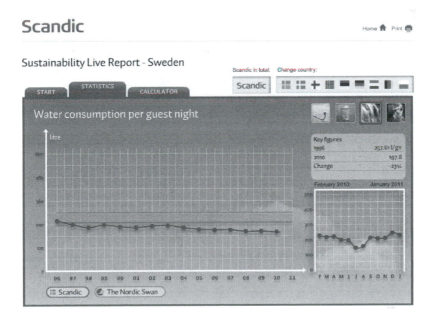

Figure 17: In-house benchmarks for water used by Scandic Hotels

Companies that use benchmarking processes include, among others:

- Accor
- IHG
- Hilton
- Marriott
- Apetito.

Introducing plant to generate fresh water/treat of waste water

In areas where access to fresh water is an issue, hospitality businesses often take steps to provide their own water. For these businesses, the options are limited, but they include:

- The installation of waste water treatment plants that clean and recycle waste water. In some cases, these treatment plants recycle the water for reuse in specific functions (such as toilet flushing). Technically, even sewage can be treated in some cases to drinking water quality. However, few if any hospitality businesses take this route;

- The installation of equipment that generates fresh water from sea water (known as reverse osmosis or desalination) or river water. Reverse osmosis is generally an energy-intensive process and so its use has significant implications for both energy costs and carbon emissions. Where water is being desalinated, the salt residue can also cause problems if disposed of inappropriately.

- In some cases, importing water on ships for use by the business.

Where water shortages are an issue, it is relatively difficult to justify the use of any of the latter technologies on the basis of environmental sustainability. This is especially the case when customers of hospitality businesses use much higher volumes of water than residents. In some instances, the argument can be made that the economic benefits of bringing hospitality businesses into the area outweigh the environmental costs, but in many instances where water is an issue excessive use by hospitality businesses is difficult to justify and can cause community anger. Indeed many of the protests against tourism related development in some countries arise because of concerns about or inequitable access to water resources (see Figure 18).

The issue of waste water treatment (whether using conventional waste water treatment technologies or more sustainable alternatives such as reed beds) is rather easier to defend and there are instances where hospitality businesses have made their waste water treatment processes available to local community groups, thus reducing the risks of pollution.

Water management for hospitality businesses is an issue that is likely to escalate in importance over the coming decades. Those with genuine responsible business practices will differentiate themselves from the crowd not just by their actions to minimise water consumption, but also by their decisions about where they operate, especially when it comes to areas where water resources are very scarce and cannot be equitably managed to serve a local community and hospitality function.

Figure 18: Water – a cause for concern

Source: www.climatechangecorp.com/content.asp?ContentID=5357

The 'throw away' culture

Waste minimisation is often viewed as less important than energy and water management by hospitality companies. This is a view that is borne from the relatively low costs of waste disposal in comparison to other utilities. It is, however, the issue of waste that most frequently demonstrates to customers the relative seriousness with which responsible business commitments are taken. It is also on the issue of waste that hospitality businesses are most frequently caught out for non-compliance with regulations (in developed countries at least). This is especially the case in EU countries such as the UK (with its very complex web of waste regulations) and Sweden where companies using inappropriate means to dispose of wastes that can be recycled or burned to generate energy face hefty fines.

Hospitality businesses are significant producers of waste. Figure 19 demonstrates the typical composition of waste from different establishments in the profit sector.

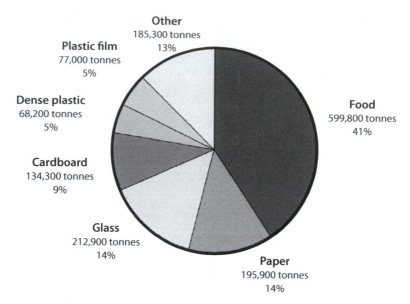

Figure 19: Typical waste compositions from different UK profit sector hospitality establishments
Source: WRAP (2011).

As is the case for energy and water, the processes for waste minimisation are clearly understood and demonstrated in Figure 20 in what has become known as the 'waste minimisation hierarchy'.

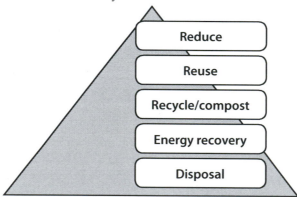

Figure 20: The waste minimisation hierarchy
Source: Michaels (2009).

The steps in this hierarchy include:

♦ Reducing waste at source by implementing just-in-time purchasing processes, effective ordering of stocks, specifying that items should be delivered with a minimum of packaging and so on;

♦ Minimising packaging or asking for packaging to be reusable;

♦ Reusing items wherever possible (such as reusable mugs in place of polystyrene ones);

- ◆ Recycling and or composting as many items as possible;
- ◆ Identifying options for energy recovery from what remains;
- ◆ Disposing of any remaining wastes responsibly.

While such examples are outstanding, they are certainly not the norm within the hospitality sector. Evidence of wasteful practices is one of the issues that customers most frequently pick up on when selecting responsible hospitality options (see Text box 17).

Text box 17: Delivering waste and resource savings

Thorough implementation of this hierarchy has produced some amazing results. Strattons Hotel (Swaffham, UK), for example, sends only 2% of its total waste volume to landfill. It has allowed some major conglomerates, including Marks and Spencer and Sodexo in Australia to make a commitment to zero waste to landfill objectives. Many hospitality businesses also ensure that food waste goes to a good cause. Pret-a-Manger, for example, donate 1.7 million food products to the homeless each year (http://www.bbc.co.uk/news/magazine-10915739), further underpinning the responsible business message.*

* Not all businesses can donate unsold food to charities. Food that is wholly packaged can be donated, however, hot food or food that is not packaged fails to meet health and safety requirements in many countries and so cannot.

Benchmarks for waste production are now becoming available (see Table 2) and the issue of food waste in particular is pricking consciences (spurred in part by the obesity epidemic makes portion size an issue).

Table 2: Estimated waste production per employee for UK hospitality businesses. (Average total waste per employee (tonnes/year) using DEFRA data by size band mid point - grey shade denotes missing survey data.)

Sector	Employee size-band mid-point					
	1-9	10-19	20-49	50-99	100-249	250+
Hotels	2.2	2.1	1.2	1.7	0.9	1.4
Restaurants	1.7	2.6	2.8	0.3	0.4	1.0
QSRs	1.2	1.2	1.5	1.5	1.5	1.5
Pubs	4.7	4.1	1.5	1.5	1.5	1.5

Source: WRAP (2011).

It is the issue of waste that is likely to focus minds in the coming decades. This is partly because of the costs of waste disposal and the fact that forward-looking companies are coming to view waste as a resource, but more because of the impacts that rising commodity prices are having on businesses and the way these are combining with the new fashion for austerity. It is likely that above all else, therefore, the strategy that a company adopts to tackling waste will dictate how it is perceived by many of its stakeholders.

Customer attitudes and perceptions of responsible business

Nicky Fisher, head of sustainability for Pret, '… initiatives [to provide unused food items to homeless charities] 'are good for the brand' and help to provide a feel-good factor for customers.'
Source: http://www.bbc.co.uk/news/magazine-10915739

We were browsing the menu when I found the following dish on offer: 6oz steak, 6oz pork chop, 2 lamb cutlets, 6oz gammon, sausage and fried egg. I was trying my best to picture how much food this was and imagine what sort of person could possibly eat it all.
Source: http://myzerowaste.com/2010/11/the-average-uk-restaurant-produces-nearly-half-a-kilo-of-waste-per-diner/

Five indicators for business

☐ The business knows how much energy and water it consumes (in volume and not cost) and how much waste is produced.

☐ Consumption of resources is declining per unit of production year on year.

☐ Consumption targets are challenging and achieved in all business units that are managed by the businesses as a minimum.

☐ The senior management team are judged not just on meeting financial but also resource consumption/waste reduction targets.

☐ Decisions on new technologies are made not just on short-term payback, but also on their contribution to reducing carbon emissions and/or waste.

The tools of the trade

As environmental management has become a mainstream concern for hospitality businesses, the number of tools that can be used to reduce consumption, measure performance or target reductions has grown hugely. Over the course of writing this text, the authors have found reference to more than 100 different management manuals, benchmarking or video-based toolkits in the English language alone – and almost all of these primarily or exclusively target the environmental impacts of hospitality businesses.

Management manuals

Management manuals have played a crucial role in supporting hospitality businesses in the implementation of environmental management practices ever since Inter-Continental Hotels & Resorts shared its prototype with the industry via the International Hotels Environment Initiative in 1992. Management manuals have now been produced by many of the major hospitality brands including:

- Radisson with its *Responsible Business* manual.

- Marriott with its *ECHO* manual.

- Compass Group with its *Environmental Handbook*.

- Fairmont with the *Green Partnership Guide* (which was drawn from the earlier guide of the same name developed by Canadian Pacific Hotels and Resorts;

- Taj with its EcoTaj initiatives (supported through a series of newsletters rather than a bespoke manual).

- The updated version of the *International Hotels Environment Initiative Manual* which was published in 2008 under the title *Environmental Management for Hotels – the Industry Guide to Sustainable Operations*.

- Manuals and fact sheets produced by international agencies like United Nations Environment Programme (UNEP), WWF and the UNWTO.

- Information produced by national governments, including in the UK, the Carbon Trust and WRAP and in the US Environmental Protection Agency.

- Manuals and fact sheets produced by the industry's representative associations, including among others, the International Hotel & Restaurant Association, the Caribbean Hotels Association, the American Hotel & Motel Association and the Hong Kong Hotels Association.

These manuals have provided invaluable 'how to' advice to thousands of hospitality businesses. The guidance frequently covers the basic elements required to establish an environmental management system as well as advice on techniques and technologies that provide rapid paybacks on the issues of energy, waste and water management. In recent years the scope of many of these manuals has expanded to include the identification of ways in which businesses can support communities, engage with the third sector and protect the environment. They also often provide advice on monitoring consumption of energy, waste and water, etc. and sometimes give guidance on industry benchmarks (or standards) for energy consumption, water consumption and waste production.

Tools to benchmark energy, waste and water performance

As we have seen in the preceding pages, benchmarking is the process of comparing performance between different organisations; different units undertaking similar processes within a single organisation; or within the same unit in a single organisation year-on-year.

Benchmarking is, of course, not unique to recording responsible business practices within hospitality businesses in general and hotels in particular. Hoteliers have long had an obsession with Revenue per Available Room (RevPAR) and a large number of hotel business both participate in and purchase the results of benchmark surveys. Benchmarking for environmental or responsible business performance seeks to apply the techniques used by organisations such as TNS within a responsible business context. Some specific services now claim to support benchmarking of specific environmental issues, including the CAREPAR scheme that claims to measure the volume of carbon emissions per available room.

As is so often the case, benchmarking which sounds so simple in theory can be fiendishly difficult in practice. Nevertheless, the pursuit of effective benchmarks for environmental performance criteria at least has been something of a Nirvana for some hospitality businesses and the trade and professional associations that represent them. For these organisations it is thought that effective benchmarking will engage businesses in responsible activities by highlighting the level of financial savings that can be achieved, and establishing a 'league' table of good and poor performers, thus providing an incentive to deliver environmental and social improvements.

For most hospitality businesses, benchmarking will typically be used to monitor consumption as regards energy (usually recording consumption of both electricity and gas, oil, or other fuels) and water (sometimes also recording the volume of waste water produced). Less frequently, it is used to log performance as regards the weight or volume of waste disposed of, the amount of supplies that are purchased from the local community, the value of the economic contribution to the local community and so on. The critical difference between benchmarking and simply recording this data is that effective benchmarking requires a business to compare performance either with competitor businesses of similar characteristics or with itself over time and seek to make consistent improvements.

Tools that have sought to provide quantitative 'benchmarks' across the whole sector (or single elements of it) include:

♦ The International Tourism Partnership's SPOT tool, (http://www.tourismpartnership.org/PracticalSolutions/Practical_Solutions.html)

♦ FHRAI Energy and Environment E2 Benchmark for Hotels, (http://www.devalt.org/Newsletter/mar02/of_1.htm)

♦ US EPA/DOE Energy Star Portfolio Manager (http://www.energystar.gov/index.cfm?c=evaluate_performance.bus_portfoliomanager)

Benchmarking tends to be confined largely to environmental issues within a hospitality context and is typically used in one of three ways:

♦ First, it is used by single businesses to monitor consumption of resources over time. A business will chart performance against a standard indicator of business success,[3] highlight key differences between years (for example, a significant increase in energy consumption in January 2010 over January 2009 due to a more severe weather conditions) and investigate the causes of these changes in consumption. This is the context within which benchmarking is most reliable

---

3   Typically in hotels, this will be the number of guest nights recorded, in restaurants the number of meals served and so on

and can make the greatest contribution towards responsible business initiatives. Businesses can also establish their own baseline and measure against this. Data from the UK's Carbon Trust indicates that simply the process of recording consumption and tracking performance can deliver savings in the region of 2–3%.

♦ Second, it is used by a business with multiple units (such as a corporate hotel company or a catering provider with multiple outlets spread across a wide geographical area) to log performance of different units, target good and poor performers and guide decisions about investments in new plant and facilities. In an ideal world, units that lie at the very bottom of the league table would be released from the portfolio rather than being refurbished, for example, because of their relatively high energy consumption. Using benchmarking systems, best performers can be rewarded. For example, at Scandic best performing hotels receive funds for a team member event/activity.

♦ Third, it is used by an individual business (usually privately owned and managed) to compare performance with similar businesses in the sector. This approach can be as a tool to give a hospitality business (generally a small one that does not have the capacity to do its own comprehensive benchmarking) a snapshot of how well it is performing against industry norms, and to provide an incentive to improve (for those that are logged as poor performers) in the form of a 'rule of thumb' calculation of the level of savings that can be accrued. The difficulty with using benchmarking in this way is that properties that do not exactly match the 'average' property descriptor will get an inaccurate picture of their performance.

As the decade has rolled on it has become evident that effective benchmarks with relevance across the sector (or even specific segments of it like hotels) and across continents are not as easy to establish as it at first seemed. This is because:

♦ The base data used to provide the benchmarks is invariably collated using a range of different methodologies.

♦ Those benchmark tools that rely on businesses entering their own consumption data are often plagued by poor data entry – ample evidence that, for many in the sector, even apparently simple tasks like reading energy meters and recording results can be challenging (anyone who has tried to read energy meters in different parts of a historic building will be aware that this apparently simple task can require some expertise and this is frequently not available to those hospitality business managers that have sought to use benchmark tools).

♦ There are difficulties in taking account of the different characteristics of establishments when seeking to make comparisons. For example, even small variations in weather conditions such as exposure to the wind can make a considerable difference to energy consumption in two apparently similar buildings. Differences between facilities, type of equipment installed, type of customers served, level of occupancy, building size and date of building construction can all be difficult to factor into benchmarking systems (although some do seek to provide mathematical correction factors to account for some of these issues).

♦ For global benchmarks to be reliable too many business sub-categories would be required, or extensive databases would need to be created.

In essence, a decade of effort has demonstrated that no cost-effective system or methodology of data collection and monitoring has been devised that is universally accepted or applicable throughout one sector of this vast industry (for example, hotels which have been the focal point of many benchmarking exercises).[4] Instead, a number of reporting/benchmarking tools have been developed by various bodies and each of these has some flaws.

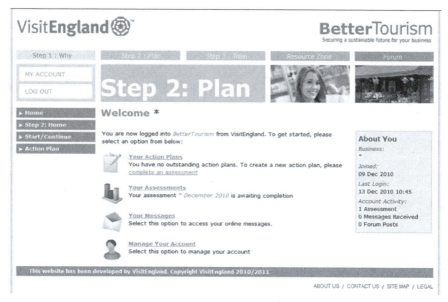

Figure 21: Green Start Benchmarking and Reporting System (www.better-tourism.org)

That is not to say, however, that benchmarking does not have some value. Many of the corporate businesses do now use internal benchmarking processes to evaluate the performance of their own premises with great success (see for example the Scandic programme, and the Green Engage programme of IHG). These internal processes are in some instances supported by developments in technology – such as devices that allow for the remote reading of energy consumption and the development of Building Management System technologies. As we have noted, large corporate hotel businesses now usually benchmark their estate for energy and water consumption at least, and many now produce league tables of good and poor performers. These processes have a number of uses, for example, highlighting to responsible business managers those units that have yet to implement effective energy management

---

4   Although progress is now being made on this issue for carbon at least – see information on the Carbon Disclosure Project above.

programmes.

The search for generic benchmarks that can be provided across the sector has moved focus. Where once quantitative measures were sought, benchmarking tools now focus on identifying the range of 'processes' that are in place to track environmental performance. These often emulate the processes within the Deming Cycle. Many tools now exist to support this development, the more recent among them being VisitEngland's Green Start programme that asks businesses a series of questions about the characteristics of their business and provides a comprehensive action plan to start implementing environmental improvements.

Environmental management systems

The introduction of ISO 14001 (the international standard for environmental management) had a revolutionary impact upon the environmental management practices of many hospitality business. It is this standard – and its cousins BS 8901 and many of the tourism certification schemes such as the Green Tourism Business Scheme and Green Globe – that have set the processes that are used both to assess the impacts of tourism businesses and to set in chain the management measures to reduce them.

These management systems are all loosely based on the Deming Cycle (see Appendix 2) using a process that demands continual improvement. These processes are not without their critics.

Conclusion

There is no question that corporate hospitality businesses have enthusiastically embraced resource efficiency programmes and the reductions achieved for individual businesses are impressive. There is, however, a fly in the ointment (isn't there always?). Despite the very impressive programmes that have been introduced by the major corporate businesses in this sector the total level of emissions of carbon (and probably consumption of water) is still going north.

This inconvenient truth reflects the growth in the size of the sector overall, the inability of even major corporations with complex responsible business programmes to deliver on those commitments universally throughout all business units, and the increasing demands that customers are placing on their hospitality experiences. It also reflects the preoccupation within the sector that any investments must deliver short-term payback periods – and generally these are expected to be of five years or less.

To date, the commitment of the global brands to reducing their environmental impacts and resource consumption have been in the vanguard when it comes to eco-efficiency. Those businesses with a longer term vision, however, have realised that the time has come to move beyond eco-efficiency and to invest in options that are not dictated by the conventional notions of short-term payback. It is these businesses and their stakeholders that are honing their responsible business strategies now to provide competitive advantage in the long term. For these businesses, questions are being raised about whether the development of hospitality businesses in areas blighted by water shortages fits within the responsible business strategy. They are also the businesses that are establishing prototype outlets that are not mainly dependent on fossil fuels and setting targets to send zero waste to landfill. It is also these businesses that recognise that their responsible business promises will seem hollow if they are propped up by a few narrowly defined environmental initiatives, while ignoring the other social and environmental consequences of their actions. As we shall see in the pages that follow, the brands that have moved beyond simple environmental management alone are those that can truly lay claim to responsible business initiatives.

References

Apetito (2011) *Annual Report*, Apetito, UK.

Becken, S., Frampton, C. and Simmonson, D. (2001) 'Energy consumption patterns in the accommodation sector – the New Zealand case', *Ecological Economics*, **39** (3), 371–386.

Bohdanowicz P., Zientara P., Novotna E. (2011), 'International hotel chains and environmental protection: An analysis of Hilton's *we care!* Programme (Europe, 2006-2008)', *Journal of Sustainable Tourism*, 19(7) 797-816.

Bohdanowicz, P. and Zientara, P. (2008) 'Corporate social responsibility in hospitality: issues and implications. A case study of Scandic', *Scandinavian Journal of Hospitality and Tourism*, **8** (4), 271–293.

Daily Telegraph (2011) 'Green growth: Mitchells and Butlers cut energy bills', 21 March, available at: http://www.telegraph.co.uk/sponsored/business/workingforchange/8396260/Green-growth-Mitchells-and-Butlers-cuts-energy-bills.html

Green Tourism Business Scheme (2009), communication at business meeting, October.

Hawkins, R. (2006) 'Accounting for the environment, in P. Harris and M. Mongielo (eds) *Accounting and Financial Management: Developments in the International Hospitality Industry*, Oxford: Butterworth-Heinemann, pp. 262–281.

Hotel Online (2010) Hilton Unveils LightStay Sustainability Measurement System, 20 April, http://www.hotel-online.com.

ITP (2008) *Environmental Management for Hotels*, 3rd edn, Oxford: Butterworth-Heinemann.

Kleanthous (2011) 'Eating Earth', a presentation made to FDIN, February 2010

Lawson, F.R. (2001) *Hotels and Resorts – Planning, Design and Refurbishment*, Architectural Press.

Marriott (2010) *Sustainable Report Update*, Marriott, USA, http://www.marriott.com/Multimedia/PDF/CorporateResponsibility/Marriott_Sustainability_Report_Update_2010.pdf

Martinac, I., Murman, H., and Lind af Hageby, A. (2001) 'Energy-efficiency and environmental management in a Swedish conference facility – case study', Sånga-Säby Courses & Conferences The 18th Conference on Passive and Low Energy Architecture – PLEA 2001, 7–9 November 2001, Florianópolis, Brazil, pp. 325–329.

McDonald's www.aboutmcdonalds.com/mcd/csr/about/environmental_responsibility.html

McKinsey (2007) *Curbing Global Energy Demand Growth: The Energy Productivity Opportunity*, MicKinsey & Co, USA, http://www.mckinsey.com

Michaels, T. (2009) *Waste not want not – the facts behind waste to energy*,The Energy Recovery Council, UK, http://www.wte.org/userfiles/file/Waste%20Not%20Want%20Not.pdf

RGA Consulting (2007) reported in www.ion.icaew.com/Tourismandhospitalityblog/19990

Shah, H. and McIvor, M. (2007) *A New Political Economy*, London: Compass.

US Energy Information Administration (2010) *International Energy Outlook 2010*, available at http://www.eia.gov/oiaf/ieo/world.html

Whitbread CSR Report (2009/10) *Good Together – Corporate Environmental Report Summary*, www.cr.whitbread.co.uk/downloads.aspx

WRAP (2011) *The composition of waste disposed of by the UK hospitality industry*, WRAP, Banbury, UK, available at www.wrap.org.uk/hospitality/report_the.html

Yum! (2008) *Serving the World – Corporate Responsibility Report*, www.yum.com.

Principle 2: Prepare for the (un)expected

The unexpected

We are playing Russian roulette with features of the planet's atmosphere that will profoundly impact generations to come. How long are we willing to gamble?

David Suzuki – eminent environmentalist

The title of this chapter is a little misleading. None of the issues described in the text that follows are unexpected. They are often discussed by scientists, academics, politicians, environmentalists and others. Most are not new. For some businesses, however, planning for the scale, likely implications, timescales and outcomes of many of these issues is entirely lacking. What is focusing minds now is the growing evidence that the implications of some of these issues are becoming evident and are already having an unwelcome impact on businesses and economies.[5]

In the text that follows, the range of issues is presented as if they are separate. In truth, of course, they are closely related. For example, climate change exacerbates water scarcity in some parts of the world and over-abundance in others. Water scarcity and over-abundance undermines agricultural productivity. Crop failure puts additional pressure on mineral resources as food imports increase. Equally, shortages of mineral resources (and oil in particular) have impacted upon the availability of land for food production as pressure has increased to produce bio fuels. Increases in oil costs also impact on food costs because of the energy intensity of modern food supply methods.

It is rarely a single issue that pushes businesses into a crisis, but a number of smaller interconnected issues. As the number of potential issues increase, so does the likelihood that they will combine to produce crisis conditions for companies.

Climate change

Of the sustainable development issues, climate change is probably the best known.[6]

---

5   There are a number of commentators – including James Stacey of Earth Capital Partners – who state that some areas of Kenya is not suffering from a drought but from climate change. Statements such as this can make investors reappraise the conditions they place upon loans or review the geographical areas in which they are willing to operate.

6   Contrary to popular opinion, there is broad-based consensus – even among many climate sceptics – that climate change is happening. A few commentators do deny that climate change is occurring, but most of the debate on this topic relates not to the existence of the phenomenon but to the cause, scale and implications of climate change.

Scientists predict that it is necessary to halve emissions of CO_2 from 1990 levels by 2050 to prevent catastrophic global warming. This is thought likely to keep global temperature increases to around 2°C (the lowest threshold of anticipated temperature change). Even within this threshold, it is thought that 20–30% of species could face extinction and there are predicted to be serious effects on the environment, food and water supplies, and health (UK Metrological Office, 2010). One of the biggest problems with climate change is the fact that the science is uncertain and while there is general consensus of the fact that the world is warming, there is little consensus of the scale or impacts of that change or of the strategies required by businesses to adapt and thrive.

Climate change has had a very high profile within the media, but the level of debate about the likely impacts has been a deterrent to action. Many businesses have taken measures to reduce their carbon emissions (this is known as mitigation in the jargon and these are described in Principle 1), but fewer have recognised that there is a need to adapt current business operations to continue to thrive throughout the period of change (this is known as adaptation).

Information about business adaptation strategies is lacking

> We need to open up the 'black box' of what the private sector is doing ... We know things are happening, but we need to pull them into the debate, before the world meets to determine its climatic fate ...
>
> Kallhauge (2009)

Food security

Food security has emerged as a significant issue on the agendas of countries from China to the UK over the last decade or so. Headlines such as 'Africa – China's new rice bowl' demonstrate the seriousness with which some governments take this issue. It has also recently become an issue of concern for many food service businesses and the major contract caterers in particular.

Food security and food wastage

> As food security rises up the agenda, so does the issue of food waste. Within the profit outlets in the UK hospitality sector, it is estimated that 400,000 tonnes of avoidable food waste were disposed of. That food had an estimated value of £722 million. Much of it could have been avoided by improvements in food storage, preparation and portion control systems.
>
> Source: WRAP (2011)

Food security concerns are driven by a range of factors, including: population growth (and the significant increase in the number of middle class who are able to afford to include meat regularly into their diet), biodiversity decline, soil degradation, desertification, water shortages and competition for land – including areas that were formerly employed to grow crops but are now used for bio-fuel production. The net result of these pressures is an increase in food prices. These have driven an additional 44 million people into poverty (World Bank, 2011) and have been felt keenly by food service businesses some of whom report price increases on some commodities of 20 per cent or more over the last five years. Perhaps because the cost of food has increased and combined with a political agenda that is increasingly focussed around vulnerabilities to do with food, a number of businesses in the hospitality sector (and especially within the major catering businesses) have begun to engage in the process of planning for greater food insecurity. This in itself has raised difficult ethical questions, including that of whether crops produced using Genetically Modified Organisms or other intensive modes of food production that are frowned on by some consumers should be utilised.

Water scarcity

The issue of water shortages has received much less attention than the related topics in this chapter. However, it will in all likelihood have more immediate effects. Water is a commodity that is already in short supply and one person in five currently lacks access to fresh drinking water (BBC, 2010). A combination of climate change, increased damming of rivers to provide hydro electric power, pollution of water courses from industrial and chemical manufacturing processes and irrigation, are changing patterns of water supply and leaving some places in a position of critical water shortages.[7] As patterns of water supply change, it is likely that some areas of the world will experience more drought and others greater risk of flash flooding.

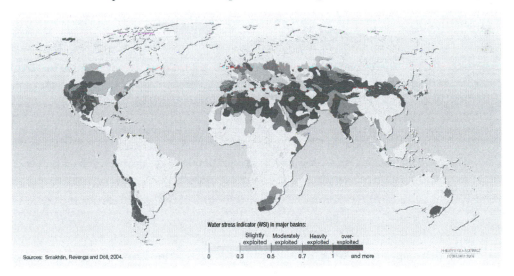

Figure 22: Areas under water stress

Source: http://maps.grida.no/go/graphic/water-scarcity-index

---

7   For example according to Inder Poonaji of Nestlé, there is already a 50% supply gap for water in parts of India. Communication at Foodservice Footprint event, 10 June 2011.

The issue of water shortages is politically charged and this is because water is fundamental to nearly all other human activities and particularly to the maintenance of food supplies.[8] Changes in patterns of precipitation are likely to reduce food productivity in some areas. In others, water shortages are already increasing the costs of food production (see Figure 22 for a graphic representation of areas at risk of water scarcity). It is expected that the yields from rainfed agriculture in some areas will decline. In Southern Africa, for example, it is thought that rainfed agricultural yields could be halved by drought by 2020 (United Nations, 2009). In others still, it is likely to reduce the availability of fertile land either as a result of accelerated erosion or as a result of more frequent heavy rainfall or from leaching of salt minerals to the surface through the process of irrigation (see for example, the experiences of Australia).

Text box 18: Water shortages likely to become critical in coming decades

The World Water Council believes that by 2020 we shall need 17% more water than is available if we are to feed the world (BBC, 2010).

To produce a kilogram of vegetables with present methods takes 2000 litres of water. A kilogram of beef takes 15,000 litres (Rees, 2010).

In China it takes 1000 tonnes of water to produce one tonne of wheat (BBC, 2010).

Depletion of mineral resources

Burgeoning populations and the demands of the global economy are placing greater pressures on a diminishing bank of resources. Timescales may be hotly debated, but there is no doubt that global oil and gas reserves as well as other minerals such as lithium (essential for batteries), precious metals such as platinum, palladium and rhodium (essential in all electronics as well as car catalysts) and silica (a vital component in photovoltaic panel production) will run out.

Oil is a particular concern. Oil is currently the world's major source of energy, it is fundamental to almost every function of modern life. It fuels 95% of land, sea and air transport, so the efficient movement of raw materials, food and goods, as well as personal mobility, is almost entirely oil-dependent. Food production relies heavily on oil to run farm machinery and to make fertilisers, herbicides and pesticides as well as to process, preserve and manufacture the resulting food products. Oil generates 40% of the world's commercial energy, provides heating fuel, and drives industry and commerce. Moreover, it supplies feedstock for many thousands of manufactured products as diverse as plastics, medicines, clothing and building materials (http://www.odac-info.org/peak-oil-primer).

---

8   Somewhere around 60% of all fresh water withdrawals are used for agricultural purposes and there are high levels of leakage/over-watering that exacerbate the issue.

Text box 19: Mineral resource shortages

The severity of issues associated with mineral shortages vary around the world. A major issue for Europe is natural gas. Global natural gas consumption is expected to rise 47% by 2030 (KepisandPobe, 2011). The supply of recoverable gas using conventional technologies in Europe will be exceeded by this date, making it dependent upon piped gas from Russia and other areas (ibid.). (Although there is the potential to recover gas from shale and other technologies which may provide a short-term reprieve for some countries.) As with water and food security risks, the increase of population exacerbates the problem.

Many countries, such as Australia and China, have an abundance of coal supplies that can be used to generate electricity. Governments in these countries, however, face complex challenges. The burning of coal to create electricity releases higher volumes of carbon dioxide than using gas. The introduction of market mechanisms to redress the environmental implications of using coal are unpopular in many of these countries. See for example the furore in Australia over the decision by the Government to slap a carbon tax of AUS$23 per tonne on its worst 500 polluters.

Source: (www.reuters.com accessed 14 August 2011).

Global demand for oil has increased sevenfold over the past half-century and demand is expected to continue growing at an annual rate of 1–2%. Despite significant awareness that oil production will start to decline (and that oil prices will continue to rise), most businesses have been ineffective at engaging in the development of alternatives.[9] Those who rely on governments to play this role should beware. In the USA, only around 7% of all energy is generated from renewable sources and in the EU the comparable figure is around 8%.

What the responsible business guidelines say

Most of the responsible business guidelines embrace this principle to some extent. Of themselves, these guidelines are strategies to support businesses through the process of mitigating against global environmental change and to stay in business for the long term. The guidelines that are the most far reaching (e.g. CERES) encourage businesses to play a transformative role in the global economy, thus adapting their own business practices to manage these issues whilst also engaging other stakeholders in the process of adaptation. Through its Business Innovation for Climate and Energy Policy (BICEP) initiative, for example, CERES seeks to engage governments

---

9   Many renewable sources of energy do not have the convenience or reliability of fossil fuels. Wind generators can only generate electricity while the wind blows, solar collectors only operate when the sun shines and so on. Many of these technologies also achieve low conversion efficiencies, and are highly site-specific. These issues are all barriers to business take up as is the fact that no one source can be used in isolation – a mix of sources are needed – often also including carbon-based fuels.

in passing meaningful climate and energy legislation that helps companies make a rapid transformation to a low carbon economy. It is these declarations that are a long way in advance of the regulatory bar.

Governments (or their agencies) in partnership with industry have also been proactive in this regard. A number have produced voluntary agreements that exceed regulation. These include the Federation House Commitment in the UK for water and numerous agreements for climate change. These are the Greenhouse Challenge in Australia, AERES negotiated agreement in France, the Agreement on Climate Change Protection in Germany, the Benchmarking Covenant in the Netherlands and New Zealand's Negotiated Greenhouse Agreements.

Text box 20: What is adaptation?

Under the definition adopted by the United Nations Framework Convention on Climate Change (UNFCCC), adaptation is a process through which societies make themselves better able to cope with an uncertain future. Adapting to climate change entails taking the right measures to reduce the negative effects of climate change (and exploit the positive ones) by making the appropriate adjustments and changes (World Business Council for Sustainable Development, 2008: 3).

The fundamentals

Some businesses have begun the process of assessing what changes will be required to adapt and survive to the challenges inherent within these issues. Given that planning for the unexpected is in no way alien to the culture of most, it is surprising that more are not active in this regard. Contingency plans for issues such as computer failure, terrorist attacks or power outages are commonplace. Risk and crisis management strategies are available in all of the largest businesses and staff are routinely trained to manage such instances. Businesses that are in the vanguard of the responsible business movement are increasingly starting to view the issues associated with the changing global environment within these existing risk and crisis management frameworks. Within these businesses, the aim is to build resilience, thus ensuring that the businesses can adapt, survive and thrive through the period of change. In some cases (for example Unilever), there is a realisation that these strategies may be delivered at the cost of immediate short-term gains. Often (but alas not always) these strategies go hand in hand with the initiatives described in Principle 1 to reduce the contribution that the business makes to global environmental change.

As Figure 23 illustrates, a relatively small number of global hospitality businesses have started the process of contingency planning to adapt their business models to the implications of global environmental change. As we shall see in the text that follows, those that have are largely addressing issues in an ad hoc way rather than within a strategic framework. Business continuity, within the sector in the long term will depend in part upon the extent to which businesses do embrace the issues above and the opportunities that they derive from them.

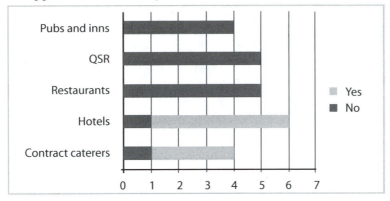

Figure 23: Hospitality businesses making explicit reference to climate change adaptation within websites and business literature

Notes: Adaptation not mitigation – nearly all companies are involved in at least some mitigation activities.

Data compiled from published data on websites or in corporate reports from 24 large hospitality businesses (see Appendix 1 for a list of companies included).

Some companies have interests that cut across sectors – for example some businesses that are primarily pub operators (and are included in the pub category) also operate a small number of hotels.

Some companies may be involved in climate change adaptation activities that are not included within public documents.

There are four main responses to these issues among businesses in general and hospitality businesses in particular. These can be categorised as:

♦ Head in the sand

♦ Developing ad-hoc single issue responses

♦ Developing comprehensive adaptation strategies

♦ Transforming the whole business strategy.

Most of the data that is available is on the topic of climate change, therefore, the information that follows has a bias towards this issue.

Head in the sand

According to UK Trade and Investment, around one in ten global companies thinks that no changes are required to adapt to the challenges of global change (Brown *et al.*, 2011). This is despite the fact that around nine in every ten companies claim to have suffered climate related impacts in the last three years (ibid.).

Global data is not available for hospitality businesses. However, a report by the now defunct Tourism Southwest in the UK found that 56% of hospitality businesses in the South West of the UK considered that they had been affected by extreme weather in the past and 63% expect their business to be affected in the future; 59% of businesses thought that they would need to adapt to climate change and 50%

considered planning for this issue as a medium to high priority; 29% of businesses questioned, however, planned to do nothing about the issue of climate change in particular (Cheng, 2010). A study by Hall in New Zealand in 2006 among rural tourism operators also found that climate change ranked a long way down the issues that concerned tourism businesses (Hall, 2006). Businesses that do not consider climate change an issue often do not have adequate insurance to cover them in the event of unexpected events. A lack of insurance – alongside a failure to plan – can be critical to a business and can prevent it from getting back on its feet.

That said, current research is beginning to reveal significant barriers to adapting for the range of issues addressed in this chapter. A research project on the topic of climate change (Hawkins *et al.*, 2011*)* is revealing that these may include:

♦ The long timescale in which significant impacts are expected to occur (20 years plus) compared to the relatively short planning horizons for most hospitality businesses (5 years or less).

♦ For companies, strategic issues such as climate change and water shortages are dealt with at a head office, yet the implications are felt regionally and locally.

♦ Strategies to support adaptation to these issues do not deliver immediate and tangible benefits to the business (and sometimes incur costs) and are thus difficult to 'sell into' the board.

♦ Strategies to support climate change adaptation, address water shortages, etc. require engagement with agencies that have unfamiliar working practices and different modes of targeting achievements (including in some instances the agencies involved in delivering development aid).

♦ The lack of portability of the hospitality infrastructure for owned facilities.

♦ Conversely, the portability of the tourism product for large corporate organisations. A climatic/water shortage/food crisis event in one destination may impact upon profitability of a specific hotel/restaurant within that destination. However, customers shift preferences to a similar destination (often using the same hotel operator), thus the net loss of profitability is small.

♦ The shift in ownership patterns for hospitality facilities – especially accommodation – into non-owned modes. This makes it (a) relatively easy for the operating company to move to another destination in the event of an unexpected incident and (b) relatively unlikely that the operating company will invest in adaptation responses that have a long-term pay payback because they have no guarantee that they will be operating that facility when the payback is achieved.

♦ A lack of knowledge or understanding about the destinations that are most likely to be affected by climate change, water shortages, food shortages and so on.

♦ A lack of knowledge about effective adaptation mechanisms.

♦ A lack of willingness to engage with consumers about the issues associated with climate change, etc. either because of (a) a fear of losing business to other modes or (b) a fear that customers will be 'turned-off' by 'moralistic' messages about climate change when on enjoying their leisure time;

♦ A lack of urgency/leadership within the industry to adapt to – as opposed to mitigate against – climate change.

Business continuity planning pays dividends in the long term

A study by Aon (2003) showed that: 92% of organisations without a business continuity plan do not survive a major disruption in the long term; 40% never re-open, 40% re-open but fail within 18 months, 12% re-open but fail within 5 years and only 8% actually survive in the long term.

Source: The Aon European risk management and insurance survey 2002/03

The barriers may be significant. History, however, has taught us that those businesses that have developed crisis management and business continuity procedures are much more likely to survive in the long term (see Text box 21).

Text box 21: Business continuity planning at the Old Mill Hotel, Bath

Climate change adaptation actions

- Installed temporary flood boards for use in the event of heavy rainfall.
- Tanked the underneath of the restaurant, i.e. sealed it so that water would not rise up from below.
- The catering facilities and staff are prepared so that managers are able to move the working kitchen and restaurant to a second kitchen and function room upstairs, enabling trading to continue even in the event of a flood
- Management are briefed on how to install flood boards and respond to a flood
- The laundry store was moved from the basement to an area behind the lodge
- Close contact is kept with the Environment Agency, to monitor the level of risk so that the hotel is continuously aware and prepared

Benefits

- There is now minimal disruption to the business from flooding, thereby avoiding loss of earnings
- The hotel managers have greater peace of mind and confidence that the property, staff and customers are protected
- Following discussions with their insurers, the adaptation measures taken resulted in lower insurance premiums
- Adaptation measures add to the value of the business, as being protected means that it is easier to sell the property on
- The measures all help to reassure customers that they are protected, as staff are frequently asked about whether the hotel and restaurant are at risk

Source: www.climateprepared.com

It is this realisation that is engaging businesses in the process of developing adaptation plans. These businesses often realise that adaptation to these issues is not always as complicated as it may at first seem. The South West Climate Impact Programme have been working with a number of businesses to help them adapt to climate change. The Old Mill Hotel in Bath, for example engaged with the South West Climate Change Impacts Partnership and implemented the measures listed in Text box 21 to ensure business continuity should an extreme weather event occur.

Developing ad hoc single approach responses

One step up from the head in the sand approach is that of commissioning (usually from an external agency) an adaptation plan for the business for one specific issue (typically climate change). When adaptation plans of this nature are commissioned, all too often they are not integrated into mainstream business continuity planning.

A failure to place sustainable development issues within a business continuity plan has two impacts. On the one hand, if the risks and responses are not presented within the same framework as other business issues, then these issues can either be allocated too much or too little emphasis. On the other, a failure to integrate sustainability issues within continuity planning means that they can fail to be integrated into the staff training, stakeholder engagement and other processes that surround that planning.

Data to indicate how many hospitality businesses are developing these approaches is not available in the public domain.

Building comprehensive adaptation plans

Those businesses that integrate sustainability adaptation alongside other businesses continuity issues are well placed to respond – and grasp the opportunities that arise from those issues. These businesses will typically include each issue within an impact matrix both to identify the likelihood that it will happen and the implications should it happen in the short and long term.

Planning horizons within business continuity procedures are fundamental – those that have planning horizons of five years or less are unlikely to be able to respond to the longer-term implications of issues included within this chapter. A small number of businesses have now begun to incorporate sustainability issues within their risk and crisis management procedures. These include:

♦ Unilever, for example, has undertaken a detailed assessment of the implications of a range of environmental issues for its business model. It now has comprehensive maps that identify areas in which its operations are at risk from a range of issues. In the case of water, for example, areas of water paucity are correlated with those in which agricultural products are sourced or consumers are based. A series of measures are being implemented in these areas, to build partnerships to reduce water stresses. These include partnerships with consumers (to engage them in using less water when utilising Unilever products), with producers (to reduce water use in the production process and to adapt products to alternatives with a lower water requirement) and so on. Metrics are used to ensure that strategies are effective and integrated into the mainstream planning process.

♦ Nestlé are also proactive in this arena with stretching and centrally agreed targets for water, climate and other issues. On the topic of water, for example, there is an aim to reduce water abstraction by 33% despite increasing production by 63%.

♦ Wyndham Hotels and Resorts has a suite of measures and targets for carbon reduction and actively participates in the Carbon Disclosure Project (http://www.wyndhamgreen.com accessed June 2011);

♦ IHG also reports into the Carbon Disclosure Project for two years and has improved its ranking year on year.

♦ Sodexo also participates in the carbon disclosure project.

Developing long-term business strategies that transform the business model to embrace change

It is the transformational companies that have taken their business continuity planning one step further to ensure that they maximise the benefits in the long term. These businesses are few and far between. They are developing strategies to adapt to use renewable or non-carbon energy sources, working with consumers to reduce the impacts of product use, working with suppliers to engage them in the process of adaptation and so on.

Table 3: Risks and opportunities to tourism businesses

Business risks	Business opportunities
• Stranded assets in former tourist regions • Winter sports destinations facing challenges as snowfall lessens and becomes unpredicatable • Obsolescence of destinations as they become too hot, water scarce or at risk from wild fires and the spread of formerly tropical dieases	• A pole-ward shift in conditions favourable to many forms of tourism is likely

Source: World Business Council for Sustainable Development (2008)

Table 4 indicates the adaptive strategies that have thus far been developed by tourism stakeholders to the issue of climate change (data for hospitality alone and other issues has not been found).

Table 4: Strategies for adapting to climate change by tourism companies

Type of Adaptation	Tourism Operators/ Businesses	Tourism Industry Associations	Governments and Communities	Financial Sector (investors/ insurance)
Technical	-Snowmaking -Slope contouring -Rainwater collection and water recycling systems -Cyclone-proof building design and structure	-Enable access to early warning equipment (e.g. radios) to tourism operators - Develop websites with practical information on adapta- tion measures	-Reservoirs, and desalination plants - Fee structures for water consumption -Weather fore-casting and early warning systems	-Require advanced building design or material (fire resistant) standards for insurance - Provide information material to customers
Managerial	-Water conservation plans -Low season closures -Product and market diversification -Regional diversification in business operations -Redirect clients away from impacted destinations	-Snow condition reports through the media - Use of short-term seasonal forecasts for the planning of marketing activities - Training programmes on climate change adaptation - Encourage environ-mental management with firms (e.g. via certification)	-Impact manage-ment plans (e.g., 'Coral Bleaching Response Plan') -Convention/ event interruption insur-ance -Business subsidies (e.g., insurance or energy costs)	-Adjust insurance premiums or not renew insurance policies -Restrict lending to high risk business operations
Policy	-Hurricane inter-ruption guarantees - Comply with regulation (e.g. building code)	-Coordinated political lobbying for GHG emission reductions and adaptation mainstreaming - Seek funding to implement adaptation projects	-Coastal manage-ment plans and set back requirements -Building design standards (e.g., for hurricane force winds)	-Consideration of climate change in credit risk and project finance assessments
Research	-Site Location (e.g., north facing slopes, higher elevations for ski areas, high snow fall areas	- Assess awareness of businesses and tourists and knowledge gaps	-Monitoring programs (e.g., predict bleaching or avalanche risk, beach water quality)	-Extreme event risk exposure
Education	-Water conservation education for employees and guests	-Public education campaign (e.g., 'Keep Winter Cool')	-Water conservation campaigns -Campaigns on the dangers of UV radiation	- Educate/inform potential and existing customers
Behavioural	-Real-time we- bcams of snow conditions -GHG emission offset programs	-GHG emission offset programs - Water conservation initiatives	-Extreme event recovery marketing	- Good practice in-house

Source: Simpson (2008)

Five key indicators for business

☐ Resource depletion, climate change, changes in water avaiability and the associated issue of food security are discussed at board meetings.

☐ Geographical locations in which the business operates that are likely to be adversely affected by these issues are identified.

☐ Risk, crisis and business continuity strategies include contingency planning for climatic events, water shortages and so on.

☐ Staff understand the implications of these issues at their locations and the responses that are expected of them.

☐ Contingency planning is undertaken with full consultation of other stakeholders within the areas affected.

The tools of the trade

The tools that are available to help businesses address these issues are not always easy to source. Information about responding to single issues – and especially climate change – is prevalent and relatively easily accessible to many businesses. Information about other issues – or the implications of the range of issues as a whole – is found in a number of different disciplines including change management, risk and crisis management and sustainable development literature.

♦ Some hospitality/tourism specific tools do exist, for example the wealth of information developed by the United Nations Environment Programme (much of it in collaboration with academics such as Murray Simpson) on the issue of climate change adaptation in specific environments (notably the Caribbean). There are also some very useful tourism specific tools, such as the materials developed in the UK by the Climate Impacts programme (UKCIP) and the Climate Prepared website (www.climateprepared.com), the Climate Change Adaptation Resource in Finland (http://www.climatechangeadaptation.info) and the Business Continuity Planning tools available from the Australian Government (Tourism and Climate Change – A Framework for Action).

♦ The World Business Council for Sustainable Development also provide a wealth of information on adapting to climate change and other sustainability business risks including the Global Water Tool. This is targeted primarily at global companies and focuses largely on the issue of adaptation.

♦ WBCSD are always working with CERES to urge the investor community to engage in the debate and have tools such as the corporate water risk investor framework.

- The Global Water Partnership Toolbox, which provides free access to a database of case studies and references that can be used by anyone who is interested in implementing better approaches to water management (www.gwptoolbox.org).

- One the topic of water, WWF have worked with SAB Miller to produce a range of guidance for businesses.

- On the topic of climate change, the UN has produced an online toolkit to evaluate energy consumption, find renewable resources and improve energy management for hotels in particular (known as the Hotel Energy Solutions e-toolkit).

- Professor Tim Laing of City University, London, has provided a great deal of UK specific advice on food security and the UN Food and Agricultural Organization also has a range of data available (although adaptation options to this issue are relatively rarely discussed, partly because of the political ramifications of reengaging in some of the debates around increasing crop productivity).

- Driven no doubt by the cost of failure and risks to their own business models, a number of insurance companies have also produced guidance for businesses about adapting to at least climate change and water scarcity. These include AXA among others.

- Some of the design guidelines such as LEED also take climate change and other issues into account within their specifications for new build and renovations (see Principle 3 for details of the LEED and similar initiatives).

Conclusion

The spectre of climate change and other global environmental issues has long hovered over hospitality businesses. However, it is evident that many have yet to really integrate their responses to these issues into risk and crisis management or adaptation plans. History has taught us that a failure to address these issues can result in significant difficulties for businesses. Moreover, those business that do address these issues (in partnership with their stakeholders) are finding that implicit within them are new business opportunities as well as risks.

It is perhaps the lack of focus on the implications of global environmental change (and the fact that these deliver opportunities as well as risk) that has deterred so many global businesses from playing a transformational role in society. Readers will notice that from this stage in the book on, we move away from the areas that have traditionally been included within the responsible business agenda and that broadly map onto 'business as usual' practices.

References

AON (2003) *The AON European Risk Management and Insurance Survey*, AON www.aon.com

BBC (2010) World Water Crisis, http://news.bbc.co.uk/hi/english/static/in_depth/world/2000/world_water_crisis/default.stm

Cheng, M. (2010) Results of the SWCCIP Tourism Group's Tourism Business Survey, February 2010, South West Tourism, Exeter

Economist Intelligence Unit (2011) *Adapting to an Uncertain climate – a world of commercial opportunities*, UK Trade & Investment, available from http://www.ukti.gov.uk/uktihome/item/128100.html

Hall, C.M. (2006) 'New Zealand tourism entrepreneur attitudes and behaviours with respect to climate change adaption and mitigation', *International Journal of Innovation and Sustainable Development*, **1** (3), 229–237.

Hawkins, R. et al (2011) Research under development and due to be published 2012.

Kallhauge, A. (2009) 'Climate change adaptation – finding the business opportunities,' seminar, 16 Jan

KepisandPobe (2011) *Natural Gas to 2030*, available at www.kepisandpobe.com

Rees, M. (2010) 'Surviving the century', the Reith Lecture, broadcast on Radio 4, 8 June.

Simpson, M.C., Gössling, S., Scott, D., Hall, C.M. and Gladin, E. (2008) *Climate Change Adaptation and Mitigation in the Tourism Sector: Frameworks, Tools and Practices*. UNEP, University of Oxford, UNWTO, WMO: Paris, France.

UK Metreological Office (2010) *Climate Change – Who Does What*, available at http://www.metoffice.gov.uk/climatechange/guide/quick/evidence.html

United Nations (2009) *United Nations Human Development Report*, available at http://hdr.undp.org/en/reports/global/hdr2009/.

World Bank (2011) Global Food Crisis, available at web.worldbank.org/WBSITE/EXTERNAL/NEWS/0,,contentMDK:21928797~menuPK:34480~pagePK:64257043~piPK:437376~theSitePK:4607,00.html.

World Business Council for Sustainable Development (2008) *Adaptation – An Issue Brief for Business*, Geneva: WBCSD.

WRAP (2011) *The Composition of Waste Disposed of by the UK Hospitality Industry*, Banbury: WRAP, available at *www.wrap.org.uk/hospitality/report_the.html*

Principle 3: Develop products that are responsible and can be operated responsibly

Don't follow trends – start trends.

Frank Capra (film-maker)

Any organisation that has sought to graft responsible business principles into an existing operation will comment that their task would have been easier had these principles been integrated from the outset. It is significantly easier (and in most instances cheaper) to design responsible business or sustainability principles into products from the outset than to retrofit an existing product/property to maximise sustainable development credentials. It is the failure to acknowledge this issue and to view all new products through a responsible business screen that bred widespread consumer mistrust in business. A continuation of this failure will leave businesses ultimately unable to play the transformative role in society promised by organisations such as the World Business Council for Sustainable Development.

Killing the goose that laid the golden egg

In some areas – and especially where hospitality is associated with leisure tourism – excessive development has destroyed whole destinations. As early as 1973, Sir George Young (Tourism: Blessing or Blight) noted the potential for tourism and rapid hotel development to 'kill the goose that lays the golden egg'. Despite the 30 or so years that have passed since that publication, over-zealous tourism development continues to result in a high volume of obsolescence. For example, around 15% of Caribbean properties closed facilities wholly or in part in 2009/10 as a key element of their economic survival strategy (KPMG, 2010).

Within the hospitality sector as a whole – outside a few trial products targeted at the eco sector and one or two forays to trial sustainable design criteria – it has not been the norm for new products to be screened to ensure their match with responsible business criteria (although some will be reviewed for reputation risks). Given that success in the sector is predicated on growth in the number of units (i.e. adding to or building new facilities rather than increasing sales into existing ones) this failure may fatally flaw the image of the sector as one that is compatible with social justice, environmental protection and economic prosperity.[10]

---

10 This may not be a view that some specialists in sustainable tourism and/or sustainable development recognise. However, many in the NGO, conservation and government communities view hospitality – especially when associated with tourism – as one of the key industries that can deliver these benefits.

The growth statistics for the hospitality sector provide some urgency to the need to start reviewing new product development (including refurbishment as an alternative to new build) through a responsible business lens. According to the International Tourism Partnership, the hotel sector alone is expected to double in size over the next 15 years (ITP, n.d.). Much – but by no means all – of this increase will take place in the BRIC countries and properties built now will have a life expectancy of around 40 years (Rushmore, 2006).

There is an emerging body of evidence to demonstrate that conventional business benefits can flow from developing responsible products that can be operated responsibly. For example buildings that are constructed/refurbished even to the relatively modest LEED standard (Leadership in Energy and Environmental Design) can expect to deliver: a 30–50% reduction in energy use; a 35% reduction in carbon emissions; a 40% reduction in water emissions; and a 70% reduction in solid waste expenses (US Green Building Council, 2008: 240). Perhaps as significant for a sector that is increasingly moving to a leased (as opposed to owned) mode of operation, a survey by McGraw Hill (FM Link Group, 2011) found that the businesses that are designed and managed according to sustainable criteria anticipate a 4% higher return on investment, 5% increases in building value and occupancy, 8% drop in operating costs, and a 1% rise in rental income.

The same survey reported that 79% of owners believe eco-friendly buildings help them attract and retain tenants and competitive advantage, especially in tough financial times. Respondents also cited benefits to occupants' health, productivity and satisfaction, with 10% of green building tenants saying they have noted improvement in worker productivity, and none reported decreases. Also, 94% of managers said they have noticed higher satisfaction levels after green projects and 83% of tenants believe they have a healthier indoor environment as a result of green efforts.

It is pertinent at this juncture to bring into the discussion the issue of refurbishment. Many hospitality businesses grow through the process of developing new facilities. The development of new buildings is, however, hugely resource-intensive (significantly more resource-intensive than refurbishment). What's more, hospitality facilities are often located in fragile environments and can be built with little or no consideration for the beauty and integrity of their surroundings, whether from the environmental or socio-cultural perspective. The resulting effects can be highly visible and undermine the environmental quality of the destination. Many hospitality businesses seek to build (or occupy) new facilities, when the opportunity to refurbish existing properties would be preferable from a sustainable development perspective. The costs of a major refurbishment can often match those of new build (and perverse incentives by governments and international agencies do little to encourage those businesses that seek to refurbish rather than start afresh[11]) and

11 See for example, the range of IMF incentives to develop new hotel facilities, taxation mechanisms such as that in the UK that applies a zero tax on new build and yet applies Value Added Tax to extensions and refurbishments.

can significantly improve operational performance. Nevertheless the environmental benefits of retrofitting existing building fabric (or at the very least recycling and reusing materials from one) will often outweigh those of new construction when a full lifecycle analysis is implemented.

At the current time, responsible business considerations are laid aside when new product development decisions are made (outside the minimum required to keep the regulators at bay). The reasons for this are multiple and, in large hospitality businesses, partly influenced by the growth in popularity of leased, franchised and managed patterns of ownership. These combine with ignorance and fear about the ability of less conventional buildings/technologies to deliver service quality. Thus, those charged with implementing responsible business programmes once facilities are constructed find themselves doing battle with among other things: outdated technologies (even in new buildings), building fabric that cannot be insulated against heat or cold, buildings that are poorly located to benefit from natural heating and lighting, spaces that cannot accommodate waste recycling, spaces that have excessive air conditioning provision, intransigent property owners or facilities management companies that are unwilling to invest in post-construction improvements that will enhance eco-efficiency let alone responsible business credentials.

Subway build eco-restaurants as a part of corporate commitment

According to Subway Marketing Director, the company's commitment to developing new eco-restaurants reflect the brand's commitment to social responsibility and sustainability. The move comes in a bid to make a real difference as America's largest franchise chain.

www.triplepundit.com accessed Wednesday, 7 September 2011

As is the case within this chapter, the focus of much of what is written about developing responsible products that can be operated responsibly in the hospitality sector focuses around the issue of new buildings. It is important to remember, however, that this agenda is much broader than building projects alone. For a sector that also provides the nutritional needs of vulnerable people, there is a significant responsibility for those involved in developing new products in the catering sector to review these for relevance across the responsible business agenda. The legislative framework for decisions in this area (vis-à-vis food safety, nutritional standards and so on) is relatively well advanced in developing countries, but this does not mean that products do not occasionally fall through the net. Those of UK origin may recognise the pitfalls at the mention of the humble Turkey Twizzler! All of the major hospitality businesses have well advanced procedures for checking the health and nutritional characteristics of new food products. It is for this reason that they are not commented on in the text that follows.

> **Text box 22: Integrating responsible business principles at the design stage delivers significant benefits**
>
> Rezidor opened the Radisson Blu Waterfront Hotel and Congress Center in Stockholm in 2011. Integration of responsible business considerations at the design stage have delivered significant benefits, including:
>
> - Stockholm Waterfront is more than twice as energy efficient as the EU standard 'Green Building';
> - The double glass façades are 1040 m² solar collectors that on average gather 1 MW of heat energy on a daily basis. This is equivalent to 90,000 normal low energy bulbs.
> - The building is cooled by water drawn from the lake, stored in 250 tonne ice tanks in the basement.
> - About 20,000 m³ of material has been reused from the building previously occupying the site.

When it comes to new buildings, hotels and restaurants are well ahead of the field with most specifying minimum criteria – albeit largely based around the environmental issues of energy and water efficiency and waste management, (see Figure 24).

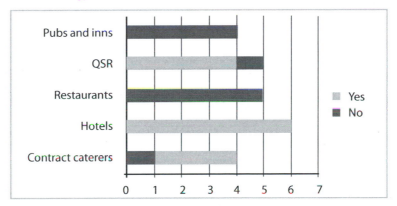

Figure 24: Does the company integrate sustainability issues into design criteria for new build and refurbishment processes

Notes: Data compiled from published data on websites or in corporate reports from 24 large hospitality businesses (see Appendix 1 for a list of companies included).

Some companies have interests that cut across sectors – for example some businesses that are primarily pub operators (and are included in the pub category) also operate a small number of hotels, a number of hotel operators also run restaurants and so on.

Most businesses recommend LEED criteria within their sustainable design specifications.

Pubs and inns and restaurants are much less likely to specify design criteria in UK materials. This is in part a reflection of circumstances – most pubs and inns are UK–based and in the current economic climate focusing on reducing the size of the estate rather than building new properties. Most hotel reports, on the other hand, are international in scope with considerable building activity in areas such as China.

It is interesting that one contract catering organisation has started focusing on the issue of sustainable design – seeking to pass the cost savings associated with good environmental design on to the client premises in which they operate.

What the responsible business guidelines say

The responsible business guidelines all recognise the need for business to play a responsible role in society. Some, however, do not make specific recommendations about new products and services (outside the fact that they should meet regulatory criteria).

As one would expect, the CERES principles are rather more prescriptive, specifying five core criteria for products and services as follows:

♦ **Business Model Innovation**: Companies will innovate business models to reduce material inputs and prioritize a transition to sustainable products and services.

♦ **R&D and Capital Investment:** Companies will use sustainability as a primary filter through which all R&D and capital investments are made – 50% of the R&D investment will be focused on developing sustainability solutions.

♦ **Design for Sustainability**: Companies will approach all product development and product management decisions with full consideration of the social and environmental impacts of the product throughout its life cycle.

♦ **Marketing Practices**: Companies will align their marketing practices and product revenue targets with their sustainability goals, and will market their designed-for-sustainability products and services with at least the same effort as their marketing of other products.

♦ **Strategic Collaborations**: Companies will collaborate within and across sectors to innovate and scale sustainable products and services, and contribute to the development of open source solutions (CERES, 2011).

The fundamentals

Within the hospitality sector – in most instances – there is a clear relationship between the physical property in which it operates and the success of the business. This makes the fabric of hospitality buildings especially important. Customer satisfaction will depend upon a range of factors that are associated with the building, including:

♦ The physical design of the building and the extent to which it complements its surrounding environment;

♦ The functioning of the mechanical systems installed into the building to ensure customer safety and comfort;

♦ The physical age of the building and its state of repair;

- The level of noise in the vicinity of the business;
- The nature of the environment (including the extent to which the community express hostility to the business) in and around the premises.

Many global hospitality businesses have responded to the link between the physical property in which they do business and customer satisfaction by developing standardised design specifications. These define everything from the colour scheme used throughout the property to the type of mechanical systems that should be installed, the paint that should be used, the size of space allocated to each individual function and so on. It is these design specifications that have led to accusations within some circles of the homogenisation of urban and destination spaces and devaluation of cultural norms regarding food (see the essay by George Ritzer on the McDonaldization of society for a fuller view on some of these issues). As a reaction, some hospitality businesses are moving away from such heavily standardised design criteria to ensure that their facilities can to some extent match local cultures.

Many critics of the sector have thus far reserved the greatest ire for unsustainable practices to specific product types. Notable among these within the restaurant sector are fast food outlets and in the accommodation sector the development of integrated or gated resorts. We suspect that these are shortly to be joined by super-luxury hotels and restaurants, especially when they are located in areas where poverty is pervading. Harold Goodwin has strong view on this.

Too much of the debate is characterised by prejudice and a misplaced focus on the form rather than the impacts of hospitality businesses. Businesses that lay claim to operating responsibly and then actively damage the environments, economies or communities in which they are located should be named and shamed, whether operating at the budget or luxury end of the market and whether they are global corporations or small independent operators. It is not the nature of the business but the extent to which it does good or causes harm that counts. The issue of inequality (and it is an issue) is revealed by conspicuous consumption not created by it. A super luxury resort operating in a poor community can choose to accentuate conspicuous consumption or to act as an agent of change. Those that choose the latter path (usually within a responsible business framework) by underpinning urban redevelopment, providing economic opportunities for a wide range of the population, underpinning essential infrastructure (including electricity and potable water for wider community use) and stimulating pride in local cultures whilst protecting environment are those that will ultimately demonstrate their value in society. We need to take a grown up approach to judging each business on its merits rather than branding specific types of business as fundamentally bad. (Harold Godwin, in conversation, 18 May 2011 – see also www.irresponsibletourisminfo/)

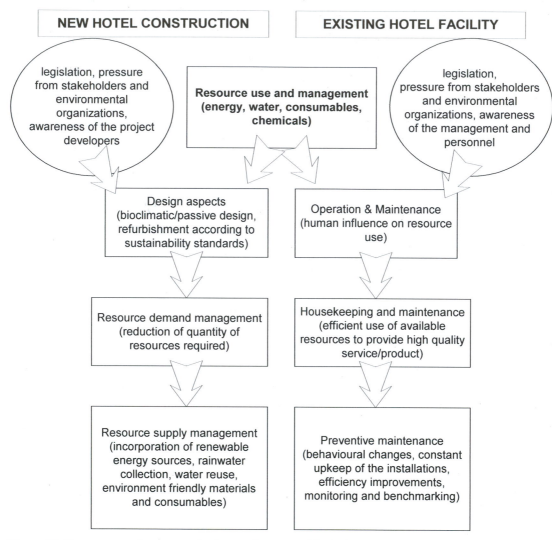

Figure 25: The pressures that engage businesses in responsible choices at new product design and operational stages

Source: Bohdanowicz (2006).

Businesses that claim to be developing responsible products that can be operated responsibly have generally adopted four strategies (these are not mutually exclusive):

♦ Install a handful of 'sustainable' technologies that are proven to deliver cost savings alongside environmental benefits;

♦ Ensure that all new build projects (and in some case refurbishments) comply with sustainable building standards;

♦ Sustainable building showcases;

♦ Transforming the business model.

Specification of sustainable technologies

It is the corporate hospitality businesses that have led the field when it comes to changing design specifications to favour a minimum threshold of environmentally efficient technologies. Few of the major corporate businesses now construct facilities that use anything other than LED lamps, make extensive use of sub-meters for energy (if not water) consumption, have building management systems that continually monitor performance, ensure insulation meets or exceeds national or local standards, integrate the latest in water efficient toilet technologies, low flow taps and so on (see Text box 23). These businesses – by working with their architects, designers and suppliers – have honed the technologies that are available to ensure that they can meet both environmental and service quality within very strict cost criteria. As a result, few guests can now differentiate between service and operational quality in a hotel that has been developed to be environmentally efficient and one that has not.

Text box 23: Sustainable technologies commonly specified into new/refurbishment projects

- Film or double glazing (especially in hot countries) that protect windows and doors from heat gain and solar glare;
- High thermal mass construction materials (that keep heat in and/or cold out);
- LED lamps;
- Timer and motion/occupancy sensors to switch lights, etc. off when not in use;
- Solar hot water heating;
- Guestroom energy management system (for hotels);
- Sensors to disable heating/cooling when external window and/or doors are opened;
- Sub-meters and/or building management systems;
- High levels of insulation (against heat and/or cold) in walls, roofs, heating pipes, water pipes for chilled water distribution, refrigeration lines;
- Energy efficient appliances (from cookers to chillers);
- Low-flow shower heads;
- Tap aerators;
- Dual/low flush toilets;
- Waste water treatment plant/grey water reuse systems;
- Areas for recycling;
- Energy efficient cooking equipment (e.g. induction);
- Installation of devices that recover hot or cold air for recirculation/reuse.

These environmentally efficient technologies collectively deliver a significant saving to operational costs and have been widely integrated into design manuals for most businesses. They are hardly revolutionary (and would not satiate the appetite of many in the sustainable development world for change) but, if adopted through-out the sector, have the potential to significantly reduce impacts. The fact that they have become mainstream within corporate businesses in a period of 20 years or less is to be applauded.

The fatal flaw in extending the universal adoption of these technologies by major corporate businesses extends to the ownership issue (that old chestnut!). More and more corporate businesses are operating on a lease-back or non-owned manage-ment model. For the thousands of hospitality units that operate in premises owned by others the installation of sustainable technologies is still an aspiration rather than achievable goal. The level of control that those in these business units have over the physical equipment that is installed when the unit is constructed – and more to the point how often it is refurbished[12] – is very limited and a great frustration to many in the sector. Developers are rarely willing to engage in the installation of technologies that have a high capital cost and that will deliver savings to property managers rather than property owners. Architects often lack the skills to specify sustainable design criteria. The time has come for corporate businesses to actively engage the in-vestment and development community in this debate (anyone who has been to one of the hotel investment fora will recognise that 'sustainability' is all too often a side show rather than a part of the main event). Declarations by a small number of large corporate organisations about the fact that they will only operate properties that meet minimum environmental criteria would no doubt rapidly engage developers' minds about the benefits of ensuring buildings are constructed to at least operate environmentally efficiently.

Ensure new projects comply with minimum voluntary standards

In some cases stimulated by regulation,[13] some of the major hospitality companies have gone one step further than specifying a handful of technologies to agreeing that their properties will meet minimum voluntary building standards such as LEED (from the USA, but with global application) or BREEAM (from the UK but with global application), Greenstar (in Australia) or CASBEE (in Japan). The companies that have taken this approach have largely made the LEED criteria their standard of choice, because it adapts easily across countries rather than having its foundations within the government policy framework of a specific nation state.

The businesses that have agreed that at least some new (and in some cases refur-bishment) projects must meet LEED criteria include, among others, Marriott, Hilton,

---

12 Refurbishment in many contract catering outlets takes place much less frequently than in hotel businesses and the companies that operate into these units have little say about when it will be commissioned. It is not uncommon to find the kitchens utilising equipment that is 20 years or more old. Given that the efficiency of technologies like heat pumps and air condition-ers has increased by over 50% in the last 30 years, replacement can offer real energy savings.

13 For example, the EU Energy Performance of Buildings Directive that requires buildings to display information about their energy performance.

Fairmont, KFC and Starwood. Some of these business have set challenging targets within the portfolios. Marriott, for example, has set a target of 300 LEED certified hotels by 2015. In seeking to meet such standards these hospitality businesses are making a voluntary commitment globally to exceed minimum building standards on environmental if not economic and social criteria. They are also beginning the process of engaging architects, designers and property owners in developing responsible products.

There are many who would claim that these standards are not as rigorous as they should be (see Text box 24). Nevertheless, they represent a significant leap forward to many conventional hospitality designs and if implemented in every new hospitality development have the potential to significantly reduce resource consumption. Perhaps the main concern with using these standards is not whether they are able to deliver change, but the extent to which they introduce complacency within hospitality businesses. Such certifications can only deliver change on a small number of issues (primarily energy and water management) and essential though these issues are, they are just two of the portfolio of issues embraced within the responsible business agenda. Other aspects that require consideration include whether or not new hotel developments within a destination are required, the social impacts of those developments and so on.

Text box 24: Building standards such as LEED have their critics

The LEED-NC standard (version 2.1 is the most recent issue) is rigid with respect to points, categories, and ratings and as is the case with the other LEED standards, takes a 'one size fits all' approach to green building assessment. There is no weighting system based on climate, bioregion and similar factors. Consequently buildings in Alaska and Florida are rated in virtually the same fashion, although the majority of the energy points are a function of location. Buildings in desert climates such as Nevada and those in relatively water-rich states such as Louisiana have a maximum of 5 points allocated for water efficiency. LEED-NC is not based on a scientific approach for its structure. The categories, points, and ratings are based on the consensus of the committee that developed it. The points within each LEED category are also highly arbitrary. In the Materials and Resources category, for example, the point structure is based primarily on materials reuse, use of recycled content materials and of local materials. It does not use life-cycle assessment or other technical approaches to assist in the decision-making process. Although it does at least partially address closing materials loops, it falls far short in this respect. It does not, for example, address the future extraction of resources from buildings and it barely addresses the composition of the products that comprise them. Although sustainable forestry is certainly an important issue, this and several others, are subject to a certain amount of gamesmanship in which products are specified solely for the purpose of achieving this point. The strength of LEED is its relative simplicity and ease of use. Unfortunately this is also probably its major shortcoming. Using LEED, a green building can be designed and built with no understanding at all of the rationale for green buildings.

(Kibert and Grosskopf, 2006)

Sustainable building design showcases

A small number of businesses have made impressive progress in sustainable design that extend way beyond those embraced within voluntary building standards. In some cases, these design innovations are hosted in a virtual environment (see, for example, IHG's Innovation hotel at http://www.ihgplc.com/innovation/). More and more, however, including within IHG they are real.

One of the greatest advances has been on the issue of carbon. For over a decade now, there have been show case examples of zero-net energy buildings (although in developing countries, many people live in buildings without energy out of necessity and not choice). Recently, there have been a number of hotel developments that also operate on a net-zero energy basis, including the Boutique Hotel in Stadthalle Vienna, the Hotel Campo del Fiori in Munich, Sen5es restaurant in Toronto among others. Industry publications such as *Green Hotelier* provide many other examples of businesses operating on a zero-net energy basis.

Less common are business units that have significantly reduced impacts across the board and genuinely addressed the full range of social and environmental impacts. Some of the corporates have now built test kitchens/hotels as showcases of the living application of their responsible business commitment. Some of these show cases demonstrate the real potential for hospitality to play a role in transforming society. They include in their number, Whitbread, who have developed both a hotel and restaurant that operate according to responsible business principles.

It is a shame that commercial realities mean that some of the key lessons of sustainable design do not pay back within the very short time horizons of most of these businesses (five years maximum) and, therefore, are not integrated into mainstream business. Indeed, the showcases are usually one-offs because the entire model cannot be replicated within current financial regimes. Thus these businesses are confined to remaining as show cases or to cater to the eco-niche. The success of them is their ability to mainstream technologies into hundreds of properties that even a decade ago would have been considered quirky and ineffective. Whitbread are building upon the success of their Premier Inn experience to create a sustainable restaurant and to ensure certain sustainable features become a mainstream element of all future new construction and refurbishment projects.

Responsible products that operate responsibly

Very few businesses fall into this final category. They are the businesses that are genuinely transformative. It is these businesses that have been built from a responsible business ethos and that can be operated responsibly in the long term. In hospitality, these businesses are predominantly found among the independents, although there is a very small number of larger businesses that would also claim legitimacy within this category.

Text box 25: Whitbread's sustainable design experience

A pilot Premier Inn green hotel at Tamworth, Staffordshire, opened in December 2008. It was a new 20-bed hotel, built next to an existing pub, in which various green technologies were trialled including:

- Clever lighting – very low-energy LED lights.
- Natural insulation – sheep's wool in the walls created exceptionally efficient thermal and acoustic insulation.
- Solar panels – to heat hot water.
- Greywater recycling – water recycled from baths and showers is used to flush toilets.
- Timber flooring – sustainably-sourced timber used instead of concrete floors.
- Sustainable, locally sourced materials – recycled plasterboard used for the internal walls. Materials have been specially selected for being ecologically friendly but still delivering very high thermal performance. Where concrete has to be used low-carbon cement is specified from a local supplier. The roof is finished in locally sourced clay tiles with waste tiles being recycled back to the manufacturers. Highly insulated windows: the insulation value is twice as effective as leading high specification windows.
- Ground source heat pumps – using the Earth's energy to heat and cool rooms.
- Mechanical ventilation with heat recovery – delivering fresh warm air to the rooms and still allowing room-by-room control of the temperature. The result is higher air quality in the rooms and lower energy used as the heat recovery system recovers over 70% of the energy of the extracted air.

Together with Waterscan, Whitbread designed and installed the most advanced greywater recycling system on the market. Providing water and removing the waste also consumes energy, so reducing the amount of potable water used can not only reduce cost, but also improve Whitbread's water and carbon footprint.

Some of the technologies worked better than others. An independent report to assess the site's performance during 2009 and to compare it against a similar hotel at Telford found that the Premier Inn, Tamworth had:

- Achieved an 81% reduction in operational carbon emissions during the 2009/10 period.
- A 66% water savings from low-flow showers, taps and the grey-water system.
- The solar heat exchange panels generated most of the site's hot water between 11am and 3pm and not when it is needed in the early mornings and early evenings. The contribution the panels made was not significant in respect to energy saving for the site. This technology was not deemed commercial for roll out into other sites.
- The ground source heat pump was expensive to install with a long payback period but it contributes a very significant energy saving of approximately 50% for the site. So it would achieve a much earlier payback on a 100+ room hotel making it commercial on a large scale.

The lessons from the showcase hotel are now been taken forward in a plan for the 60-bed Burgess Hill hotel which is to adopt the best-performing technologies from Tamworth to deliver 70% carbon- and 60% water-savings compared with a hotel of a similar size. Whitbread have built a 220-seat Beefeater green restaurant as part of this working R&D site.

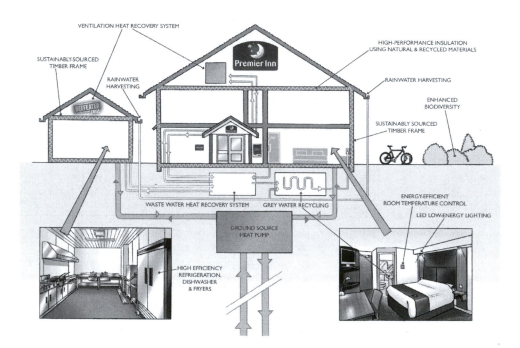

The Burgess Hill includes:

- Ground-source heat pumps using the earth's natural energy to provide heating and cooling as well as hot water.

- Rainwater harvesting and greywater recycling providing 100% of the hotel's toilet water use and saving 20% of the hotel's entire water use.

- High-efficiency thermal insulation.

- Low-flow showerheads delivering the feel and effect of a powerful shower without the associated water loss.

- Heat-recovery shower systems capturing and reusing energy used by the boilers.

- Automated light controls with intelligent sensors turning lights off when not in use.

- Sun pipes reducing the need for artificial lighting by increasing natural light.

The lessons learned from Burgess Hill and Tamworth are being incorporated into new build hotel and restaurant facilities and 25 renewable/sustainable elements from the Burgess Hill and Tamworth showcases are now routinely incorporated into such projects

http://cr.whitbread.co.uk/our-six-priorities/environment/energy-and-water-efficiency/burgess-hill.aspx

Other companies have started seeking to help other businesses address challenges by sharing their own experiences. These include TUI Travel plc with their guidelines for sustainability in hotels.

Figure 26: TUI Travel plc publish their own guidelines for sustainability in hotels. (www.tuitravelplc.com)

To be placed in this category, it is critical to not just build responsibility into the physical fabric of the business (and that alone is hard enough) or engage in environmental management. The essence of being placed in this category lies in longevity and breadth of engagement. The businesses that fall into this category do not have built-in obsolescence dates or five-year operating horizons. They have been developed with a view to contributing positively to the societies in which they are based for the long term. It is the businesses that take this leap of faith and – in the words of Paul Polman (CEO) of Unilever have 'made it clear to investors that if they are looking to make a quick return, then Unilever is not the best place to put their money' – that have the potential to play a transformative role.

Within the hospitality sector, businesses that are playing this transformative role will typically:

♦ Operate in or from buildings that have a small ecological footprint, usually delivered by a combination of renewable energy technologies, highly efficient mechanical systems, water efficient technologies, waste minimisation strategies, can be maintained with a minimum of chemical inputs and so on (when businesses do not build their own facilities, they will have rigorous criteria that all new development must meet – and these extend to siting and design considerations).

♦ Operate in areas where they can have a high and positive impact on society and local economies. For these businesses, sharing their experiences is a part of their ethos, supply chains are typically short local and ethical and nurturing others to transform is second nature.

♦ Engage customers in the process of change – whether by helping them to select responsible modes of transport to get to the business or enthusing them about sustainable lifestyles once they are there.

♦ Often have undertaken lifecycle assessments of their own operations and have a full awareness of their own impacts from the wallpaper used for the restaurant to the carrots served within it.

♦ Refuse new opportunities to establish facilities in locations or deal with partners that cannot meet their responsible business requirements. Thus businesses in this category would not be involved in the development of a facility in an area of extreme water scarcity unless – through its activities – it could improve access for local communities to affordable potable water alongside development opportunities.

♦ Sit at the heart of their communities.

These are not the businesses that talk the language of short-term payback and return on investment. For them costs and benefits are viewed in a long time horizon (although they need to remain profitable to stay in business). It is the necessity to engage in a long-term financial game (and the short-term demands of shareholders) combined with a model in which profitability is predicated on the growth of new sites that excludes all but a few global corporations from this category. This category is, therefore, dominated by small groups and independents, including:

♦ The **Scarlet Hotel**, developed with a simple brief 'to create a unique and sustainable building that blends with and enhances the local environment, utilising the fabulous cliff top location to construct a feeling of space and light'. It uses the very latest in clever technologies, has high levels of insulation, air tightness, utilisation of solar orientation and natural cooling, the provides a sound base for the managerial handling of green issues. All major options for sustainable energy creation were considered before settling upon a combination of different energy sources including a wood chip boiler. The local community and economy was not forgotten. The design facilitates the use of local products and arts and crafts, employs local people and makes a significant contribution to the local economy and is one of the few tourism businesses that stay open all year round.

♦ **Hotel Mocking Bird Hill**, Jamaica which is built on the concept of 'guiltless indulgence'. Based in – and committed to conserving – a unique area of the Jamaican countryside, the hotel utilises solar energy and rainwater harvesting, provides ventilation from natural sources, treats its own waste water, doesn't use chemical pesticides and seeks out organic products from local people wherever possible. It is also a significant local source of employment and supports local people in gaining access to tourist markets.

♦ A number of businesses offering dedicated eco experiences, including Siwash Lake Ranch in Canada, Lanzarote Retreats, La Cusinga Ecolodge in Costa Rica and Eco Camp Patagonia.

♦ A small number of restaurant businesses of which sadly only the UK operators are well enough known to the authors to name and include Venus Café in Cornwall, Acorn House in London, Due South in Brighton, Penrhos in Herefordshire and Konstam in London.

It is difficult to place corporate businesses within this category as few genuinely implement sustainable criteria for all development decisions. Those who could potentially cut the mustard (even though they have some properties in their portfolios that will fail to make the grade), include Scandic, Leon Restaurant Group, Pret-a-Manger, Rezidor, Fairmont (for its CO_2 saver pledge with WWF) and caterers like Apetito who are reviewing the sustainability credentials of product lines.

The sparsity of large corporate hospitality businesses and our uncertainty about placing them in this category is an issue, especially for those organisations involved in leisure tourism. The unwillingness of large corporations to influence the design process[14] (especially when new facilities that are intrinsically unsustainable on siting or operation grounds) in tourism destinations that are not adequately protected by regulation (there are many) leaves many of the world's most precious environments vulnerable to over-development. This in turn calls the long-term prosperity of many hospitality businesses into question. The responsible business practices that are embraced by most corporate businesses to effectively minimise energy consumption or water consumption will do little to change this fact. The only solution for businesses is to review new opportunities through a responsible business lens – and this includes being prepared to refuse to operate into areas or premises that cannot or do not meet minimum responsible business criteria.

---

14 Many would claim that they are unable to influence these processes. However a collaboration between a few of the largest corporate hospitality operators to exert pressure on developers and tourism authorities to meet minimum standards combined with a refusal to operate properties that do not meet those standards would without doubt have an impact on development practices.

Five indicators for business

☐ The responsible business team/criteria are central to all new product development decisions;

☐ The design manual and building specifications are reviewed regularly to ensure compatibility with responsible business criteria;

☐ The business actively discusses its responsible business initiatives and requirements with property developers, the investment community and others involved in new development decisions;

☐ Opportunities to take on the management of new facilities or to operate into facilities that conflict with responsible business criteria are refused;

☐ Minimum and measurable performance criteria are specified for all new build and refurbishment projects, including the use of renewable energy technologies.

The tools of the trade

When it comes to developing responsible products that can be operated responsibly, there is no lack of guidance available. The problem for many hospitality businesses is separating the good from the bad. The tools that have been developed fall into the following categories:

The regulatory bar

In some countries, there is a regulatory bar for responsible design. In EU countries, tools like energy performance certificates are designed to raise this bar alongside regulatory tools such as Part L of the Building Regulations in the UK that specify minimum performance criteria for all new buildings. In some instances these criteria specify renewable energy technologies must be a part of the design brief. In some countries, there are also regulation or taxation mechanisms in place to – for example – deter construction waste from going into landfill rather than reuse.

Regulation sets an important framework from which to go forward and – in countries where it is enforced can play an important role. In the case of leisure tourism – regulation does not apply purely to Governmental regulation. The requirement of organisations such as UNESCO that World Heritage Sites must apply minimum standards within new facilities (and develop visitor management plans) have also played a valuable role.

Environmental impact assessments

Environmental impact assessments are required by regulation for new developments and when hoteliers are responsible for their own developments, they must specify any mitigation measures in which they will engage to counter negative impacts. Strategic environmental assessments when used by planners can also play a role – ensuring that a series of developments do not have detrimental effects on a whole area.

Design manuals

Alongside the design manuals developed by many of the large corporate hospitality businesses, a number of green building and design manuals exist in the public domain. Among the better is the International Tourism Partnership's *Sustainable Hotel: Siting, Design and Construction Manual*. Others include the Green Globe sustainable design guidelines and those developed by specific governments, such as the *Green Hotel Design Guidelines* in Abu Dhabi. These manuals provide guidance on a range of issues from selecting the initial site to orientation of the building, appropriate mechanisms to engage with local community members about the development, choice of materials and technology to selection of alternative (non-fossil fuel based) energy sources and so on. Some of the most useful information is available within the design manuals hosted by the major companies themselves – but these are rarely available in the public domain.

Aside from these there are a number of generic publication, such as the *Green Building Handbook* (Woolley *et al.*, 2005) and BRE's *Green Guide to Specification*.

As with any publication, there are difficulties in keeping these manuals up to date and an increasing number of these tools are now being converted into websites associated with product guides, supplier lists and so on.

Certification schemes for 'green' building

When to comes to building standards – unpronounceable acronyms abound. The main schemes are LEED (Leadership in Environmental and Energy Management – developed in the USA but of global applicability), BREEAM (Building Research Establishment Environmental and Energy Assessment Method – developed in the UK but of global applicability), Greenstar (largely confined to Australia) or CASBEE (largely confined to Japan).

Typically these schemes provide different levels of award (certified, silver, gold and platinum in the case of LEED), allocated on a points-based system undertaken through a formal assessment. The criteria typically embrace:

♦ Siting issues (orientation, location and so on)
♦ Water efficiency
♦ Energy efficiency and emissions
♦ Selection of building materials and resources used in construction
♦ Indoor environmental quality (in some standards only)
♦ Innovation
♦ Design

These standards without a doubt have a role to play in helping building specifiers set a minimum bar that a building should reach or exceed. Those using them should be aware that they have a prejudice towards the environmental impacts of a property and do not in themselves provide any reassurance that the property will meet an organisation's own responsible business criteria. These standards are characterised by the same flaws that affect all other standards – that is that they have a need to generate income and, therefore, have to set their minimum requirements at a scale that is achievable by most businesses. There are critics who would prefer a 'higher bar' (LEED delivers energy efficiency reduction of 25–30% over conventional build and some critics think that 50% or more should be specified). The fact that these standards do deliver efficiencies over conventional designs is what really matters and thus, they have an important role to play in reducing emissions if nothing else. A number of hospitality businesses now specify them as a minimum standard for their new build properties and this is a significant step forwards.

Life cycle analysis

An assessment of the impacts of a product from raw materials extraction through manufacture use and final disposal (often called cradle to grave). Some businesses – including the Scarlet – have used life cycle analysis for all of the main components of their build. This is, however, unusual with the technique being applied to only a small number of components. Caterers have also used the technique on food products when trying to define the best environmental option. However, it is fiendishly complicated and costly so a relatively little used tool.

Conclusion

There is ample evidence that global hospitality businesses are embracing the principles of eco-efficiency within new product designs. There is much more limited evidence that they are really ensuring that the new developments in which they have become embroiled match their own responsible business criteria. In this area there is a conflict between the need to expand and remain competitive (according to the conventional rules of business) while at the same time being seen to operate responsibly. Some opportunities within the sector have been lost – for example that to influence the investment and developer community.

Showcases have amply demonstrated what can be achieved within the sector. The extent to which the technologies and knowledge embedded within these becomes the norm over the coming years will dictate whether or not the sector emerges with its non-polluting image in tact.

To date the ire of the those who seek to criticise the lack of application of responsible business practices to new product development (whether in buildings, food products, etc.) has been targeted at very specific types of development (fast food restaurants, integrated resorts, etc.). In the future we suspect that it will refocus to target those businesses that conveniently abandon responsible business claims when seeking to expand into as yet unexplored territory. In the case of hotels, those that fly the flag for net zero carbon in their buildings and provide air freighted exotic fruits or personal helicopter transport may bring a cynical smile to the faces of customers and critics.

References

Bohdanowicz, P. (2006) *Responsible Resource Management in Hotels: Attitudes, Indicators, Tools and Strategies*, Stockholm: Royal Institute of Technology.

FM Link Group (2011) Survey: Sustainable buildings reap income, productivity benefits, available at http://fmlink.com/article.cgi?type=Surveys&archive=false&title=Survey%3A%20Sustainable%20buildings%20reap%20income%2C%20productivity%20benefits&mode=source&catid=1000&display=article&id=28310, accessed 13/05/2011

ITP (2008) Sustainable Hotel Siting, Design and Construction, available at http://www.tourismpartnership.org/Publications/SDCGuidelines.html

Kibert, C.J. and Grosskopf, K. (2006) 'Radical sustainable construction – envisioning the next generation of green buildings', CCE White Paper, University of Florida.

KPMG (2010) *KPMG's 2010 Caribbean Hotel Benchmarking Survey*, KPMG.

Ritzer, G. (1993) *The McDonaldization of Society*, Pine Forge Press, USA

Rushmore, S. (2006) quoted in *Insiders Perspective – Land Use*, Winter 2006 – 7

US Green Building Council quoted in Butler, J. (2008, August). 'The Compelling Hard Case for Green Hotel Development'. *Cornell Hospitality Quarterly*, **43** (3), 234 – 244.

Woolley, T. Kimmins, S., Harrison, R. and Harrison, P. *Green Building Handbook*, New York: John Wiley & Sons.

Young, G., (1973) *Tourism: Blessing or Blight*, London: Penguin.

Part 3: People and communities

Embraced within this theme are the range of issues associated with ensuring that the operations of the business engage with and respect the rights and views of the range of individuals and communities at a global and local scale. All too often businesses develop with scant regard to people and communities, especially when those people and/or communities are perceived to be: tangential to the purpose of the business, opposed to the operations of the business or subservient to the business as a downstream supplier. Those businesses that have challenged mainstream thinking and have sought to put people and communities back into their business model have generally reported a range of benefits and these are described in the pages that follow.

The principles embraced within this theme relate in part to developing mechanisms to take account of the views of people and communities locally and globally (these are often called stakeholders). They then move on to focus on strategies that have been refined to work with those stakeholders (aside from shareholders) that have particular significance to hospitality businesses. These are: suppliers, employees and customers and public policy makers.

Principle 4: Develop mechanisms to take full account of the views of people and communities

There must be a long-term commitment to CSR activities, which must be supported at senior management level, taking into consideration the issues that are salient to the brands' stakeholders. There also must be sufficient resources to support actions and provide robust measures of performance.

(Polonsky and Jevons, 2006)

Almost since the invention of the firm, shareholders have been 'promoted' as the dominant decision makers and maximising shareholder value as the ultimate objective of a business. Milton Friedman (the award-winning economist) is probably the best-known proponent of this view, often quoted as stating that 'the purpose of business is business'. For most capitalist economies, it would be naïve to suggest that this reality has reversed. It would also be misleading to claim that it remains unchallenged. One school of thought that has gained credence in the business world suggests that those organisations that address the interests of their stakeholders (as opposed to shareholder interests alone) will somehow perform 'better' than those that do not (Polonsky and Scott, 2005).

The failure of a number of high profile companies in recent years and the associated scandals have brought the dominance of the shareholder model of doing business under increased scrutiny. A wide range of business leaders and thinkers have made statements about the significance of companies in broader society (see, for example, Henry Mintzberg's statement that 'Corporations are social institutions. If they don't serve society, they have no business existing' and the thoughts of Demos about the Future of the Firm). In essence, these acknowledge that the future resilience of many businesses depends, not just on the willingness of shareholders to invest, but also on the 'good will' of a large range of organisations/individuals quite apart from shareholders. These *stakeholders* include among others employees, suppliers, customers, clients, sub contractors, financial institutions, third sector organisations, government agencies, the communities in which the business is based and so on.

Business leaders, policy makers, commentators and citizens have begun to reflect on what alternative types of capitalist structures might be more inclusive of all stakeholders, be more resilient in the long term and reduce the risk of future crises.

(Davies, 2009)

In knowledge and service economies, canny organisations – including a number of hospitality businesses – have come to the realisation that a number of different stakeholders are vital to their future success. In the words of William Davies, they recognise that:

> the value of a contemporary business consists largely of intangible assets, rooted in people, relationships, intellectual property (IP) and reputation, none of which is easily captured in the quantitative calculations of external investors. Treating these assets like physical items of property – tradable, dispensable, swiftly exploitable – can do great damage to their long-term value, as so much evidence on mergers and acquisitions suggests.

(Davies, 2009)

In short, businesses are coming to realise that the value on their balance sheets has as much to do with the nature of their relationship with employees, customers, clients, suppliers, communities and so on as the physical assets on which they are based. As Principles 5, 6 and 7 illustrate, hospitality businesses are not ignorant that within this people oriented sector, the quality of their links with stakeholders is crucial to their success[1], and many already have strategies to address key issues.

The power of the stakeholder

Stakeholders have the potential to help a business achieve its aims or to damage it. A handful of businesses have found their name in the press in recent years for all the wrong reasons, often as a result of the actions of one or more stakeholder groups. In most cases, these stakeholder groups are very small in comparison to the businesses that they tackle, but their media savvy approach makes size irrelevant. These groups tend to focus attention on a small number of issues that have the potential to fatally damage the reputation of a brand. The main issues are listed below:

♦ **Employment practices** – whether justified in a complaint or not, disaffected employees have access to a huge number of mechanisms through which to publish their views. These extend from the apparently innocent blog to blatantly controversial websites like fuckedcompany.com that seek to spill the beans on ill-doing by large businesses. Naomi Klein, for example, documents how employment practices of Nike and Gap were exposed by a small group of verbal activists and used to undermine trust in the brand (see Klein, 2000).

♦ **Treatment of suppliers** – suppliers can mobilise like never before and communicate with each other about poor company practices. Websites like Tescopoly (http://www.tescopoly.org/index) abound with support from powerful players (in the case of Tescopoly, the Small and Family Farms Alliance and GMB trade union among others) with the potential to disrupt the supply chain or reduce

---

1   Many hospitality businesses, such as those serving leisure tourists in rural areas have long been aware that a key element of their appeal is the environment and community in which they are based.

the pool of suppliers willing to bid for contracts. With the cheap and easy access to the Internet and mobile phones, formerly unempowered groups (such as employees working for a subsidiary company supplying food products in sweat-shop conditions) can mobilise, impact on brand value and change the practices of a multi-national company almost overnight.

♦ **Attitudes towards customers** – the customer voice has always been of primary importance to companies and never has information about customer service been so crucial and yet so difficult to control. Those who listen to the debates about websites like TripAdvisor will be only too well aware that many hospitality businesses question the lack of external verification of the views quoted on the site (in many cases with some justification). Nevertheless, the site boasts that it hosts over 40 million travel reviews and opinions and is used by 1.3 million visitors per month (http://www.tripadvisor.co.uk/PressCenter-i47-c1-Press_Releases.html, accessed 15 October 2010). In essence it has at least some influence over the decisions of thousands of customers each year.

♦ **Its approach to corruption** and the way in which the company engages with local governments and organisations when negotiating contracts. Transparency International, for example, reports on the strategies of 500 leading companies as regards corruption, and consultancies such as Deloitte warn hospitality businesses of the danger of falling foul of US anti-corruption laws as they seek to expand their global footprint (see, for example, Campanelli and Georgiou, 2010).

♦ **Its emissions** to land, atmosphere and water, its attitudes towards communities and so on. A host of commentators, blogs, websites, government agencies, consultancies and third sector organisations from the Environment Agency in the UK to Sustainability, Greenpeace, Friends of the Earth, AVAAZ and the Ecumenical Coalition on Third World Tourism publish regular information on those businesses that either make claims that cannot be substantiated in fact, or that actively pollute, or that permit the rights of women or children to be abused on their property (whether knowingly or not).

Working with stakeholders – what the responsible business guidelines say

Stakeholder 'engagement' is a vital element in all responsible business standards and guidelines. As a result, any business making claims to responsible business values will inevitably also make reference to its stakeholders.

Most of the codes that seek to guide business in the development of responsible business initiatives take a relatively narrow view of stakeholders. Within their *Business in Society publication*, for example, the ICC, define stakeholders as 'those constituents that have a direct stake in the company'. It does go on to say that 'a company may also wish to broaden its consultations to include other participants in the production chain such as Government authorities, the media and non governmental organisations'. Stressing that 'Companies should be mindful of the differences that may exist within stakeholder groups, such as local communities who are becoming increasingly emphatic about their concerns and with whom it may be useful to establish a dialogue' (ICC, 2002.). Many of the commentators of responsible business practice take a wider view of stakeholders, often using this definition as their baseline: 'a stakeholder is any group or individual who can affect or is affected by an organisation's activities'.

The exception to this rule is the CERES roadmap for a sustainable development that provides comprehensive information about the nature of stakeholder engagement if not the identification of stakeholders (see Figure 27).

For hospitality companies – whose business model is dispersed, and depends upon the good will of communities around the globe – the use of a narrow definition of stakeholders may be a hostage to fortune. For these businesses, key risks relate, for example, to employee practices within the supply chain, and in the case of accommodation businesses, to the attitudes of government agencies and communities in the vicinity of properties.

STAKEHOLDER ENGAGEMENT

S1 FOCUS ENGAGEMENT ACTIVITY

Companies will systematically identify a diverse group of stakeholders and regularly engage with them on sustainability risks and opportunities, including materiality analysis.

S2 SUBSTANTIVE STAKEHOLDER DIALOGUE

Companies will engage stakeholders in a manner that is ongoing, in-depth, timely, and involves all appropriate parts of the business. Companies will disclose how they are incorporating stakeholder input into corporate strategy and business decision-making.

S3 INVESTOR ENGAGEMENT

Companies will address specific sustainability risks and opportunities during annual meetings, analyst calls and other investor communications.

S4 C-LEVEL ENGAGEMENT

Senior executives will participate in stakeholder engagement processes to inform strategy, risk management and enterprise-wide decision-making.

Figure 27: CERES recommendations for stakeholder dialogue. *Source:* CERES Roadmap for sustainability 2010 (www.ceres.org/ceresroadmap)

The fundamentals: identifying stakeholders

A small number of global businesses have invested significantly in (a) identifying who the core stakeholders of the business are; (b) assessing which of these are primary and which are secondary stakeholders;[2] (c) understanding stakeholder perspectives on the business; and (d) engaging stakeholders in a genuine and open dialogue.[3] Widely quoted examples include Nestlé (see the information in Tapscot and Tiscoll's *Naked Corporation*), Puma, MMO2 (a telecommunications company providing fixed and mobile products) and Unilever.

Almost all of the hospitality businesses that have made a formal commitment to responsible business issues have also begun to make strides in the area of engaging with stakeholders. Each business will approach the issue of stakeholder engagement differently.[4] A key element to defining the approach is business size and management style. Most of the larger hospitality businesses that directly manage their facilities tend to take a formal and broad approach to identifying the wide range of stakeholders and hosting formal meetings (often facilitated by external consultants). Businesses that operate primarily on franchise or leasehold models tend to have more limited or less formal stakeholder engagement processes and often claim that they find it difficult to influence the practices of their franchisees vis-à-vis simple issues like environmental management let alone stakeholder engagement.

A handful of hospitality businesses have sought to engage with the widest possible range of stakeholders. Sodexo, for example, identifies stakeholders as illustrated in Figure 28 – and includes employees, local communities and international organisations within their scope. Other hospitality businesses, however, are more cautious either about engaging with those stakeholders that are likely to be more critical of the business or prioritise their early stakeholder engagement processes to target very specific groups with whom they can build partnerships that will yield rapid results. Yum!, for example, do not identify stakeholders per se, but recognise that they have commitments to 'people, the environment, and society as a whole' (http://www.yum.com/responsibility/default.asp). They focus their attention, however, on their franchisees – i.e. the group with whom they have the greatest shared purpose. They are now in the process of working with these stakeholders to deliver changes.

---

2   There are various views as to how to define primary and secondary stakeholders. Gago, Antolín (2004) and Eleanor et al (2006), for example, talk about the concept of 'salience' when it comes to defining stakeholders, arguing that some inevitably have more power and legitimacy than others to impose sanctions (or provide rewards). Mitchell et al. (1997) discuss the concept of stakeholder power and other authors talk about concepts of legitimacy (see, for example, Phillips, 2003) and proximity (see, for example, Driscoll and Starik, 2004).

3   Among those businesses with the most extensive and multi-way stakeholder engagement processes are a handful of those that have experienced greatest reputational damage from a CSR related issue.

4   Although a number of UK-based businesses that use the Business in the Community Framework to guide their responsible business initiatives may have similar approaches.

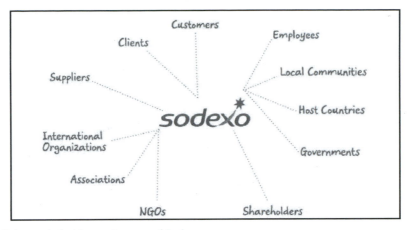

Figure 28: Defining stakeholders – the case of Sodexo

Table 5: The range of stakeholders that are generally identified by different types of hospitality businesses

Hotels	Restaurants
Employees	Employees
Suppliers	Suppliers
Customers	Customers
Clients	Clients †
Local communities	Local communities
Local authorities	Local authorities
(Tour operators)	NGOs
NGOs	Government authorities
Government	Shareholders
Shareholders	Property owners ‡
Property owners ‡	
QSR	**Contract caterers**
Employees	Suppliers
Suppliers	Employees
Customers	Clients †
Communities	Customers
Local authorities	Local communities
Local communities	Host countries
Host countries	Governments
Governments	NGOs
NGOs	International organisations
Shareholders	Shareholders
Property owners ‡	Property owners/facility management companies ‡

* Stakeholder groups are listed in no particular order of importance.

† For many hospitality businesses – and especially those in the cost or business and industry sectors – the customer is not the primary client. The food services of these businesses are purchased by clients (typically a school, hospital, or large corporate company such as Barclays Bank or BT) and are then consumed by customers (in the case of a school the pupils, a hospital the patients, a company the employees). For businesses in these situations, it is the decisions of the client that dictate the level, cost, nature of service rather than the customer. Increasingly client companies are asking food service businesses to provide evidence of responsible business policies and programmes as a condition of contract.

‡ This stakeholder group is only relevant to those businesses that are operated on a lease or franchise basis.

There is a remarkable level of consistency between the stakeholders identified by different businesses in the hospitality sector. For most hospitality businesses, stakeholder engagement processes have focused on three specific groups (suppliers, employees and customers and governments/policy makers) and these are the subject of Principles 5, 6 and 7 respectively. The broader process of engaging stakeholders in general is the subject of the remainder of this chapter.

It is of course, vital for any business that aims to act responsibly to understand the full range of stakeholders with which it will need to engage. Seeking to engage with all of these stakeholders as soon as they are identified, may appear on the surface to be a good thing. However when it comes to fulfilling on the expectations of those stakeholders, this is not necessarily the case. As Dawkins (2004) points out:

> 'stakeholders, internal and external, expect different types/levels of CSR activities. Failure to deliver on stakeholder expectations, whether unintentional implied or not, will result in reputational damage. As such managers need to keep all the stated and implied "promises" made (Kitchin, 2003).'

Differentiators of good and poor engagement processes

The key differentiator between a good and a poor responsible business programme is not the range of stakeholders that are identified, but the nature of the dialogue in which they engage. Genuine dialogue can help stakeholder groups express concerns as well as hopes for engaging with a company. These concerns may not be easily resolved, but the process dialogue can help to build trust and explore avenues through which improvements can be made. There are some stakeholder groups that will not willingly engage with the business. For example, some stakeholders (such as Baby Milk Action) have remained reluctant to engage with Nestlé despite the significant strides it has made to improve its responsible business performance. Nestlé has responded to these groups by developing working groups that seek to 'create shared value' (Tapscot and Tiscoll, 2006).[5]

No-one gets it right all the time!

In today's world no-one 'gets it right' all the time. Whatever your interactions and strategies are with stakeholders, they can always be improved.

(Freeman et al, 2006)

Regardless of how good an initiative is, the failure to actively engage one or more stakeholder groups often results in accusations of 'greenwash'. See, for example, the accusations levelled at McDonald's by marginal groups over changing the colour of its logo (http://www.thegoodhuman.com/2009/11/25/greenwash-of-the-week-mcdonalds-europe-logo-going-green/). This is despite the good that is being achieved and the potential to replicate it internationally.

---

5   See the Shared Value area of the Nestlé website for more information.

Identifying the appropriate mechanisms to engage with different stakeholder groups can be complex and companies are often rightly fearful that attempts at engagement may be misconstrued. It is this fear that has brought about a culture of *green hushing* within some organisations. Many international businesses, however, do seek to work with all stakeholders (including those that are likely to take a negative view of the organisation). No-one pretends that dialogue will always be easy – indeed many of the companies that have got the most effective stakeholder engagement processes have had to engage with their fiercer critics to address key areas of discord and have had to go that extra mile to build trust and transparency into their processes.

Green hushing

A term brought into being by Treehugger (a prominent business and environment website) to describe the phenomenon whereby companies that are authentically 'doing good' stay silent, for fear that they'll be tarred with the same brush as those that are carrying on with business as usual but making green claims.

Those businesses that have used stakeholder engagement to best effect have found that it can hone a responsible business strategy and deliver brand value, but only if there is scope for imaginative solutions on both sides. Gap, for example, used stakeholder engagement processes to rebuild the company image and to transform the way in which it approached ethical trading issues (see Smith *et al.*, 2011). Starbucks recognise the significance of stakeholders within their mission statement … 'to inspire and nurture the human spirit – one person, one cup and one neighbourhood at a time'. The chairman widely acknowledges that 'managing a brand is a lifetime of work' and that stakeholders have a fundamental role to play in the process of continual renewal. It is no coincidence that Starbucks has conquered the Web with over 700,000 followers on Twitter and 5 million followers on Facebook – these social media tools are used as a core element of the company's stakeholder engagement process and add value to the brand (www.starbucks.co.uk).

These companies have found that stakeholder engagement is an ongoing process and one that needs to be underpinned by a genuine multiway communication process. This requires different communication mechanisms to build relationships with each stakeholder group. Even a single stakeholder group (for example customers) may require a range of communication mechanisms to take account not only of the specific needs of, but also the differences within, the group (e.g. to account for different priorities in different geographical areas).

Text box 26: Listening to the voices at the fringe

Many hospitality businesses are aware that their stakeholders – including the voices on the fringe – are important and some have started the process of engaging. Some, such as Whitbread have found that, when done well, broad-based stakeholder engagement processes can be invaluable – providing an opportunity to gain a different perspective on the business. To do it well, it is essential that the objectives of stakeholder meetings/communications are clearly established, the purpose of the meeting/communication understood, the terms of reference agreed and roles and expectations set. It is also important that the tone for the meeting/dialogue is set at the outset.

More than **60%** of our customers and people were 'very concerned' about environmental issues and expected companies to take action.

Whitbread community engagement process – Good Together
cr.whitbread.co.uk/our-strategy/stakeholder-engagement.aspx

Stakeholder engagement does not mean bowing down to stakeholder demands but discussing and agreeing on a common direction or on principles that are common and can be used to deliver change. The characteristics of stakeholder engagement processes that deliver the greatest benefits to companies are summarised here.

The elements of stakeholder dialogue that make a business stand out from the crowd

This list is adapted from Freeman *et al.*, 2006.

Element 1: Genuine multiway dialogue with stakeholders to ensure that the responsible business positioning adds value to the main brand positioning for the company and to each stakeholder group.

Examples: In the case of MMO2, for example, help lines have been established that take questions from concerned members of the public about the health impacts of mobile phone masts, thus keeping the company abreast of current issues and providing a forum through which information can be disseminated back to those groups. For the most part, stakeholder dialogue within the sector has been limited in its approach to multiway dialogue.

Hospitality sector examples: Sodexo captures the significance of stakeholder engagement within the third pillar ('We Engage') of its 'Better Tomorrow Plan' sustainability strategy, which also defines the company's mechanisms for engagement with each of its various stakeholder groups. The aim is to give everyone a say – even dissenters – because the company firmly believes that it is better placed if it has a firm handle on the views of those it engages with.

Element 2: Recognise stakeholders as individuals with needs and values rather than an amorphous group with homogenous needs.

Employees, for example, will have a range of needs (including career advancement) but will also have values that they will wish their employer to meet.

Examples: Unilever samples the views of employee via the Global People Survey. Feedback is accommodated within the company's mission and values taking account of the needs of some employees for family friendly working hours (as described in the value statement, *Living our Lives*); and others for leadership development. It has different mechanisms for each customer group and for suppliers in individual tiers of the supply chain and so on.

Hospitality sector examples: Principles 5, 6 and 7 demonstrate that hospitality businesses have been adept at recognising and responding to the needs of stakeholders in some specific groups (employees, suppliers, customers – especially corporate buyers, and public policy makers). They have, however been less adept at understanding and responding to the needs of specific groups, including in some instances their own franchisees.

Element 3: Seek solutions that satisfy multiple stakeholders.

Examples: Companies need to find solutions that can meet the needs of multiple stakeholders. In the case of Unilever, for example, this has enabled it to make three big commitments for 2020, each of which satisfies a number of stakeholder groups, including those environmental groups that have a tendency to be critical of the business, customers who wish to buy products that do not damage the environment and employees who wish to work for a company that reflects their values.

Hospitality sector examples: Hospitality businesses thus far have been most effective at finding solutions that satisfy the needs of shareholders, alongside those of customers, employees and suppliers. Some companies have, however, found solutions that meet the needs of wider ranges of stakeholder groups. Apetito, for example, with its 'Sourcing with Integrity Procurement Policy' which ensures that all suppliers meet minimum Ethical Trading Standards, builds profitability, provides support for staff nominated charities, meets customer demand and meets business to business sustainability criteria.

Element 4: Engage in dialogue with stakeholders who are hostile as well as those who are friendly.

Examples: It is challenging to meet with critics and this can only be achieved once the rules of engagement are agreed. The rewards, however, can be significant. In the case of Nestlé, dialogue has meant convening working groups and seeking to engage some of the vocal critics of their products in working within these groups to discuss these issues and identify potential routes forward even if issues that cannot be immediately resolved are parked.

Hospitality sector examples: Hospitality businesses have started engaging with their critics. Compass Group, for example, engaged with the Marine Stewardship Council to ensure that sustainable fish is served throughout its premises. Scandic has followed the campaign of SNF (Society for Nature Conservation) and removed tropical shrimps from its menu across the Scandinavian portfolio. Hotels have also engaged with critics on issues such as prostitution. However, critics of new development projects are often excluded from stakeholder dialogue processes, as are communities that do not approve of the business model.

Element 5: Use stakeholder groups to keep ahead of the wave of regulation.

Examples: In democracies, stakeholders provide pressure on regulators as well as companies. Canny organisations use their stakeholder dialogue process to gauge the social mood music and ensure that their activities are in tune. Puma, for example, have used stakeholder engagement to drive their sustainability programmes, including the environmental profit and loss account and the launch of PPR Home to take their sustainability efforts to a new platform. In so doing, the company is identifying the geographical areas in which specific impacts are of greatest concern and adapting the business model to reduce those impacts in consultation with stakeholders.[6]

Hospitality sector examples: On some issues, hospitality businesses have been proactive at gauging the mood music (e.g. health, alcohol and to some extent carbon management). On others they have been less proactive (e.g. water, waste disposal, cultural homogeneity).

Examples: On the health agenda, hospitality companies have been particularly proactive. In the UK, for example, they have worked with the government in what is known as the Responsibility Deal for public health outcomes. Voluntary energy efficiency and waste agreements with government agencies are other examples of ways in which the sector has engaged with stakeholders to ensure action is in advance of regulatory need.

Element 6: Use stakeholders to take the pulse of the companies' reputation.

In the world of Internet-based seller and user reviews, there are few businesses that don't understand the power of stakeholder feedback in building brand reputation. Companies such as Google keep a firm eye on user reviews and actively use these in the product development process.

Hospitality sector examples: The customer feedback form has long been a staple of any hospitality businesses market research programme. Those companies with an eye to the future have extended customer feedback into loyalty schemes, social media and other mechanisms that get feedback from suppliers, customers and other partners to hone the service. Those businesses that have done this effectively have found new business opportunities. Starbucks has made extensive use of Twitter and Facebook to engage with customers and nurture its reputation as a caring brand.

Element 7: Refuse to trade off the interests of one stakeholder group for another.

Examples: Shareholder interests are important but will only be sustained if the brand trust and reputation remain intact. Innovative solutions can help to ensure trade-offs are not required. In the case of Unilever, therefore, the needs of environmental NGOs have been met through commitments to halve the environmental footprint of products, and those of shareholders have also been met by delivering on

---

6   There have been critics of Puma's environmental profit and loss account (primarily around the accounting method).

this commitment by improving efficiency.

Hospitality sector examples: Within hospitality businesses, programmes to utilise ethical beverages ensure the needs of multiple stakeholders are met and are carefully implemented to ensure that quality, price and other customer concerns can be met whilst also meeting the needs of the supplier and ethical trading community.

Element 8: Negotiate with powerful and less powerful stakeholders.

Examples: Engaging with less powerful stakeholders can be particularly challenging, but gaining an understanding of the 'voices at the fringe' can be a fundamental part of any successful stakeholder strategy. For some companies (for example Nestlé and Monsanto) this means accepting that some organisations will never engage with the product or ethos of the company. These stakeholders are not excluded from the dialogue but effort to engage is focused on other stakeholders who, while critical of the company and/or its products, are willing to work in partnership to develop imaginative solutions. The trick for companies is to identify the critical but positive groups from the critical but negative ones to avoid a swarm mentality that allows a number of less powerful stakeholders to come together and attack.

Hospitality sector examples: This is an area in which scant progress has been made. Communities in the vicinity of proposed new hospitality developments, for example, are not often given a true voice. This is especially the case where these developments are remote from head office and perhaps commissioned by a developer who is separate to the company that will operate the property. Finding mechanisms to hear the voices at the fringe can be a challenge but it is one that networks of small social enterprises, such as CoaST in the UK, are helping to tackle.

Element 9: Stakeholder engagement is a process of continual update and learning. Dialogue with stakeholders is ongoing and must be regularly revisited and redesigned.

Examples: All of the companies mentioned above refine and revisit their stakeholder process on an ongoing basis. In so doing, they build trust and strengthen the value of the process and also engage in a greater level of learning about their business and its interactions with society.

Hospitality sector examples: Hospitality businesses that have started the stakeholder dialogue process have, for the most part, found their initiatives rewarding and do seek to extend these processes further over time.

Element 10: Act to fulfil the company's purpose and stakeholder aspirations.

Examples: It is the *job* of businesses to generate a profit. It is rarely the *purpose* of business to generate a profit. Often the *purpose* of a business is aspirational. Those businesses that have as their purpose an aim that is also an aspiration for stakeholders will find the process of engagement less difficult. In the case of Unilever, for example, the purpose of the business is to develop new ways of doing business, with the aim of doubling business whilst reducing the environmental footprint.

Hospitality sector examples A few hospitality businesses have managed to embrace as the purpose of the business something that benefits them and their wider stakeholders. Rezidor for example express their intent within their business values of which openness is one 'we are frank and transparent, accessible, flexible, keen to listen and consider all options (www.rezidor.com).

The hospitality sector is certainly not ignorant of the benefits of stakeholder dialogue. In the words of UNEP:

> Hospitality companies, like all businesses, answer to a variety of stakeholders, including investors, customers, employees, suppliers and the local community. Increasingly, they are experiencing demand for greater participation in decision-making, which may translate into a heightened need to obtain voter approval for planning and development, for example, by carrying out an environmental impact assessment. In this new regulatory context, corporations are being pressured into making a higher community commitment through charitable involvement, a trend mirrored in the corporate marketing techniques increasingly used for the generation of brand awareness.
>
> (WTTC, IFTO, IH&RA and ICCL, 2002: 40)

There is a downside to stakeholder engagement. This has resulted in an element of 'green hushing' within some hotel businesses. Companies like Rezidor (one of the hotel groups that has firmly embraced the responsible business message, but which does little to publicise its initiatives and is quoted by the Ethisphere Institute as one of the world's most ethical companies) for example actively resist the temptation to publicise their responsible business initiatives, preferring instead to develop and hone their strategy and undertake their dialogue with stakeholders with a minimum of publicity. It is easy to understand the reticence of businesses to divulge the details of emerging stakeholder relationships. However, a demonstration of engagement with stakeholders is increasingly taken as one of the signs that a business is serious about its commitment to society and the environment.

Stakeholders and transparency

Apetito, state a desire to 'engage with wider stakeholders' as an important element of its quest to ensure transparency. The means to engage with stakeholders are multiple and include: training for sales staff, the development of brochures, hosting open days and participating in third sector initiatives such as the Courtauld Commitment, the Federation House Commitment and Fareshare charity.

Hospitality businesses will, in the words of *The Economist*, need to ensure that their initiatives continue to develop and engage a wider group of stakeholders in ever more sophisticated dialogue, to avoid falling into the trap that their stakeholder consultation exercises are seen as little more than a smug form of public relations. It goes on to say that those businesses that use their stakeholder exercises as a form of PR may find that 'A bad name has seldom been more expensive, especially when there is a war for talent and customers can look at your supply chains in Vietnam on YouTube' (*The Economist*, 2008). The indicators from those hospitality businesses that have begun to engage are positive with evidence that – for many – stakeholder engagement is far more than a smug form of PR.

Five indicators for business

☐ The business knows who its stakeholders are.

☐ The stakeholder list extends beyond the boundaries of suppliers, customers, investors and regulators to include non-governmental organisations and agencies that have been/may be critical of the business model.

☐ Someone in the organisation is responsible for managing stakeholder dialogue.

☐ Engagement with stakeholder is multiway – providing multiple methods for stakeholder feedback.

☐ Stakeholder views are considered by the management team and incorporated into business strategy as appropriate.

The tools of the trade

Given the significance of stakeholder dialogue in much of the responsible business literature it is surprising that information on the topic is largely absent from the tools that have been developed to help hospitality managers grapple with responsible business issues. If one looks at handbooks like the International Tourism Partnership's excellent and otherwise comprehensive text *Environmental Management for Hotels* – the industry guide to sustainable practice, stakeholders gain barely a mention. Many of the other generic tools also fail to provide managers with the information they need to engage in a meaningful dialogue with stakeholders.

Some of the broader tourism planning tools, such as Community Based Tourism Planning, do actively engage with the concept of stakeholders, but all too often tip the balance to provide one group (in this case communities) with undue weight in the tourism management process. Some authors have commented that this over-reliance on communities in the planning process often leaves communities struggling to offer tourism and hospitality experiences that meet the expectations of international visitors. See for example, the work of Nicole Häusler of Mas Contour for more information.

Those businesses that seek the services of one of the organisations like Business in the Community or an experienced responsible business auditor may fare a little better. For these organizations, stakeholder dialogue is a crucial part of the process, and many will help businesses identify which organizations they should seek to engage. Even for these organisations, however, identifying the most appropriate mechanism to engage in dialogue is far from simple and often lies under the control of companies themselves.

Conclusion

It would be foolhardy to state that hospitality businesses have flocked away from the generation of profit as their reason for being in favour of building cohesive and effective partnerships with stakeholders. Such a move would be absurd, not to mention very bad for the achievement of environmental or societal ends. (Let's not forget that economic prosperity is one of the oft-quoted legs of the three-legged sustainability stool and businesses that fail to make a profit lose their potential to have any positive influence on society.) But it is true to say that many of the global hospitality leaders have come to recognise that the ongoing resilience of their businesses is at the behest of stakeholders. As yet, the means to engage with those stakeholders – and especially those who are disengaged from the process – are under-explored and poorly understood. The leading hospitality businesses are not ignorant of the significance of this issue and many are aware that a failure to engage may make hospitality businesses vulnerable to scandals of similar nature to those that have been focused on clothing manufacturers and petrochemical companies to date. Some are now leading the way in honing their approach to stakeholders.

Moreover, in ever more competitive markets, hospitality businesses are only too well aware that loyal customer bases have to be strategically nurtured and defended, talented employees wooed and protected, increasingly verbal non-governmental organisations at least placated and supply chains managed (adapted from Leadbeater, 1997). As Principles 5, 6 and 7 show, hospitality businesses have started the process of working with the stakeholders in these areas. Engagement is, however, only one part of the equation – moving from engagement and into action that supports the approach towards people and communities is rather different.

References

Campanelli, A. and Georgiou, C. (2010) 'Hotels beware – do not check in corruption', Deloitte Touche Tohmatsu.

CERES Roadmap for sustainability 2010 (www.ceres.org/ceresroadmap)

Davies, W. (2009) *Reinventing the Firm*, London: Demos.

Dawkins, J. (2003) *The Public's Views of Corporate Responsibility*. MORI White Paper, February, http://www.ipsos-mori.com/publications/jld/publics-views-of-corporate-responsibilty.pdf

Driscoll, C. and Starik, M. (2004) 'The primordial stakeholder: advancing the conceptual consideration of stakeholder status for the natural environment', *Journal of Business Ethics*, **49** (1), 55–73.

Eleanor, R.E., O'Higgins, J. and Morgan, W. (2006) 'Stakeholder salience and engagement in political organisations: who and what really counts?', *Society and Business Review*, **1** (1), 62–76.

Fernández Gago, R. and Nieto Antolín, M.(2004) 'Stakeholder salience in corporate strategy', *Corporate Governance*, **4** (3), 67.

Freeman, R.E., Ramakrishna Velamuri, S. and Moriarty, B. (2006) 'Company stakeholder responsibility – a new approach to CSR', Bridge Paper for the Business Round Table – Institute for Corporate Ethics.

ICC (2002) *Business in society - Making a positive and responsible contribution. A voluntary commitment by business to manage its activities responsibly*, ICC Paris

Kitchin, T. (2003) 'Corporate responsibility: a brand extension', *Journal of Brand Management*, **10**(4-5) 312-326.

Klein, N. (2000) *No Logo*, London: Flamingo Press.

Leadbeater , C. (1997) *A Piece of the Action: Employee Ownership, Equity, Pay and the Rise of the Knowledge Economy*, London: Demos.

Leadbeater C and Meadway J (1997) *Attacking the recession: How innovation can fight the downturn*, NESTA, London

Mitchell, R. K., Agle, B.R. and Wood, D. (1997). 'Toward a theory of stakeholder idenification and salience: defining the principle of who and what really counts', *Academy of Management Review*, **22** (4), 853–886.

Phillips, R. (2003) 'Stakeholder legitimacy', *Business Ethics Quarterly*, **13** (i), 25–41.

Polonsky, M. J. and Jevons, C. (2006) 'Understanding issue complexity when building a socially responsible brand', *European Business Review*, **18** (5), 340–349.

Polonsky, M. J. and Scott, D. (2005) 'An empirical examination of the stakeholder strategy matrix', *European Journal of Marketing*, **39** (9/10), 1199–1215.

Smith, C., Ansettm S, and Erezm L, (2011) 'How Gap Inc. engaged with its stakeholders', *MIT Sloan Management Review*, available at http://sloanreview.mit.edu/the-magazine/2011-summer/52415/how-gap-inc-engaged-with-its-stakeholders/

Tapscott, D and Ticoll D (2003) *The Naked Corporation* Free Press, New York

The Economist (2008) 'How good should your business be', *The Economist*, 17 January.

WWTTC, IFTO, IH&RA and ICCL (2002) *Industry as a Partner in Sustainable Development*, Paris: UNEP.

Principle 5: Embed responsible business practices throughout the supply chain

Purchased products and services account for more than 60% of the average company's costs. When your supply chain's environmental and social footprint equals or exceeds your company's, the business' resulting exposure to supplier activities becomes enormous – as does its vulnerability to adverse environmental and social impacts caused by any suppliers.

(Vassallo et al., 2008:3)

Text box 27: Storm clouds on the horizon?

According to the World Resources Institute (2008), the world has experienced a remarkable rise in the price of vital commodities, including energy and agricultural products. For example, between 2006 and 2008, the average world price for oil rose by 110%, rice by 217%, wheat by 136%, maize by 125%, and soybeans by 107%. For all businesses, the corollary of these price rises has been felt immediately and painfully in the form of an increase in costs. Some businesses (including a number of hospitality businesses) have responded to this rise in commodity prices by entering into heated discussions with suppliers, cutting margins and forcing some to the very edge of the financial abyss (see www.tescopoly.com for a flavour of the heated nature of the debate that can follow aggressive price reduction strategies for suppliers and the public relations furore that follows in its wake). In all too many instances, suppliers respond to pressure to cut costs by passing harsher conditions on to employees and suppliers further down the chain (especially when they are located in countries without rigorously enforced human rights/employee standards). It is the employees in these companies who bear the brunt of longer working hours or poorer rates of pay. As many of the world's international companies have found out, such strategies may offer the opportunity for cost reduction in the short term, but they can be costly for corporate reputations, and rarely lead to long term and resilient supplier relationships.

The responsible business initiatives for most hospitality companies focus on the direct impacts of the organisation. The vast majority of impacts for hospitality companies lie in the supply chain. There is a clear dichotomy between these two positions. Forward looking companies have realised that this dichotomy could damage their reputation in the short term and, in the long term, place their future under threat, especially when it comes to the issue of food security. In the words of Paul Polman (Chief Executive Officer of Unilever):

> We must start viewing food security as a part of the larger question of sustainability and the need to live within the natural resource constraints

of the planet. For big companies, like Unilever, this will mean developing new business models which will allow them to uncouple growth from their environmental impacts. With this mindset we should advocate and, where possible implement, … practical approaches'.

(Institute of Hospitality, 2011: 20)

Those companies that can legitimately claim that responsible business is a part of their DNA have recognised the need to fundamentally change the nature of their relationships with their supply chain. These companies are few and far between and none of them would claim to have completed their responsible business journey as yet. Most, however, are committed to continue building constructive partnerships with their suppliers to jointly pursue responsible business objectives. The reasons that they embark upon this journey are occasionally based on a genuine desire to save the world. Usually they are more pragmatic and include a combination of the following:

♦ The need to protect reputations as third-sector organisations increasingly investigate corporate responsibility initiatives (especially in global companies) and target supply chain weaknesses as a key means of undermining credibility. To understand the power of the media see, for example, the recent experiences of Unilever (who played a leadership role in the Round Table on Sustainable Palm Oil and had a commitment to source all its palm oil from certified sustainable sources by 2015. A documentary, screened by BBC programme *Panorama* on 22 February 2010, was investigating whether this claim could be met.

♦ The dwindling stock of many commodities and the need to achieve security of supplies. This is the case for not only oil, but in current market conditions, also wheat,[7] soya beans, cocoa and corn, as well as minerals. Global climatic conditions, combined with competition for land (not aided by the increase in use of land for production of biofuels), have led to reduced output, and driven prices up. Businesses with supplier arrangements that are dependent on more than price alone have demonstrated that they are more able to weather such storms and secure access to suppliers.

Supply chains at risk

The financial crisis and a number of other large events that have happened in the past five years have definitely prompted companies to start looking at the true costs of supply chain disruption risks.

Paul Kleindorf (quoted in the Financial Times, http://www.ft.com)

---

7   The USDA said wheat stocks in 2010 would fall from just under 194 million tonnes to 174.8 million tonnes. (http://www.bbc.co.uk/news/business-10956219)

- A rapidly growing population that is driving an increase in demand for products from rare earth[8] to foodstuffs;

- The need to develop the unique selling proposition of the brand. As more and more hospitality businesses are finding, the plethora of brands that seek to demonstrate responsible business practices have confused the consumer (see Principle 6). This is especially the case when dealing with complex products (such as accommodation choices or a whole meal as opposed to a single item on a supermarket shelf). Real success in brand differentiation lies in demonstrating responsible business practices throughout the organisation, and nothing demonstrates trust and responsibility better than mutual reinforcement of the brand image by suppliers. See, for example the way that Cadbury's has repositioned its Dairy Milk brand via its partnership with Fair Trade and a range of catering businesses use their fair trade products and relationships with organisations like the Marine Stewardship Council. This effectively enables the brand to reassure consumers of its 'moral convictions', gain publicity from the partnership, and guarantee access to raw materials for its products in the long term.

- The need to manage carbon outputs of food production/processing and services, to minimise the likelihood that this will become the focus for regulators' attention (see Figure 29).

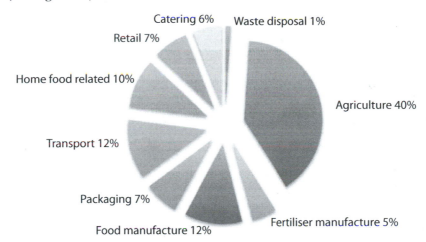

Figure 29: Greenhouse gas emissions from food
Source: WWF/FCRN (2010).

Within hospitality businesses, supply chains are of particular importance. They provide the blueprint for cheap food. Historically, within the sector, contracts have been negotiated to reward suppliers that can: meet bulk order requirements, meet

---

8   Chemicals used in a range of products (especially electrical products and solar technologies) are in the lanthanide series that are regularly found in the earth's crust, but rarely in concentrations that makes it economically viable to mine them. Those areas in which they are sufficiently concentrated for viable mining are found mainly in China and prices for these chemicals have increased significantly in recent years.

rigorous externally imposed health, safety and risk criteria, match quality standards for a global audience, organise logistics and cut margins to the quick. These arrangements favour suppliers that can produce large volumes, using standardised production processes (or cheap labour) at a low unit price. In essence, these relationships have promoted dependence upon a tiny number of suppliers for a large proportion of product. They have also given those intermediaries with the potential to provide large volumes of products from a number of primary producers disproportionate power over those producers. Previous experience in the sector engendered a belief that the failure of one primary producer to deliver on its commitments could be easily resolved by switching to a competitor producer. The range of threats that are now facing global supply chains in general and food supply chains in particular are calling this conventional wisdom into question. The result? Many businesses (and especially businesses for which food is a central component) are realising that their supply chains are dangerously exposed. The nature of this exposure is wide-ranging and has resulted in particularly heated discussions about food supply chains in general and food security in particular. The buzzword of the moment is 'resilience' and a number of food service businesses are now reviewing their supply chain with a view to building it.

Working with suppliers – what the responsible business guidelines say

Many of the guidelines acknowledge the growing significance of supply chains in the achievement of responsible business ambitions. For example, the International Chamber of Commerce in its *Business in Society* booklet, states:

> Supply chain responsibility is an issue of growing concern for companies, particularly in those sectors in which production is largely outsourced …. While, in most cases, companies cannot be held legally accountable for their suppliers' conduct, a responsible business approach encourages companies – where reasonable and appropriate – to engage in a constructive dialogue and direct cooperation with their suppliers and subcontractors, especially in developing countries. Companies should encourage their suppliers to abide by the same business principles that they themselves uphold, thereby promoting good practice throughout the supply chain. This can be done using several incentives, including information and training, as well as audits of the supplier's practices. Corporate buyers increasingly request their suppliers to provide comprehensive social and environmental information on the products and materials that they purchase.

(ICC, 2002)

The Caux principles set out guidelines for managing stakeholders, and suppliers are one of the stakeholder groups identified (see Text box 28). In the Roadmap for

Sustainability, the CERES principles do not make explicit recommendations about suppliers and the supply chain. Broad targets for the supply chain are instead integrated into direct business responsibilities, stating that 'Companies will ensure that at least 75% of the company's Tier 1 and Tier 2 suppliers and 50% of Tier 3 suppliers meet the company's standards for sustainability performance' (CERES, 2010: 11). This ensures that suppliers are central to stakeholder dialogue and integrated into the company's main responsible business values. They support these ambitions by a requirement to ensure that suppliers are treated fairly and provided with support in meeting the responsible business guidelines of the company.

Text box 28: Caux Principles and supply chain responsibilities

A responsible business treats its suppliers and subcontractors with fairness, truthfulness and mutual respect. Business therefore has a responsibility to:

- Pursue fairness and truthfulness in supplier and subcontractor relationships, including pricing, licensing, and payment in accordance with agreed terms of trade.

- Ensure that business supplier and subcontractor activities are free from coercion and threats.

- Foster long-term stability in the supplier relationships in return for value, quality, competitiveness and reliability.

- Share information with suppliers and integrate them into business planning.

- Seek, encourage and prefer suppliers and subcontractors whose employment practices respect human rights and dignity.

- Seek, encourage and prefer suppliers and subcontractors whose environmental practices meet best practice standards.

Source: Caux Round Table Principles for Responsible Business (www.cauxroundtable.org/)

The fundamentals: reengineering supply chain relationships with a responsible flavour

Reviewing supply chains to ensure that they reflect (or at least do not contradict) responsible business priorities may sound simple. In the words of David Nestle, it requires adopting processes to 'work with suppliers and customers in a collaborative way to create shared value and to ensure CSR is built into the foundations of the core business principles – after all, CSR isn't a destination; it's a journey.' (http://www.caterersearch.com/Articles/2009/10/02/330196/going-beyond-the-greenwash.htm). It may sound simple, but don't be deceived. The nature of the hospitality sector, its legacy of supplier arrangements and health, safety and quality requirements, makes the integration of responsible business criteria into the supply chain fiendishly complicated. For those businesses that do it properly, it is a process that requires continual update and review. Thankfully, many suppliers to the sector are a little ahead of most hospitality businesses when it comes to responsible business requirements, which does ease the pain of integrating suppliers into responsible business programmes (see Text box 29).

Text box 29: Wholesalers to the sector are ahead when it comes to supply chain management

Wholesaler 3663, for example, has already taken steps to reduce packaging within the supply chain by:

- Introducing reusable trolleys to replace crates or boxes. All outer packaging is now 100% recyclable.

- The company actively works with customers in hospitality businesses to reduce the number of deliveries and fuel consumption associated with those deliveries has declined by 6.6% over the last year.

- The company also passes responsible business issues throughout its own supply chain, for example, requiring all of its print and stationery suppliers to meet ISO 9001, ISO 14001, the PEFC Programme for Endorsement of the Forest and Forestry Stewardship Council certification.

Source: 3663 Sustainability Report 2009/10

For most hospitality businesses, the supply chain is not a single amorphous entity, but a complex array of primary and secondary producers, processers, packers, logistics teams, wholesalers,9 other intermediaries and so on. Most hospitality businesses keep accredited supplier lists that overlay these procurement arrangements and one cannot over-emphasise the importance of these lists within the sector. They are closely guarded and are the formula for cheap food. Suppliers on the list typically offer hospitality companies rebates for purchases over and above a critical threshold. Purchasers who exceed these critical thresholds are rewarded in their annual bonus. The catering companies that exceed volume purchasing thresholds stand to be able to either improve profitability or sell food at a lower cost. These rebate systems are central to the 'business as usual' model for food service companies, but they present a significant barrier to small and medium-sized food production businesses (who are not able to produce in sufficiently large volumes to have rebates applied to their products) and, thus, they (alongside due diligence procedures as currently reflected in Hazard Analysis and Critical Control Points – HACCP – processes) encourage the perpetuation of mass production systems and global supply chains. The business practices that perpetuate these lists are in many ways contrary to conventional thinking about responsible business.

---

9   In total, wholesalers account for around 71% of the food and beverage supply market for food service companies in the UK (source – Rawlingson Lane Publicity).

Nevertheless, collectively, hospitality organisations use these lists to procure thousands of product lines that account for many millions of pounds of expenditure. Text box 30 demonstrates the typical range of product categories purchased within hospitality businesses.

Text box 30: Typical range of products purchased by hospitality businesses

- Bakery
- Beverages (alcoholic and non-alcoholic)
- Butchery
- Catering equipment
- Cleaning products
- Dairy products
- Decorating
- Dry goods
- Financial services
- Facilities management
- Fish and seafood
- Fresh produce
- Furniture and furnishings
- Grocery
- Guest amenities
- Guest entertainment
- Hot beverages
- Lighting
- Linen
- Paper products
- Professional services
- Property management software
- Property services
- Retail goods
- Snacks
- Soft drinks
- Tableware
- Telecoms
- Uniform and workwear
- Washroom services
- Waste management
- Wines and spirits
- Utilities (electricity, fuels and water/waste water)

Any changes to the hospitality supply chain to meet responsible business criteria have to be made in the short term at least, whilst ensuring that: supply lists can continue to function, quality, health and safety and other criteria are met, and costs do not rise significantly.[10] This is a complex process and gives those hospitality businesses that have grown from a sustainable ethos (e.g. Pret-a-Manger, Leon and to some extent the smaller caterers like Vacherin) a distinct advantage. For them, supplier relationships will have been built, pricing proposition based and brand position won on 'sustainable' product credentials. Designing responsible supplier relationships to support an existing product is tough, little researched[11] and can take

---

10 In western economies, there is considerable pressure to keep costs to a minimum. This is especially the case for caterers servicing the public sector where the combined impacts of recession and food price rises are squeezing many catering functions.

11 As Keating et al. (2008) note, 'While numerous scholars have noted the importance of incorporating CSR into the purchasing decisions of firms … the literature provides little guidance on how best to pursue this objective'.

many years to deliver. That is not to say that it cannot be achieved or deliver benefits to the bottom line. But the challenge extends way beyond nurturing the interest of procurement professionals within hospitality businesses in selecting a few products that have been fairly traded or produced using fair trade, organic or free-range systems. Outside the organisations for which the business model is predicated on a sustainable ethos, few of the international corporations have really started down the route of 'sustainable' supply chain management. Even among those businesses that are predicated on a sustainable ethos, few will claim to have 'completed' their work in this regard. This is hardly a surprise when one looks at the magnitude of the task of engaging suppliers in the responsible business debate and the uncertainties about the best environmental option for many products.

Those businesses that have made most progress in engaging suppliers in their responsible business programmes have generally followed the processes below:

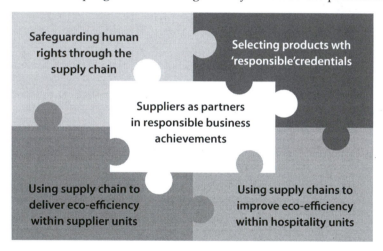

Figure 30: The steps in engaging suppliers in responsible business initiatives.

These processes should be viewed as inclusive (i.e. businesses need to make progress in each stage). Hospitality businesses have made some progress in implementing these steps. A number have developed codes of conduct that they ask their suppliers to comply with. The aim of these is to ensure that suppliers meet their businesses own values. Many of the businesses that don't yet have these codes of conduct in place are in the process of developing them.

When it comes to integrating responsible business credentials throughout the supply chain, QSR, hotel and contract catering business appear to have generally made better progress than restaurant or pub companies. As a general rule, however, for hospitality businesses the mechanism to integrate responsible business credentials throughout the supply chain is through a process of asking suppliers to provide a copy of their environmental/responsible business policies as a part of the procurement process and then organising site visits or audits for a very targeted number of premises. While this approach may be simple to implement, it rarely extends beyond primary suppliers, does not always help the supply chain to gain access to resource efficiencies and does not uncover potential human rights abuses among secondary or tertiary suppliers. Nor does it creatively open up new mechanisms for supply in a world that is likely to be become more resource poor.

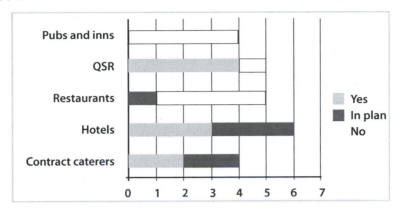

Figure 31: Hospitality businesses that actively seek to engage suppliers in responsible business initiatives.

Notes: Data compiled from published data on websites or in corporate reports from 24 large hospitality businesses (see Appendix 1 for a list of companies included).

Some companies have interests that cut across sectors – for example some businesses that are primarily pub operators (and are included in the pub category) also operate a small number of hotels.

Codes of conduct for suppliers are not available for all businesses.

Using the supply chain to drive eco-efficiencies in the hospitality business

Most of the businesses that have started down the path of reviewing supplier credentials have done so for the same reasons that they adopted responsible business practices in the first place – because they recognise that it can reduce costs.

This approach has also been a popular starting point for the responsible supply chain strategies of many hospitality businesses, but those who think that it is also an end point should beware. In the words of Sustainability, 'Supply chain strategies that focus narrowly on the cost- and time-efficient movement and coordination of goods and materials from upstream suppliers to downstream consumers do so at their peril. Smart business strategists must equip themselves to anticipate and manage an array of dilemmas and trade-offs – such as the degree to which their particular supply chain may deplete natural resources or the challenge of delivering accountability for good labour practices, not just among first tier suppliers in emerging economies, but among their suppliers' suppliers and in tiers beyond that' (Sustainability, UNEP and UNGC, 2008: 1). Those businesses involved in the provision of food should be aware of the significant risks of seeking to gain the reputational benefits of responsible business whilst applying their new found ethics only to initiatives that produce cost savings in the first tier of the supply chain!

Text box 31: Driving supply chain and eco-efficiencies

Sodexo's Tillery Valley food production business started working with its suppliers to source larger pack sizes for raw materials. One example is tinned chopped tomatoes – a high volume raw material for the company.

In 2008, approximately 27,000 4-kg tins of chopped tomatoes were purchased which resulted in 12,500 kg of waste steel. Contamination meant that it could not be taken away for recycling by a waste contractor. By January 2009, Tillery Valley had renegotiated with the supplier to optimise the size of raw material packs so 200-kg drums of chopped tomatoes were purchased, significantly reducing labour requirements and the weight of steel waste. Steel waste has reduced by 78% and a contract has been secured to recycle it.

Bohdanowicz *et al.*, (2005) describe how Scandic successfully persuaded producers and suppliers to make their products more environmentally responsible so that they met the value of the hotel group. Suppliers that were influenced included low energy lamp and chemical manufacturers. In some cases, they even managed to engage suppliers in the process of eco certification.

Using responsible business programmes to drive eco-efficiencies through supplier companies

For most businesses, it is a small step to move from using the supply chain to deliver cost efficiencies to the procurement organisation to working with it to also deliver efficiencies into first tier suppliers. These efficiencies are generally a direct result of initiatives that reduce: emissions of carbon, water consumption and waste production. For food service companies, where the majority of impacts lie in the supply chain, such strategies can be powerful motivators of change and can help businesses to achieve corporate ambitions and – perhaps more importantly – to make a substantive contribution towards ameliorating the impacts of global environmental change. Companies leading in this field include:

The power of many – the supply chain leadership coalition

Companies including Procter and Gamble, Unilever and Dell are all members of a group called the Supply Chain Leadership Coalition, encouraging suppliers to release reports about carbon emissions and strategies for battling climate change.

♦ Unilever which is taking a whole supply chain approach to reducing the impacts of primary, secondary and tertiary suppliers and also driving efficiencies and impact reduction throughout logistics, etc. (see Figure 32).

♦ Marks and Spencer have moved all their whole fresh turkey, duck and geese to free range and have introduced clothing ranges made from organic linen and cotton; wood and wood products are being swapped for FSC certified alternatives and changes to logistics have achieved a 20% improvement in delivery fuel efficiency to stores, with a target to increase this to 35% by 2015 (http://annualre-port.marksandspencer.com/operating-and-financial-review).

♦ Wal-Mart aims to deliver a reduction of 20 million metric tonnes of greenhouse gas (GHG) emissions by the end of 2015 with help from its suppliers. This trans-lates into 150% of the retailer's estimated global carbon footprint growth over the next five years (www.environmentalleader.com/2010/02/26/walmart-pledges-to-cut-supply-chain-emissions-20m-metric-tons-by-2015/). Wal-Mart is now screen-ing all Chinese suppliers for environmental practices to ensure its supply chain commitments can be met.

♦ PepsiCo (responsible for Walkers Crisps among other brands) is working with a UK environmental consultancy, to deliver a Sustainable Potato Project com-mitment. Four areas are identified as crucial to manage along the supply chain: carbon, water, agrochemicals and direct energy. For each of these issues, PepsiCo are identifying the financial and environmental impact on the potato supply chain and establishing key performance indicators (KPIs) to drive environmental progress at farm level. KPIs on potatoes were developed in 2009 and extended to oat growers in 2010. (http://www.pepsico.co.uk/purpose/environment/reports-and-updates/20089-environment-update/sustainable-supply-chain)

A few hospitality businesses are now engaging with their supply chain to drive resource efficiencies. Contract caterer Sodexo, for example, have asked their sup-pliers to provide packaging data about items purchased (it currently holds data for more than 7000 individual line items) by material type and whether primary, secondary or tertiary packaging. The suppliers also provide annual purchasing data so that the weight of all packaging can be calculated. One supplier is now providing data on what is used for sales packaging and what is back-door waste. Reports are prepared on the average packaging weight per stock keeping unit (SKU) and Sodexo is now looking at the embedded carbon of packaging. This data is used to target packaging waste reductions and to improve the resource efficiency of deliveries and so on with significant carbon and waste minimisation benefits to Sodexo and first tier suppliers.

Sodexo is now working with its largest three suppliers (all leading global brands) to redesign packaging for the benefit of all. Sodexo's initiatives dovetail with those already underway within many of its suppliers. Unilever, for example, already have a comprehensive range of supply chain procedures underway including initiatives within factories to send zero waste to landfill and achieve 40% reductions in emis-sions in logistics related CO_2 (see Figure 32).

Figure 32: Unilever approach to driving supply chain efficiencies and reducing impacts

Some governments have cottoned on to the potential to develop relationships with a small number of powerful companies to deliver change. For example, WRAP (The Waste & Resources Action Programme) funded by the UK Government, has developed and supported the delivery of the Courtauld Commitment Agreement with the grocery sector, including food and drink manufacturers and retailers. Now in its second iteration, this agreement includes commitments to reduce traditional grocery product and packaging waste in the grocery supply chain by 5%. Over 50 major retailers and brand owners have signed up to the commitment. A voluntary agreement for the hospitality and food service sector to reduce packaging and food waste is now being developed. Such an initiative will – without doubt – significantly increase the number of food service businesses that actively pursue, monitor and report on resource savings throughout their supply chain.

Text box 32: Auditing supply chains

For some companies, the process of overhauling procurement processes can be huge. José Lopez, executive vice-president of operations at Nestlé, says: 'Our size and breadth mean the standards we set our suppliers are incredibly important to our business and, increasingly, our consumers.' The company drew up a set of principles for 'responsible practices' across its supplier chain, he says, with a 'rigorous supplier code of our own to set non-negotiable minimum standards that all our suppliers, their employees, agents and subcontractors, must meet.'

Harvey (2010), http://www.ft.com

Changing product choices – it's about more than fair trade coffee

The third (although in some cases only) strand of responsible supply chain strategies is related to the second and is associated with changing product choices to favour more responsible alternatives (sometimes at a higher cost – or adding a 'responsible' product to the supplier list and selling it at a premium). For a few companies, such as Nestlé (see Text box 32) this process involves undertaking an audit of all products to identify those that pose the greatest risk (to the environment, society and reputations). In many more, it relates to targeting a few high profile products and changing them, usually for options that are associated with 'doing good' (see Text box 33).

Within hospitality, the latter route has been pursued by almost all businesses. See, for example: the comprehensive adoption of fair trade hot beverages by global brands from Starbucks to Compass, the adoption of eggs from free range systems in some countries by caterers such as Aramark, to the use of beef from the UK and Ireland in UK restaurants by McDonald's, the rejection of bottled water by a range of hospitality businesses in preference for in-house purification systems and the preference for foods that are produced within the country in which they will be served (if not locally). These initiatives can have a significant and positive impact and can provide insurance when facing challenges such as food security. In isolation, however, they do not constitute a responsible approach to supply chain management.

Text box 33: Choosing products that do good

Companies have been tackling the issue of cattle and deforestation, where for example Nike and other major shoe companies have introduced new sourcing policies to not buy any beef products that come from deforested lands. In addition, Bertin (Brazil's second largest beef exporter) has also placed a moratorium on all beef sourced from deforested land, a topic becoming popular within the beef industry.

UNDP Green Commodities Facility – Beef Scoping Paper, April 2010

A legitimate claim to a responsible approach to supply chain management requires a more targeted approach that examines the impacts of a number of items in the supply chain to identify those with the greatest negative impacts. It may sound simple, but combine the hundreds of product lines that are used by many hospitality businesses with the fact that even the experts cannot agree on the most 'sustainable' option for many products and it becomes a complex process. Most businesses, therefore, choose to tackle it slowly. For those businesses that go beyond the obvious fair trade options to champion new causes (such as local or regional food, healthy and nutritious menus or processes that minimise the use of chemical cleaners) there is an opportunity to 'do good' and gain PR benefits. Vacherin, for example, have championed red meat free weeks and Scandic stopped serving giant shrimp in all of its hotels in the Nordic region and the Baltic in 2009 because of the significant environmental and social impacts caused by shrimp harvesting.[12]

The approach of targeting specific products for replacement for social and environmental reasons is not without its risks. The growth in high profile and ethical products has played a significant role in stimulating specific economic models and modes of production (fair trade, free range, etc.). Many, but by no means all, commentators see this as a positive development.[13] Oxford Analytica, for example, lists just some of the concerns over the growth in demand for fairly traded products from corporate giants like Starbucks (which recently announced that all of its espresso coffee would be fairly traded) and Nestlé. Key among these concerns are the issues of: who benefits from fair trade (there is some evidence that it is not the most disadvantaged, but the producer organisations that have become relatively organised); and the relative power that major multinational corporations have when bargaining with fair trade producers. The bulk buying power of these corporations means that they often pay less per item than customers who buy in smaller volumes (*Forbes Magazine*, Sept. 2009). No matter how well meaning, it is clear that the adoption of a few high profile ethical brands alone will not cleanse the supply chain of practices that are contrary to the responsible business ambitions of a company.

Text box 34: Buying local

A Buy Local campaign launched in Portland, USA, by independent businesses and community has played an important role in reinforcing the unique character of the local area and providing opportunities for entrepreneurs to build community economic strength and prevent the displacement of local community businesses. It provides a sense of place and authenticity to the community that engages visitors and residents as well as maintaining a healthy and diverse economy.

www.portlandbuylocal.org accessed 14 August 2011

---

12 The creation of ponds in which the shrimp can be harvested is thought to damage tropical mangrove swamps with the knock-on effect on fish populations. This in turn, destroys the local fishing industry, undermining livelihoods in vulnerable coastal communities. Moreover, the destruction of the mangrove swamps makes coastlines more susceptible to tropical storm damage. There are also questions about the use of chemicals and antibiotics within the shrimp farms and their impacts on the ecosystem.

13 Lobbyists campaigning for and against fair trade or other systems of production that lay claim to having lower environmental and/or social impacts have muddied the waters, making it very complex to identify which are the 'best' options. See, for example, the huge debate around organic systems of food production. Those in favour of these systems lay claim to their health, environmental and social benefits. Those against lobby on the basis that they cannot produce enough food to sustain growing global populations and that the health and environmental benefits are largely unsubstantiated. The range of debate and lack of clear scientific information makes it very difficult for companies to identify the 'best' option to meet their responsible business criteria.

Case study: BaxterStorey – developing a sustainable British food supply chain

BaxterStorey have built their business and reputation on a passion for using fresh, seasonal and locally sourced produce.

The senior management team recognise the importance of being a responsible corporate citizen. They operate a series of initiatives that guide all areas of practice – from recycling to waste management, ethical purchasing to community financial support and fair treatment of suppliers to ensuring chef teams are offered the sector's leading career and development opportunities.

One of the most significant commitments of the business makes is to supporting the sustainability of the environment and in particular the British farming community. Since the company started over 10 years ago, partnerships have been established with a series of farmers, producers and artisan food suppliers. Over the last three years close partnerships have been built with these groups. As a result, the business can make a commitment that 100% of fresh (non-meat) produce comes from regional suppliers with distances from unit no further than 80 miles for units inside M25; and 150 miles round trip for units outside London.

Meeting the challenge: fresh, seasonal and local

Over the past 10 years, BaxterStorey have established relationships with 1600 farmers, growers and artisan producers across the UK in order to be able to support this commitment. Annually, the company spends £80m on fresh produce including almost 30 million kilos of fresh fruit and vegetables, 1 million kilos of fresh meat and 6.5 million fresh eggs every year.

The delivery of a sustainable network of UK supply for all fresh meat has been of paramount importance to BaxterStorey and the company has always used regional butchers throughout the UK to source its meat. So much so, that by 2008, the nationwide supply network meant they had ensured that 95% of all fresh meat, with the exclusion of bacon, also complied with the company's local purchasing guidelines. The last 5% represents bacon, and the last part of the fresh meat supply chain to fall into place. Much bacon is sourced in one country and then processed in another, since UK labelling merely refers to where the meat was processed. To avoid excessive travelling for the meat and the consequent food miles this creates, BaxterStorey wanted a solution that meant that the pork was reared and then processed within the UK.

Following two years close work with the farming community, in September 2009, BaxterStorey became the first contract caterer to commit to using 100% fresh meat sourced in the UK. British consumers want to support UK farming but they remain price conscious and if there's too big a disparity, that's where their commitment ends. Amongst the UK's bacon suppliers there existed a vicious circle where the domestic price – thanks to the often forgotten fact that the UK has the highest animal welfare standards in Europe – was significantly higher than Danish rivals. Producers in the UK needed to invest to bring unit cost down but were unwilling to do so without greater volume, distributors needed increased orders from caterers, which in the main knew their clients and customers wouldn't swallow the price differential (EU bacon was 20% to 40% cheaper at the time) and therefore sourced it from abroad.

To realise its commitment to sourcing bacon in the UK, the company had to get to the start of the food chain and put its money where its mouth was. Drawing together producers and distributor Brakes, BaxterStorey encouraged a team approach to develop a UK-based supply chain which could fulfil the company's requirement for 6 million rashers of bacon every year. BaxterStorey has now been confirmed by Defra in 2009 as the first UK contract caterer to agree to conform with the newly instituted voluntary code of conduct regarding the labelling of bacon.

Finally, to ensure the quality standard of the meat and to have visibility over the quality of the animal husbandry attached to its production, they have insisted that all bacon produced must meet the standard to ensure certification by the Red Tractor quality assurance scheme.

Filling the 5% gap was not an easy process. It required extensive negotiation on BaxterStorey's part with food distributors, wholesalers and farmers. Each one along the line wanted a commitment in volume to enable BaxterStorey to achieve a price for the pork to make this project feasible. By committing to volume and committing to purchasing from British farms, BaxterStorey is helping to sustain a significant portion of the farming industry that has suffered greatly over the past decade.

As a further development in its sustainable sourcing, in October 2010, BaxterStorey committed to using only free range RSPCA Freedom Farm Assured eggs produced by chickens in conditions that exceed the current regulations for animal husbandry. The move precedes new EU legislation which is scheduled to come into force across Europe in 2012 banning the production of eggs from chickens kept in battery cages.

Sourcing free range eggs from one farm, Staveley's in Lancashire gives the people who dine in their restaurants the confidence to know that they can pinpoint the exact origins and pedigree of the food they are eating. This is a decision that benefits the consumers and the UK farming industry. In 2011 BaxterStorey were recognised with a Good Egg Award from Compassion in World Farming for this approach to free range eggs.

Nevertheless, the willingness of the hospitality sector from hotels to quick-service restaurants to host products with good ethical credentials demonstrates the desire to be seen to be doing the right thing. What started with coffee and tea is now extending to food choices, cleaning chemicals, selection of renewable energy and food waste disposal options. Having engaged supply chain professionals in the responsible business programme, the aim for most hospitality businesses must now be to ensure that sustainable procurement extends to a wider range of products and that purchasing teams are able to manage the very complex trade-offs that are necessary.

Using the supply chain to ensure that people count

The labour standards conundrum

> *For more than a decade, major American retailers and named brands have answered accusations that they exploit 'sweatshop' labor with elaborate codes of conduct and on-site monitoring. But in China, many factories have just gotten better at concealing abuses. Internal industry documents reviewed by Business Week reveal that numerous Chinese factories keep double sets of books to fool auditors and distribute scripts for employees to recite if they are questioned.*
>
> Bloomberg Business Week, 27/11/2006,
> available at www.businessweek.com/magazine/content/06_48/b4011001.htm

When it comes to ranking risks of poor PR exposure, one supply chain issue is more significant than all others. This, of course, relates to the way that people are treated by the organisations that supply major corporations. Gap, Primark and Nike are just a few of the brands whose corporate reputations have been stained by accusations of poor working conditions for employees. The response has been to develop standards for managing human rights in the workplace. Some of these standards are recognised by international certification organisations, such as SA 8000 or the Ethical Trading Initiative, the ILO Declaration on Fundamental Principles and Rights at Work, the UN Global Compact and – in the case of tourism – the UNWTO Global Code of Ethics.

These standards have been hugely successful among corporate businesses. For example, as at 2009, around 1.3 million workers were employed in SA 8000 accredited facilities globally. Some of those businesses that have adapted to rigorous supply chain employee standards have found that these alone are insufficient to keep them away from the unwelcome eye of the media. Some, such as Gap, have surprised the business community in this regard – rather than just putting details of its supply contracts online, it invites consumers to see online which factories it uses, so we can explore how their relationships work. Some companies in the hospitality sector, and hotels in particular, have been asked by their corporate customers whether they are able to comply with standards such as SA 8000 and this is beginning to drive awareness of this issue throughout the sector.

Hospitality businesses have barely scratched at the surface of this issue as yet. One early adopter was the tour operator sector, where employee conditions within hospitality businesses are a key focus of the Travelife Criteria.[14] As Figure 33 demonstrates, however, relatively few of the major catering businesses have embraced processes to ensure that people count.

---

14 Hoteliers are themselves suppliers within the context of tourism. Within the Travelife programme, it is the customers (tour operators) that are driving the adoption of environmental policies and programmes by the hoteliers that they commission.

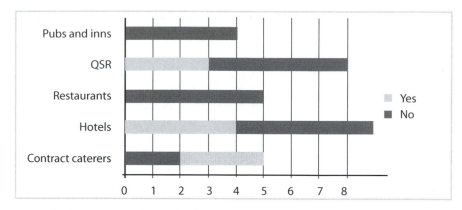

Figure 33: Hospitality businesses with a code of ethics for suppliers vis-à-vis employment conditions

Notes: Data compiled from published data on websites or in corporate reports from 24 large hospitality businesses (see Appendix 1 for a list of companies included).

Some companies have interests that cut across sectors – for example some businesses that are primarily pub operators (and are included in the pub category) also operate a small number of hotels.

Not all companies make the details of their codes of conduct available in the public domain and are therefore excluded from this analysis.

It is in this area that many in the sector will be exposed to significant future risks – especially given the complexity of its supply chains and the focus on price as a key criterion in the purchasing decision.

Building resilient partnerships

Each of the strategies described above are characterised by a conventional approach to business in which the 'purchaser' dictates the conditions to which suppliers must adhere as a condition of business. These strategies have delivered environmental benefits for thousands of businesses, cost reductions for suppliers and improved working conditions for the employees of those suppliers. A handful of companies, however, have come to realise that – in the words of Mad Eye Moody[15] – these systems require 'constant vigilance', can be costly to maintain, and can present a significant risk of exposure when suppliers are unwilling recipients of new demands from buyers.

Forward thinking businesses, therefore, have started to look at different ways in which supply chains can be managed. They have come to realise that their relationship with suppliers is about far more than ensuring the products they require are delivered to their premises at an agreed time and price. These companies are increasingly recognising that they and their suppliers are partners in each other's mutual success. By rethinking supply chain practices, they can harness the creativity of their supply community to both develop their own business and also enhance the supplier's brand. It is these businesses that have begun the process of reviewing and restructuring their relationships with suppliers and seeking mechanisms to work

---

15   If you are not a Harry Potter fan, ignore this reference.

with them to find constructive and long-term solutions. Often these solutions work from the basis that the increase in supply chain costs are in themselves a reflection of unsustainable modes of production and the solution, therefore, is to support the supply chain in adopting the mantle of sustainability. The starting point for these partnerships is often a supplier declaration (see for example, the Scandic Supplier Declaration).

Organisations that have taken this approach include a few hospitality businesses:

♦ **Cadbury's**, in establishing their Cocoa Partnership, in response to research carried out by the Institute of Development Studies, Sussex, and the University of Ghana, 'Sustainable Cocoa Production in Ghana.' The research showed Cadbury that the average production for a cocoa farmer has dropped to 40% of the potential yield and that cocoa farming has become less attractive to the next generation of farmers. The Cadbury Cocoa Partnership aims to address farmer productivity, to attract the next generation into cocoa farming, securing the future supply of a vital ingredient (*Business in the Community*, 2009).

♦ Unilever, which has developed a partnership with Oxfam to help farmers in developing countries get onto their supply lists. The programme of work helps small farmers gain long-term contracts and provides a guaranteed supply of products to the global giant.

♦ **Loews Hotels** in San Diego has launched a Buy Local mandate across its properties. Employees within the company will work with local farmers to ensure that their produce is appropriate for use by the hotel and that they benefit from the economic benefits of becoming suppliers (www.environmentalleader.com). Other similar projects have been successful in the Caribbean with partnerships including Oxfam having some involvement.

For most of these organisations, partnership initiatives have yet to extend throughout all products and suppliers. But they represent an important step forward – demonstrating the value of partnership to deliver innovative supply chain solutions.

Five indicators for business

☐ Everyone in the procurement team understands the aims of the responsible business programme and how they will affect the supply chain.

☐ The company is/has undertaken an audit of at least primary suppliers and identified the environmental and social implications of current supply chain choices (including collating data about the responsible business aspirations/policies of companies in the supply chain).

☐ All major suppliers are aware of the responsible business programme and have been engaged in a dialogue about achieving responsible business ambitions.

☐ Supply chain contracts are reviewed regularly (at least every two years) to ensure that they are keeping pace with responsible business commitments and do not pose a reputational risk.

☐ Progress in changing supply chain preferences to ensure that they are in keeping with responsible business aspirations is recorded, measured and improvements are targeted.

The tools of the trade

When it comes to supply chain management, there are very few hospitality specific resources. Those that are available include:

How-to manuals

These provide advice about generic approaches to 'greening' the supply chain. They tend to focus either around the issue of providing generic advice about integrating responsible business ambitions into procurement processes, or advice about buying specific products. Some of the better known tools that have been produced include:

♦ *Considerate Hoteliers*, Green Source directory. This provides buyers with questions that can be asked of suppliers when buying specific products. Targeted specifically at hoteliers, it aims to help procurement professionals grapple with the trade-offs that often need to be made when selecting the best environmental option. Its failure to enable procurement professionals to identify products that match specific criteria is a major shortcoming of the tool.

♦ Guidance by IGD on supply chain logistics, supply chain waste prevention and integrating local businesses into the supply chain.

♦ Guidance within the International Tourism Partnership's *Environmental Management for Hotels* publication. This provides a checklist for procurement professionals to ensure that sustainability considerations are reflected throughout the supply chain.

♦ Generic guidance issues by WRI/WBCSD in the form of a ten-question sustainable procurement framework. For more information visit http://www.wbcsd.org

♦ Guidance produced by hospitality businesses and available in the public domain, including IUCN and Accor's work on biodiversity, which includes within its scope aspects of food sourcing.

Interactive tools

A few interactive tools have also been developed to help procurement professionals make responsible choices. Prominent among these in the hospitality sector is the Green Hotel concept from Beacon Purchasing (www.beacongreenhotel.co.uk).

This tool enables buyers to explore a virtual hotel and examine the environmental credentials of a number of products and then identify suppliers of those products. While an excellent concept, and most of the options available offer the potential for cost savings, the scope of products provided is limited.

Certified products

There has been an explosion of products that now carry some form of 'eco-label'. Some of these have been readily accepted by the sector and are used to demonstrate the ethical stance of the business. The range of ecolabels available is frankly bewildering. With a few exceptions, many remain unknown to their respective target audiences. Organisations like the Global Ecolabelling Network (www.globalecolabelling.net) are now seeking to tackle some of the confusion by working to promote ecolabels and the credibility of ecolabelling processes globally as well as encouraging demand for more environmentally responsible goods and services.

Some of the certification processes that are recognised and used by the hospitality sector include:

♦ **Fair trade** – from coffee to confectionery and cotton, these labels have been broadly embraced by the sector and are now a popular way in which many businesses demonstrate their environmental credentials to customers. Indeed it is the customer recognition of the logo itself that is as important to many companies as the environmental credentials they display.

♦ **Free range/cage-free**. These terms have been readily embraced by the sector, and businesses from the contract caterer Compass to eco-specialist Pret-a-Manger have been keen to demonstrate that when it comes to shell eggs, at least all are free range/cage-free. The enthusiasm for this label in some markets has improved supply capacity, enabling many buyers to switch from battery-reared hen eggs at no additional cost.

♦ **Local/regional/national** – the food security debate has pushed the procurement of locally sourced foods up the agenda for many food service businesses.

♦ **GLOBALG.A.P.** – the GLOBALG.A.P. standard has been developed to reassure consumers about how food is produced on the farm by minimising detrimental environmental impacts of farming operations, reducing the use of chemical inputs and ensuring a responsible approach to worker health and safety as well as animal welfare. For major food service businesses, it is seen as an accreditation that can be achieved within the current business model and that provides a reasonable degree of confidence about the provenance of food products.

♦ **Organic** – in the case of food and personal care items, some businesses have differentiated themselves in the market by choosing organic products. The supply of these products and their price premium means that they cannot be accommodated within business as usual modes but for some outlets, they are an important point of product differentiation.

Other certification standards have been far less successful in the sector[16] and are hardly recognised by procurement professional and client or customer groups. These tend to be the standards that do not have a high level of consumer recognition and that tackle the less 'sexy' issues for the media. They include:

- **PAS 2050** – the carbon standard for foods. Some large caterers have experimented with this label, but found devilishly tricky to apply to a product with multiple ingredients (such as a whole meal). At the current time, most have concluded that it is not sufficiently widely recognised by consumers to provide a point of product differentiation.

- **BS8901** – the standard for sustainable events that is becoming increasingly important in the UK and is a pre-tender requirement for those businesses hoping to provide services to the Olympic Games.

- **Lifecycle analysis** – there are some who would argue that a full life cycle analysis is the only mechanism to ensure that products with the lowest negative environmental and social impacts are selected. Despite the development of an international standard to this end (ISO 14040), the costs of using the standard and complexity of applying it to a whole meal as opposed to individual ingredients mean that it is little used. Some of the eco-chic businesses – including the Scarlet Hotel in Cornwall – have, however, undertaken a full life cycle assessment for many of their product choices.

- The **SA 8000** social accountability standard, which is largely unknown to UK companies. This provides a management and reporting standard for working conditions and is widely used by textile manufacturers and other sectors recruiting high proportions of labour from developing countries. It is not much used by hospitality businesses (the authors are not aware of any that have sought to meet its requirements), although some businesses have been asked whether they can comply with its requirements.

- The **AA 1000** accountability standard (largely unknown in the UK) developed to help organisations become more **accountable**, **responsible** and **sustainable**. It addresses issues affecting governance, business models and organizational strategy, as well as providing operational guidance on sustainability assurance and stakeholder engagement. Despite its reliance on the stakeholder concept (something often talked about by hospitality businesses), the authors are not aware of any hospitality businesses that have sought to meet its requirements.

---

16 This is in comparison to in business in general, where a survey by The Economist found that 38% of companies actively meet certain standards of behaviour (Economist Intelligence Unit (2008) Global Business Barometer for The Economist).

Conclusions

In the modern world, global supply chains have been crucial to business success – providing the blueprint for secure supply and cheap products. Many organisations are, however, coming to realise that these supply chains can be their weakest critical link. The latest jargon encourages businesses and local communities to build resilience into their supply chains and often this means reviewing the amount of carbon that is embedded in food production, processing and transportation as well as the labour standards that are used. Those businesses that fail to recognise the links between food, social equity, climate and security of supply can find themselves exposed to the media or vulnerable to price rises and increased competition. Businesses that have fully engaged with their suppliers have realised that in so doing, they can unleash their combined imagination and often provide products that are not only more responsible but also more efficient, cheaper and fulfilling for the workforce. Those that have undertaken token behaviours based on cost reduction alone, or enforcing standards on suppliers, have all too often come unstuck.

In the words of the World Resources Institute *et al.* (2008), those companies that succeed and build resilience will be those that 'anticipate the implications of a changing landscape, collaborate with suppliers …, and make environmental sustainability a fundamental business principle. Hedging strategies or shifting suppliers will not be enough. We believe that in order to adapt to these challenges, companies will need to implement real structural changes, such as product innovation and restructured value chains, which will affect both the companies and millions of existing and new consumers.' (World Resources Institute *et al.*, 2008: 4).

As we shall see in Principle 6, partnership is a powerful tool, not only with suppliers, but also with consumers and employees, as businesses increasingly seek to 'nudge' them towards more sustainable behaviours.

References

3663 Sustainability Report 2009/10 available from *www.3663corporate.co.uk*

Bohdanowicz P., Simanic B., Martinac I. (2005b), 'Environmental Training and Measures at Scandic Hotels', Sweden, *Tourism Review International*, **9** (1), pp. 7-19.

Bohdanowicz, P. (2006) - 'Responsible resource management in hotels - attitudes, indicators, tools and strategies'. Doctoral thesis, Stockholm: Royal Institute of Technology

CERES (2010) Roadmap, Summary available from www.ceres.org

Forbes Magazine (2009) *Fair Trade's Rapid Growth Raises Flags,* available at http://www.forbes.com/2009/01/08/fair-trade-labor-cx_0109oxford.html

Harvey, F. (2010) 'Supply chain: responsible sourcing means focus on details', *Financial Times*, 1 October, available at http://www.ft.com/cms/s/0/e6cf80ac-cceb-11df-9bf0-00144feab49a.html#axzz1Cvzi8zy9

ICC (2002) *Business in society - Making a positive and responsible contribution. A voluntary commitment by business to manage its activities responsibly*, ICC Paris

Institute of Hospitality (2011) 'Food security in a changing climate', *Hospitality*, 21, 20–25.

Keating, B., Quazi, A., Kriz, A. and Coltman, T. (2008) 'In pursuit of a sustainable supply chain: insights from Westpac Banking Corporation', *Supply Chain Management: An International Journal*, **13** (3), 175–179.

Business in the Community (2009) How to Manage your Supply Chain Responsibly – Page 2.

Oxford Analytica, quoted in Forbes Magazine (2009).

Sustainability, UNEP and UNGC (2008) 'Unchaining value – Innovative approaches to sustainable supply', *Sustainability*, UNEP, UNGC.

UNDP Green Commodities (2010) *Beef scoping paper*, available from greencommodities.org

Vassallo, D., Cacciatore, E., Locatelli, M., Clarke, R. and Jones, M., (2008) *Green Purchasing Power – Cost reduction and revenue generation through sustainable procurement*. Arthur D Little, London.

World Resources Institute and A.T. Kearney Inc. (2008) *Rattling supply chains – the effect of environmental trends on input costs for the fast moving consumer goods industry*, World Resources Institute

WWF/FCRN (2010) *Environmental Impacts of the UK Food Economy*, Godalming, Surrey: WWF.

Principle 6: Engage employees and customers in actions that support environmental, economic and social wellbeing

A new paradigm for both brand communications and design innovation is required. This will invite consumers to participate in the creative process within a framework of global core brand concepts. In this way, real communities will grow around the brands. A brand will no longer grow because of how well it is controlled, but because of how well it is shared. Of paramount importance will be the way in which a brand's traditions and practices relate to contemporary concerns such as well-being, work–life balance, community security and environmental protection. Therefore, a brand's social and environmental depth will become an important determinant of its financial value.

(Bendell and Kleanthous, 2007)

This principle is perhaps the most contentious of the ten that we present in this book. Many businesses (including hospitality businesses) would agree that they have a fundamental role to play in engaging their employees in actions that support environmental, economic and social well-being in the work place and to some extent at home. Many would, however, disagree that it is their role to actively influence customer behaviour to favour sustainable choices. They would argue that this is a role for government and third-sector organisations. If it is, it is one in which they have failed. A decade of effort has proven that these agencies do not have access to the 'skilled group of professionals whose job it is to persuade people to change their behaviour' nor do they have the experience of the marketplace to deliver upon that behaviour change (Rose, 2002: 7). These skills reside with people who work in marketing, advertising, brand development and PR roles.

Securing behaviour change

A decade of campaigns by public sector organisations has effectively engaged the public in understanding that there is a necessity to change behaviour around issues like climate change, but has failed to 'move people from awareness and understanding to secure lasting behaviour change'.

(NESTA, 2008).

Those businesses that are leading in this field are those that recognise that the real benefits of behaviour change do not just lie in convincing employees and consumers to favour products that have 'green' or 'eco' credentials and reside in a niche corner.[17] They lie also in changing the way that employees and consumers relate to and use even mainstream products. Those companies that are leading the way on this topic are encouraging consumers to change the way they travel to, feel about and use a product or service (primarily through their advertising and branding) – even if it means they ultimately use less. Madness? Apparently not! Early evidence would demonstrate that those companies that go down this route win customer trust and loyalty and these are essential attributes for customer retention – especially in mature market economies where 'the aspirational characteristics of the global brand are less salient' (Dimofte *et al.*, 2010).

Ethics sell?

We are drawn to brands we trust, brands that are different from the rest, brands that are innovative, brands that appeal to the emotions, brands that signify something intelligent or interesting about the user, and brands whose parent company behaves well.

Gordon (2006)

What the responsible business guidelines say

Engaging in the process of changing employee attitudes towards the responsible business agenda is universally embraced by the responsible business guidelines. The International Chamber of Commerce acknowledges that responsible business programmes can 'increase morale, transparency and trust among company personnel'. They go on to state that: 'Companies must raise awareness among their own personnel and other stakeholders if business principles are to be effective and command wide support. Processes or formal management systems for developing, adopting and implementing individual principles should therefore include internal consultation and communication' (ICC, 2002).

The issue of changing customer behaviour receives rather less attention. This is partly because it is a relatively recent theme in the responsible business literature, it is a concept that is not universally embraced by businesses and it has traditionally been seen as a priority for governments and the third sector community. Most of the business guidelines recognise that responsible business programmes can play a significant role in reducing the risk of negative PR exposure and can meet changing customer needs. Others embrace this issue under the heading of stakeholder dialogue. The CERES principles in particular also embrace the concept under the topic of disclosure and product transparency, stating that 'Companies will provide veri-

---

17 It is an irony that some of the brands, particularly in the hotel sector, that sell themselves on their 'eco' credentials are actually relatively unsustainable, basing their claims around rather flimsy choice of organic spa or food products rather than a genuine commitment to responsible business or the principles of sustainable development.

fied and standardized sustainability performance information about their products at point of sale and through other publicly available channels' (CERES, 2010: 13). There is considerable debate, however, about the extent to which it is the responsibility of businesses to influence customer behaviour. There are many who think that businesses should take responsible business initiatives to reduce the impacts of customers. While there are others – including many of the think tanks such as NESTA, the New Economics Foundation and WWF who believe that business has the potential to engage customers in responsible consumption through their routine communications.

The fundamentals: engaging employees

The reported benefits of employee engagement programmes have been a powerful driver for hospitality businesses seeking to enact this principle. These benefits are multiple and are reported in a wide range of industry and academic journals. They include not only the potential to deliver cost savings to the business, but also the fact that in those companies where values and standards are widely shared, employees make better decisions, collaborate more effectively and react to opportunities (and crisis) more efficiently (Kanter, 2010: 24). There is also evidence that active engagement of employees in responsible business initiatives can make a company more attractive to work for (see Text box 35). In recent years, some hospitality-specific studies have reinforced this evidence. See, for example, Chan and Hawkins, 2010; Bohdanowicz and Zientara, 2008). In an industry that is notorious for poor staff retention, such benefits are not to be sniffed at.

Text box 35: Ethics make work more appealing

In responding to the financial crisis, Geoff Mulgan notes 'In other sectors, too, there has been a long-term trend towards more people wanting work to be an end as well as a means, a source of fulfilment as well as earnings (Mulgan, 2009).

'In my view the successful companies of the future will be those that integrate business and employees' personal values. The best people want to do work that contributes to society with a company whose values they share, where their actions count and their views matter.' (Jeroen van der Veer, Committee of Managing Directors, Shell)

Hospitality businesses that are seeking to engage employees in responsible business initiatives will, at worst, specify the roles that employees *will* play in fulfilling the responsible business agenda. Businesses that chose to take this route usually focus on eco-efficiencies alone and do little to inspire employees or make them believe that their personal values and those of the business are in any way related. These businesses will often find that their employee training programmes actively demotivate employees, reinforcing a view that responsible business initiatives are little short of cost cutting activities that engage staff in additional and sometime unsavoury tasks (such as separating rubbish for recycling). At best, staff training programmes will actively engage employees in the development of the responsible business agenda to ensure that there is a convergence of personal and business values that contributes not only to the bottom line, but also to local communities and employees' sense of well-being. Those hospitality companies with the most effective responsible business initiatives have found that the latter path is the one that delivers benefits.[18] Hence some hospitality businesses have gauged employees' personal interests, values and perceptions about social and environmental issues prior to launching specific initiatives. As far back as the early 1990s, for example, Canadian Pacific Hotels and Resorts questioned employees about the attributes that a company that they felt proud to work for would have. Working for a company that looked after the society and environment was particularly important and came to drive the development of the Green Partnership Programme that has become a core part of the company's corporate identity.[19]

Human rights

In this chapter, we do not talk about human rights and conditions of work. Any businesses that lays claim to operating responsibly whilst abusing the human rights of those who work for them – directly and indirectly – is living a lie. Within this principle, we assume that the human rights of all employees are respected as expressed in the UN Declaration of Human Rights. There remain some tourism business in which this basic right is over-looked. See, for example, the BBC documentary *Tourism and the Truth*. There are many that recognise the significance of this issue. Rezidor, for example, is a signatory to the Tourism and Human Rights Initiative and the Universal Declaration of Human Rights and more currently the Global Compact.

Businesses that have the most effective mechanisms to engage employees in supporting environmental, economic and social well-being adopt a cyclical process to this end. This is described in Figure 34.

---

18 Businesses that take a holistic approach to responsible business – that is based on good scientific principles such as those laid out by Nattras and Altoman in the *Natural Step* – are able to take a holistic approach to building capacity of the work team rather than just telling employees what to do in an educational programme.

19 Canadian Pacific Hotels & Resorts are now a part of the Fairmont group of hotels. The Green Partnership Programme now underpins the activities of the larger parent group. It is not unusual for hotel companies to extend the 'responsible business' programmes of smaller hotel groups that they acquire throughout the business. Hilton, for example, took on and developed the Scandic group's environmental initiatives when they acquired the latter in 2001 (one of the better known is Hilton Environmental Reporting or HER). They have continued to operate their responsible business and staff training programmes after the subsequent sale of Scandic in 2007.

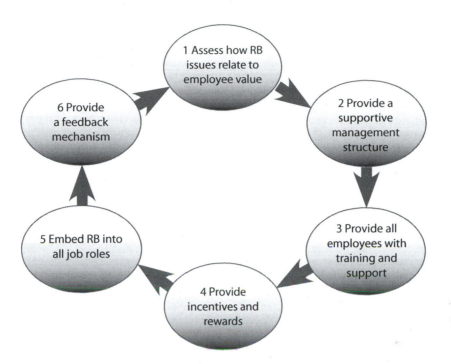

Figure 34: Engaging employees in doing good. Adapted from UNEP *Finance Initiative* (2011).

1. Assess how responsible business issues relate to employee values

For companies, the benefits of responsible business initiatives are usually experienced at head office in the form of cost savings (delivered through resource efficiency), enhanced customer satisfaction and improved employee motivation. For employees, the benefits can only be meaningful if they make a positive difference to their everyday lives and the communities in which they are based. This is especially the case for hospitality businesses with their thousands of dispersed units – many of which are in different countries and cultures to the head office operation. Responsible business programmes that are based wholly on delivering resource savings or other head office benefits are unlikely to motivate employees. In fact, when they engender sorting waste for recycling or other unattractive and mundane activities they can have the opposite effect. Those that improve the environment or community in which employees are based are likely to enhance pride in the business and deliver the other benefits noted above. Head offices need to play a balancing act to ensure that responsible business initiatives deliver on resource management priorities whilst also meeting employee values and needs. The best mechanism to do so is to actively research employee values and map these onto corporate priorities. A number of businesses have taken this route. For example:

♦ Rezidor, through its 'Yes I Can' initiative.

♦ Sandals through the work that it undertakes through its Foundation which is based entirely on reinvesting in the communities in which it is based..

♦ McDonald's, with its work with employees to help them gain formal qualifications in the workplace (especially in countries where access to such opportunities is limited).

♦ Scandic, with its 'Omtanke' and 'Scandic in Society'. The latter initiative specifically aims to contribute to the well-being of the communities in which Scandic operates. The first step in the initiative involved gathering together all employees in each hotel to discuss the how the company could help local societies. The information gathered allowed managers in each hotel to devise programmes tailor-made for particular communities. Projects include various forms of fund raising and charity, but the focus is on those activities that are based on personal involvement. (Bohdanowicz and Zientara, 2008).

Values and motivation

The factors that need to be present to create the most intrinsically motivated people are the opportunity for autonomy, to achieve mastery and to align their work to a purpose. Some corporations such as Google worked this out years ago. There are financial benefits too, those companies with employees registering a high level of engagement with their jobs had, on average, a 10% higher rate of productivity than those whose employees were actively disengaged.

(Kingaby, 2011)

2. Provide a structure to let employees engage with responsible business priorities

Those businesses that are serious about using responsible business strategies to enhance long-term economic value recognise that there is a need to shift from delegation and denial of responsible business tasks to accountability and engagement. These businesses are committed to enthusing all staff about responsible business initiatives (albeit under the leadership of one or a small team of individuals). Within these businesses, there is a clear structure for reporting on responsible business progress. In the very best cases, those employees that excel in responsible business activities will experience the same career enhancement opportunities as those that excel in quality management, PR or other functions.

Typically, the structure for responsible business issues will have the elements indicated in Figure 35.

Those businesses that fail to engage senior team members (and especially unit managers) in responsible business initiatives invariably find that their staff training is ineffective. Thus training has to focus on all levels of the organisation, rather than targeting rank and file employees alone.

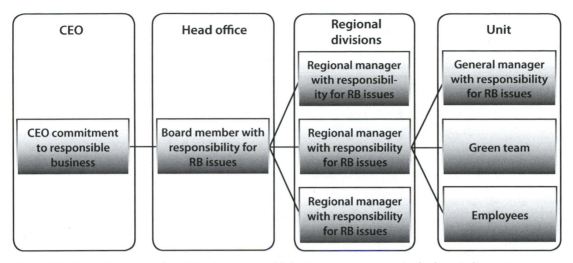

Figure 35: A typical structure for delivering responsible business programmes in the hospitality sector

Most of the annual reports that we reviewed demonstrated this type of structure (on occasion and especially within hotels and QSR with the addition of a dedicated Responsible Business Executive role). What is less clear within these reports is whether the structure is driven from head office (top down in the jargon) or employee values (bottom up). The best programmes have elements of both of these attributes (see Text box 36)

Text box 36: Vacherin – A passion for people

You won't find extravagant claims about responsible business practices on the web site of contract caterer Vacherin. But you will find a passion for good food, a desire to nurture employees, a willingness to learn and an unusual commitment to share experiences. This approach is expressed within the simple slogan Vacherin Cares.

Vacherin have long since recognised that it is the people that work for them that make their service exceptional. As a company, therefore, it actively seeks out new and exciting ways of inspiring and engaging employees (some by their own admission, madcap). It is this approach that makes Vacherin stand out from the crowd. As a company, Vacherin

- Always seeks the 'Sparkle', asking staff each year to come up with ideas, no matter how small or off the wall, about how to improve or rejuvenate their contract.

- Provides the 'Life Plan' – a unique approach to training and development that seeks to understand every member of staff's personal life and aspirations, as well as their career goals.

- Actively encourages chefs to pursue their passion for food and to seek out the very best of ingredients.

- Nurtures new entrants to the sector by taking university placement students, engaging employees in completing their studies and setting up its own apprenticeship scheme as well as offering staff access to masterclasses and other training opportunities.

■ Donates two days each year in which each member of staff can engage in work with a charity of their choice.

This strategy has emerged from a meeting of head office and employee minds:

■ The owners and senior team meet every year to review where Vacherin are as a company and set the strategy for the future. In 2011, this strategy planning meeting reviewed and consolidated progress on 2010 priorities. These included a three-year plan under the battle cry 'tastier, brighter, stronger' (echoing the Olympic motto of faster, higher, stronger).

■ Following the strategy session, staff review plans in a company meeting to get buy-in and their feedback. Feedback is integrated into the overall strategy.

■ Incentives have not been used to date (outside a bonus scheme for managers), partly because of the level of debate over their effectiveness (see, for example, Kaur, 2011: 211–225).

These initiatives have held the company in good stead: 93% of its employees claim to actively enjoy going to work and 94% to have a good work–life balance. Staff turnover levels in the company are relatively low with an annual turnover of 8% for management and 27% for other staff. Vacherin have found that their caring approach pays dividends, helping the company to provide a great quality service.

Experience across hospitality businesses has demonstrated that, while the engagement of all staff is important, the buy-in of unit managers is critical to success. Those hospitality units that are managed by teams to whom responsible business issues are not important consistently fail to achieve corporate objectives (Wu, 2010). Typically, unit managers are asked to engage by becoming the leader of the Green Team, thus demonstrating their commitment to the achievement of responsible business priorities.

3. Provide all employees with training and support

When hospitality businesses get accused of failing to meet their responsible business commitments, the root cause is most commonly a lack of staff engagement. Common failures include towel reuse policies that are not implemented in practice in hotels, water minimisation initiatives that are damned by consistently running taps in commercial kitchens, waste recycling and minimisation programmes that are scuppered by staff caught disposing of all products into a compactor skip. Hospitality businesses, from contract caterers Baxter Storey to hoteliers Rezidor and Hilton now have their own in-house responsible business training initiatives. These seek to help all staff understand why responsible business issues are important, to identify how their individual behaviours at home and at work can make a difference and start the process of embedding in staff an awareness of the steps that they can take to ensure their impact is positive.

The challenge of staff turnover

The hospitality sector is notorious for its very high levels of staff turnover (annual turnover rates in excess of 100 per cent are not uncommon for some job roles in some companies). This presents a challenge and means that responsible business training has to be delivered on a regular basis and integrated at various points of the employment cycle. Many businesses find that it is most effective to embed responsible business training in the staff induction process as well as providing bespoke training sessions at regular points throughout the year.

Providing training throughout dispersed units in different cultures can be challenging. Unlike manufacturing processes, which are likely to be confined to a small number of sites each hosting a relatively large number of employees, hospitality businesses operate over a large number of sites – each with a small number of employees. Typically, each unit cannot justify/support a dedicated trainer so on-going training support may be requested from external agencies and used to train regional or hotel based trainers (often those trained are in the HR department). In some hospitality businesses, the Green Team may be designated with responsibility for training new staff.

Embedding behaviour change

The eco-efficiency element of responsible business initiatives offers the potential for employees within hospitality businesses to make savings at home as well as in the workplace. Those businesses that seek to help staff adjust their behaviour not just at work but also at home can provide direct financial benefits and deliver the nudge to change lifestyles.

Some induction training initiatives in the sector are now relatively well tried and tested. Scandic, for example, introduces all staff to the responsible business programmes via the checkin@Scandic e-learning program at the induction stage. As their employment progresses, this training is supplemented by a range of programmes (delivered through the concept of the Compass and the framework of The Natural Step) that helps them to understand the Omtanke philosophy that underpins all of the Company's activities. Rezidor introduces all new entrants in all business outlets to its 'Responsible Business' programme through a backpack that contains information, back of house collateral and a three-hour training session[20]. The company has trained an army of hotel-based trainers to spread the message, and uses simple concepts like coloured T-shirts to communicate the 'three pillars' of the responsible business programme (Red – WE are the people; green – WE are the environment; and blue – WE are the community). Research by companies on their in-house training initiatives demonstrates that they successfully change employee attitudes towards environmental and social issues not just at work, but also deliver behaviour changes at home.

---

20 Not all franchised businesses participate in the training, though they have the option to do so.

Text box 37: The formal education sector – the weak link in the chain

Globally, businesses and NGOs complain that those that they recruit from schools and colleges have insufficient environmental or sustainable development 'literacy' to support their responsible business initiatives. Hospitality businesses have already played some role in trying to address these issues. DoubleTree by Hilton, for example, has its 'Teaching Kids to CARE' programme which teaches children to care about the local community and the the environment as well as politics/democracy. Other major companies (including hospitality businesses) have similar initiatives.

Within the hospitality sector, the level of literacy about responsible business for employees recruited from training colleges (at all levels) is shocking. If one looks across the curricula, there are a number of declarations about the significance of campus greening (see for example, Talloires Declaration (USLF, 1990), but for most higher education organisations teaching in the area of responsible business for hospitality students is at worst absent and at best tokenistic.[21] There are a few exceptions, for example Leeds Metropolitan, University which includes a module on Responsible Hospitality within its broader MSc in Responsible Tourism Management, and a small number of institutions have elective modules on environmental management. Some companies have tried to address this issue by making their materials available via websites. Scandic, for example, has made information about its Better World Campaign available to all, Accor continues to host all of its excellent training materials on its website and Hilton International have their in house ecoLearning programme. There are also some generic learning programmes, such as the Sustainability 101 GMIC and TNS e-learning programme available from www.Greenmeetings.info.

For teachers within higher and further education establishments, the inclusion of responsible business issues is difficult to tackle. Relatively few businesses in the sector have responsible business roles in their own right. Instead they expect staff across core departments to integrate responsible business concerns into their work. This means that the most effective approach to teaching responsible business issues is to embed it into the core functions of finance, operations management, marketing and communications, etc. However, many of the staff engaged within these disciplines lack access to information about how to effectively achieve this.

Just like training for any other business area, training for responsible business needs to be refreshed and renewed. To maintain staff interest, this can change to focus on different aspects of the sustainability agenda each year, and use a variety of communication tools (including classroom presentations, workshops, film screenings and adjacent discussions, on-line training sessions, social media and podcasts). Companies that are truly committed to responsible business issues make attendance at regular training sessions a mandatory item on the personal development agendas of employees, or provide incentives to encourage excellence. The best training initiatives are delivered within a supportive framework. This involves monitoring the

---

21 This is in contrast to the field of tourism, where sustainable or responsible tourism is taught within many curricula and is in many cases the subject of a Masters study in its own right.

performance of individual business units post training. Those business units that fail to meet responsible business targets at this time are then offered additional training and technical support.

Figure 36 provides an illustration of the number of hospitality businesses from the 24 that claim to train all staff about responsible business issues.

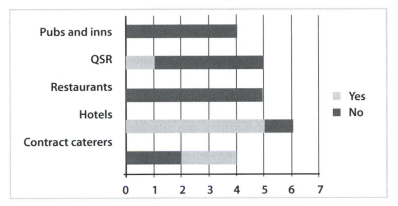

Figure 36: Businesses claiming to train staff in responsible business issues

Notes: Data compiled from published data on websites or in corporate reports from 24 large hospitality businesses (see Appendix 1 for a list of companies included).

Some companies have interests that cut across sectors – for example some businesses that are primarily pub operators (and are included in the pub category) also operate a small number of hotels.

Most companies provide training on some elements of responsible business (for example nutrition and wellness or environmental management). Comprehensive training across the responsible business agenda is, however, less common, as illustrated in the figure.

A number of independent businesses also have access to such training programmes, including that developed by the Responsible Hospitality Partnership (formerly CESHI) for VisitEngland and the Regional Tourist Board Partnership. Known as Green Edge, and using a range of interactive games and activities, this helps organisations to prepare managers for the responsible business challenge.

4. Provide incentives and rewards

Hospitality units that exceed quality or revenue management expectations are usually rewarded by head office. Managers that exceed sales targets gain high-profile recognition. Staff who make an outstanding contribution to customer care find themselves celebrated in company publications. Responsible business is no different to these other aspects of hospitality service. Those who excel require recognition and reward. Many hospitality businesses, have gone down the route of providing these rewards in terms of financial incentives (either for managers alone or for the whole of a green team). Scandic, for example, offer financial awards to hotels that exceed their responsible business targets to enable them to organise a team event and Hilton reward individuals who have made an outstanding contribution to responsible business targets with a bicycle. While these play an important motivational role, they are not necessarily the only mechanism that recognises success.

In fact there is some evidence that rewards that are linked to recognition and status have greater value to those employees that receive them (Kaur, 2011). Within the responsible business field other rewards that are effective include giving the opportunity to spend more time working on a voluntary basis for or invest in a cause about which the staff being rewarded feel passionate (for example a local community project). Many hospitality businesses have realised that this is the case. Hilton, for example, through its Hilton in the Community Foundation donates funds collected by the team members to charities nominated by local team members. Aramark provides its employees with the opportunity to give back to communities – using their skills within facilities management or wellness and nutrition to deliver community benefits (www.aramark.com). As experience in companies as diverse as Google and Procter and Gamble has demonstrated, these rewards can help a whole team of people and be more successful across the responsible business agenda as a whole than financial rewards (especially when these target managers alone). Rewards can only be successful, however, if underpinned by training and thus this is a priority at all levels of the business.

5. Embed responsible business priorities into job descriptions

Those businesses that are leading the way in the responsible business field have come to recognise that the core principles of the company in this regard need to be defined in all job descriptions from that of the CEO to the cleaning staff. Businesses that have gone down this route include UK retailer Marks and Spencer and BT. Few hospitality businesses have taken this route (see Text box 38 for the approach of Compass) but some of the hotels have developed concepts such as the 'Omtanke' initiative of Scandic. These programmes are at the core of the business philosophy and form an effective code of ethics for employees.

6 Provide a feedback mechanism

As in any area of the business, it is of fundamental importance that employee engagement for responsible business is not a one-way process. Employees and green teams are more receptive when they see their own values and priorities reflected. They are also more likely to innovate when they are given the freedom to feed ideas into the responsible business programme. Hospitality businesses typically use staff notice boards, suggestion boxes and other mechanisms to gather feedback. Feedback mechanisms are only effective if the data collected from these processes is analysed and suggestions that are feasible are logged as an action item. The employees that have suggested such ideas are often best rewarded when their ideas are taken forward if they are consulted and/or involved in their implementation.

Text box 38: Compass Group's Code of Ethics for all employees

As a world leader in our field we recognise that we have to set the very highest standards for ethical business practice. Every individual employee shares a responsibility to uphold these standards and to conduct our business in a professional, safe, ethical and responsible manner.

Our Code of Ethics, developed in consultation with our European Works Council and the Institute of Business Ethics, sets out the clear standards of behaviour that we expect all of our people to demonstrate in dealing with colleagues and those outside the company such as customers, suppliers, shareholders and other stakeholders. These are reflected in the five sections of the Code:

1 Relations with our employees

2 Relations with our customers

3 Relations with our investors

4 Relations with our suppliers and subcontractors

5 Relations with governments and the wider community

The Code underpins our social, ethical and environmental commitments and sends a powerful message to all our stakeholders of Compass Group's commitment to responsible business practice. The 10 principles of the United Nations (UN) Global Compact, to which we are a signatory, are integral to our own Code of Ethics. This UN initiative encourages companies to commit to make human rights, labour standards, environmental responsibility and anti-corruption part of the business agenda whilst maintaining competitive advantage.

www.compass-group.com/cr-code-of-ethics.htm

The fundamentals: changing consumer behaviour

Hospitality businesses have enthusiastically embraced the issue of engaging staff in responsible business initiatives. Many have also been keen to imply (if not explicitly lay claim to) the green credentials of their brand through their advertising, marketing and other promotional activities. The instances in which they have wielded their might to change consumer behaviour are altogether more isolated.[22] Indeed, there is no consensus that consumers should have responsible business issues 'thrust' upon them.

---

22 There are some examples from industry in general of organisations that have actively sought to change consumer behaviour. See, for example, the success of advertising campaigns to engage individuals in selecting equipment that has an energy efficiency rating of A or above, the 'Love Food, Hate Waste' campaign in the UK and the washing at 30°C campaign.

Text box 39: Primary or secondary drivers?

Customer demand and willingness to nudge customers to change behaviour are intricately linked. There has been much debate in recent years about consumer demand for responsible hospitality experiences, especially when it comes to holiday travel. The majority view is that responsible or at least environmental issues are secondary purchase drivers for some nationalities. This means that they lie further down the purchasing decision-making hierarchy than price, location and facilities. Even this view is by no means universal (see, for example, research undertaken on behalf of DEFRA in the UK (Miller *et al.* 2009) and in Malaysia (Kasim, 2004) which seems to indicate that most customers do not integrate environmental or social concerns into their leisure holiday-taking decisions). Whether customer demand for responsible hospitality experiences means that customers are also willing to and do change their personal behaviour in practice (even marginally) remains largely underexplored.

All of the market segmentation studies that are available demonstrate that there are some market segments that demand eco or responsible business credentials, while others remain resolutely negative towards environmental and/or social issues (see Figure 37). Any business that wishes to adopt a responsible business initiative will face the challenge of meeting the needs of customers for whom responsible business or ethics are a 'must-have' attribute alongside those for whom they are a 'waste of time'. With the exception of 'eco-chic' businesses, most hospitality businesses need to accommodate customer segments that have aspirations to sustainable lifestyles alongside those who are cynical about the concept. Too frequently, communication campaigns to change behaviour have dodged this issue by: (a) focusing on swapping consumer choice from a conventional to an ethical brand or (b) tokenistic gestures that customers are invited to buy into and more importantly that do little to address the major impacts of hospitality experiences.

There is little hospitality specific data for those businesses that are seeking to engage consumers in changing their behaviour to work with. Knowledge about effective mechanisms to engage customers in behaviour change are under-researched. When it comes to hospitality settings, the behaviour changes that will deliver the greatest environmental and social benefits are almost wholly unexplored. It is for these reasons that the concept of engaging customers in changing the way that they use hospitality experiences remains relatively radical. This is despite the fact that market research data make it very clear that a growing band of customers do – or at least say they would - prefer products and services that have good environmental and social credentials (see Figure 37). All too often, however there is a significant gap between what they claim and what they do (see Figure 38).

Within one marketplace – the business market – there is a compelling incentive to engage customers in responsible behaviours (especially vis-à-vis carbon and, in future, water). For those businesses that service other companies that have adopted responsible business initiatives of their own, responsible business initiatives are fundamental to winning contracts and are included in pre-qualification criteria. See for example, Text box 40 and the supply criteria used by PWC for all services, including hospitality (www.pwc.co.uk/pdf/Responsible_Purchasing_Policy_July_2007.pdf). For many of these businesses, the proof that a business is serious about its responsible business criteria will be in the way that it communicates and engages customers.

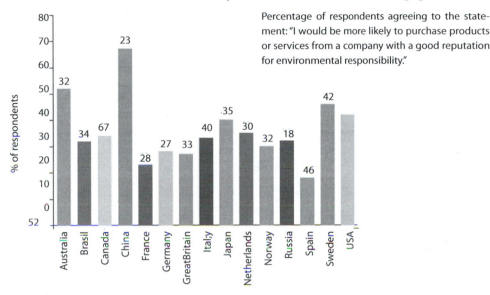

Percentage of respondents agreeing to the statement: "I would be more likely to purchase products or services from a company with a good reputation for environmental responsibility."

Figure 37: Customers would prefer to buy from companies with a commitment to environmental responsibility. *Source*: WBCSD

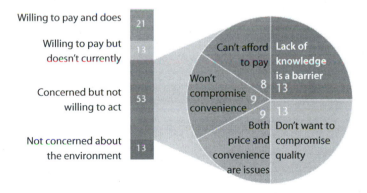

Figure 38: Actions speak louder than words. Global retail consumers segmented by willingness to pay for products with environmental and social benefits. *Source*: McKinsey Quarterly, March 2008, in WBCSD (2008)

Initiatives to involve customers in actions that support environmental, economic and social well-being are rarely recorded in environmental reports (with the exception of nutrition and health, where large companies have made a number of interventions). Outside of this area, none of the web sites or reports that we examined seek to actively engage consumers in the process of behaviour change (most prefer to talk in terms of offering customers choice). Initiatives to change consumer behaviour to favour sustainable choices fall into four broad categories:

♦ Initiatives that seek to nudge customers into using existing hospitality services in more sustainable ways

♦ Initiatives that remove specific options from the marketplace

♦ Initiatives that engage consumers into changing their own behaviour

♦ Initiatives that seek to influence choice to favour 'ethical' or 'green' options.[23]

Text box 40: Responsible business criteria count in the business market

Virgin Atlantic are based in three offices in the Crawley and Heathrow area. Following a competitive tender review, Baxter Storey were appointed to manage their catering services across the estate which consists of:

■ Restaurants service breakfast and lunch in each building

■ All day cafe bar at The Base and The Office in Crawley which are open throughout the day serving premium beverages and snacks

■ Retail shop at The Base

■ Free issue beverage vending

■ Snack and confectionery vending

Baxter Storey were chosen because they were able to establish a cultural fit, demonstrate a clear understanding of Virgin Atlantic's business requirements and demonstrate a strong commitment to CSR and strong environmental credentials.

Baxter Storey have now mobilised all three locations and Virgin Atlantic have seen operational benefits, including:

■ An increase in sales through freshly made products, service innovations and marketing strategies.

■ Developing the menu range, by creating 90% of all food using fresh, locally sourced, quality ingredients, which is noticeably better than previously offered.

■ Providing the Baxter Storey team with the autonomy to be creative and passionate about cooking, having stopped the previous format of weekly menu cycles.

■ Re-energising the team and getting them motivated and excited about the changes and training options available to them.

---

23 It is perhaps indicative of the timidity within the marketplace that there is no standardised terminology with which to describe products that are 'responsible'. The terms 'green', 'ethical', 'socially responsible' are all used within the mainstream market and 'eco-chic' tourism', 'eco-lodge' and 'responsible' have some currency in the hospitality and tourism marketplace.

Initiatives that seek to nudge consumers into using hospitality services in more sustainable ways

The concept of changing the way in which customers use products and/or services is hardly revolutionary or new. A number of highly effective campaigns, from tackling the issue of drink driving to encouraging consumers to wash their clothes at 30°C or less have changed behaviour. In the hospitality sector, customers are also not unfamiliar with signage in their rooms asking them to use their towels more than once, packaging requesting that outer food wrappings are recycled and so on.

Communicate but don't greenwash

Unfortunately, not all firms that claim to be environmentally friendly are genuinely green. Some exploit the idea to gain greater market share, jumping on the green band-wagon without making any substantive change in their environmental actions and performances (Polonsky and Rosenberger, 2001). The most quoted example is claiming to be green by dint of operating a towel and linen agreement (i.e. asking guests to reuse towels or to agree to not have bed linen changed daily). Green marketing has faced a backlash because of its failure to live up to its promises as a tool for promoting ecological and social sustainability. Those misleading green marketing claims – i.e. greenwashing – lead to consumer scepticism towards all claims, minimising the benefits to truly committed companies that seek to promote the environmental attributes of their products in the marketplace (Chamorro and Bañegil, 2006; Crane, 2000b; Polonsky and Rosenberger, 2001).

In El Dief and Font, 2010.

The initiatives within the sector to date have for the most part been fairly modest and often relatively poorly implemented (usually because they are not supported by appropriate or sufficient staff training). They have sought to change customer behaviour at the margins whilst also providing customers with a feeling that the company is engaged in 'doing good'. Initiatives that seek to nudge consumers into changing behaviour include:

- Cards in bathrooms requesting that towels are replaced on the towel rail if the customer is prepared to use them for a second day;[24]

- Initiatives to promote and encourage customers to choose seasonal, local or regional choices or those that are produced by ethical trading systems;

- Initiatives to encourage customers to select tap water or alternatives that are filtered and bottled on site rather than brought-in bottled water;

- Initiatives that encourage customers to separate specific products for recycling whilst on the premises;

---

24 Care should be taken with these initiatives. Businesses where the average length of stay is one night will find that they don't deliver savings and are a reputational risk. They should also be actively implemented and genuinely make an improvement to the environment.

♦ Initiatives that encourage customers to reduce heating or increase cooling temperatures in specific areas;

♦ Initiatives that provide choices of products such as recycled paper and biodegradable tableware (sometimes at slightly higher cost) and that actively engage consumers in making those choices on the basis that they 'do good'.

More controversial – and based on trying to identify actions that make the biggest impact – are initiatives to:

♦ Suggest consumers reduce consumption of specific products such as red meat (for example, Vacherin's campaign to encourage its customers to select more sustainable choices during Green Week in 2010);

♦ Engage customers in philanthropic giving to a local cause/charity – perhaps via a voluntary contribution over-and-above the cost of their meal/accommodation. The Green Imperative Fund (GIF) established by Banyan Tree in 2001 is typical of this sort of initiative. The fund aims to provide financial support to worthy environmental and community-based projects where Banyan Tree resorts are located. Every guest is invited to be a GIF 'partner' by giving a voluntary contribution of US$2.00 per room night.

♦ Some companies – including Hyatt – have started working specifically with event planners. Throughout March 2011, Hyatt Hotels, through its 'Meet and Be Green' programme, offered clients a 3% discount at most of its premium branded hotel properties if they agree to 10 steps that the chain claims can reduce energy and waste (http://www.triplepundit.com/2010/07/hyatt-launches-meet-and-be-green-initiative/).

A few businesses have become aware that they have to do more than the conventional customer communications. Among these are contract caterer Vacherin. They recognised that the global increase in consumption of red meat and dairy products makes a significant contribution to emission of gases implicated in climate change. In fact, they calculate that a restaurant switching from red meat and dairy to vegetarian options for one day is equivalent to localising the entire food supply chain. Staff are made aware of this issue and staff canteens now hold red-meat-free days or weeks. These are being extended to clients.

While they sound simple, the implementation of these initiatives is not without PR risk. To a cynical public, it is important (and too often forgotten) that those businesses that engage in these campaigns are able to track and demonstrate environmental and social benefits as well as economic benefits.

Many of these initiatives have now become mainstream and a large number of third sector websites host, for example, standardised towel cards for hospitality businesses to download, print out and display. The real challenge is to move these initiatives into the areas that will nudge consumer behaviour where it will make a real difference. These include choosing different modes of transport to get to/travel around the location, engaging consumers in choosing not to have access to products that are not seasonal and require air freighting, engaging consumers in reducing personal water consumption especially in areas that are water poor, reducing consumption of foods with a high carbon footprint such as red meat and so on. Helping customers to understand the rationale for such action (rather than telling them what to do) is a key mechanism to achieve, this in combination with the removal of some options from the offer. Choice editing (see below) can play an important role in the latter activity and may provide a preferable route to tackling some of these issues, especially if it can be implemented on a sector-wide basis.

Taking 'irresponsible' choices out of the marketplace

Having spent decades expanding customer choice, many businesses have discovered an amazing fact. And that is that less can actually be more! Dazed by the array of products on shelves, consumers are increasingly looking to their suppliers to filter out products that are unacceptable because of their health, environmental or social impacts. This process is known as 'choice editing'. There are many who would argue that choice editing undertaken by global corporations has the most significant role to play in changing customer behaviour and can be more powerful than regulation, as for example, Grant, in the *Green Marketing Manifesto* (Grant, 2007).

What is choice editing?

Choice editing for sustainability is about shifting the field of choice for mainstream consumers: cutting out unnecessarily damaging products and getting real sustainable choices on the shelves. In the context of high consumer concern, but low levels of action, the idea of integrating the most compelling issues of sustainable development through choice editing makes sense. Consumers benefit from the assurance that the issues they care about are considered, rather than facing the demand that they grapple with those complexities themselves.

(Sustainable Development Commission, 2006)

To some businesses, choice editing may seem counter-intuitive, but it is already a fact of every day life in many hospitality businesses. Those food service organisations that have selected to offer consumers only the choice of hot beverage products that are sourced from fairly traded or ethical sources are already practising choice editing as are those businesses that are offering the option to select only seasonal food products or local meat products.

When undertaken on a voluntary basis by large businesses, choice editing can be a powerful tool to bring about a change in consumer behaviour. It can also play a role in building trust in the brand and avoiding reputational risk. Those businesses that have engaged in choice editing in the sector have found that it is most effective if:

- The choice offered is perceived to be a better or healthier option (even if it has not been scientifically proven to be so). For example, organic vegetables as opposed to those produced by conventional means;

- The choice offered appeals to the 'inner eco-warrior' in customers themselves or in the increasing number of business clients who specify baseline responsible business principles as a condition of doing business (as is the case for Fair Trade beverages, or fish options that exclude known endangered species such as cod);

- Customers don't notice the change. While this does little to enhance corporate reputations, there are occasions when it is simply better to slip options off the supply list because they pose a reputational risk (this has been the case where products are found to have been produced by, for example, destroying virgin rain forest);

- The choices offered provide customers with simple solutions that means the issues they care about are taken care of (e.g. good animal welfare standards are applied to all product choices);

- Business acts together to provide cohesive action, rather than proposing apparently contradictory consumer advice on issues.

The process of choice editing is not always directly communicated to consumers. However, those businesses that choice edit have to be prepared to respond to those consumers whose preferred option is no longer available. Some companies have got this badly wrong. Getting it wrong is something that hospitality businesses greatly fear.

When choice editing is used effectively, it can have the effect of retaining existing customers, winning new customers and enhancing reputations. McDonald's, for example, have made some progress in rebuilding their corporate reputation by making extensive use of choice editing – initially to favour some meat products produced to high animal welfare standards and latterly by choosing to use only free range eggs in their breakfast products. When implemented across a sector, choice editing can also deliver immediate environmental or social benefits. The New Zealand Government have also made a brave choice editing decision by integrating basic responsible business criteria into the quality grading scheme for accommodation. Thus any business seeking to gain recognition and the marketing advantages of the New Zealand tourism authority must comply with at least a minimum number of criteria. Within the UK, choice editing by a customer (in this case a very large one – the UK Government) that specified that food provision in public sector settings (primarily schools) should meet minimum 'sustainable' criteria played a major role in focusing the thoughts of the contract caterers on this topic.

Text box 41: Can luxury be responsible?

There are a number of businesses, especially at the luxury end of the market, that prefer to keep responsible business programmes strictly out of customer consciousness or to imply to customers (through their corporate communications) that they will take care of the environmental and social impacts of their stay for them (for example, through their corporate philanthropy programmes). The companies that are in this category have a firm belief that the perceived quality of the customer experience may be compromised by asking customers to change their behaviour even when the change required is marginal, will have little impact upon the customer and will deliver significant environmental or social benefit.* These businesses are already choice editing. For many of them, however, a difficult balancing act will need to be performed over the coming decade: this will identify how far back-of-house and cost-saving responsible business initiatives can be taken before becoming evident within the customer experience.

At the moment, the rationale for the decisions of these luxury businesses to avoid changing customer behaviour at all costs is largely unquestioned. The hospitality businesses that make these claims will, however need to keep an eye on the emerging unease about some luxury items and experiences. In the words of WWF '… there are warning signs of a coming impasse. Titles and headlines such as "How luxury lost its luster"; "The Devil sells Prada 2; and "Has luxury's lap gotten too big?" indicate how journalists are questioning whether the corporate globalisation of luxury brands has emptied them of their meaning. Meanwhile, questions are increasingly raised about the ethics of luxury goods' (Bendell and Kleanthous, 2007: 7).

Some brands like Six Senses combine choice editing with an effective redefinition of luxury. Market segmentation tools like 'Lifestyles of Health and Sustainability' (LOHAS) help in this regard to define a market segment that is seeking both luxury and responsible business credentials.

* Ironically, it is likely to be the consumers of these businesses that have the largest per capita environmental footprint. The businesses that perpetuate this view also often don't recognise the very positive brand associations that can be made with responsible products as described by Futerra in their document Sell the Sizzle.

3. Supporting consumers in changing their own behaviour

Perhaps most radical of all is the concept of extending initiatives to change consumers practices not just in their use of the hospitality experience itself, but also in the way they behave either within a destination (for holiday leisure consumers) and at home. A few pioneering businesses are now taking this route. For example:

♦ **Marks and Spencer's Plan A** includes a commitment to 'help our customers live a more sustainable life'. This is done by selling products that meet Plan A principles, labelling, information campaigns to nudge consumer behaviour and asking consumers to sign up to a number of simple pledges. There is also help for customers to set out their own personal Plan A.

♦ **B&Q's One Planet Home** scheme has trained 'eco advisors' in store to advise customers. It provides information on its website and sells a range of independently assessed 'eco' products (http://www.diy.com/oneplanethome).

♦ **EDF Energy's 'Team Green Britain'** aims to help people reduce their carbon footprint, use less energy, live healthier lives and save money Unilever are seeking to engage customers in India in using less water when washing clothes.

While it sounds radical, this is an area in which hospitality businesses can really excel. Initiatives that make responsible business decisions a part of the mainstream for consumers and that illustrate how these issues can promote authenticity, support communities, protect the environment and so on, all make consumers more accepting of sustainable lifestyles. Perhaps more important, they also underline the way in which sustainable or responsible travel choices can improve the overall quality of the experience. Progress in this area includes:

♦ The number of hospitality businesses that have started producing Visitor Charters to engage customers in responsible behaviours within the destination. See, for example, the Fowey Visitor Charter developed by CoaST and hosted by a number of hotel businesses in Cornwall in the UK (www.fowey.co.uk/site/local-information/fowey-visitor-charter).

♦ A number of businesses offer incentives/rewards for individuals who arrive by non-car or other 'soft' transport modes.

♦ A number of hospitality businesses provide recipe cards, seasonal food advice, information about sustainable fish or other communications that customers can take and use at home.

♦ The development of green maps such as that produced by Fairmont Hotels in partnership with VisitEngland and GreenTraveller.co.uk

♦ Some businesses offer local cuisine and cooking classes involving trips to local markets and farmers in search of ingredients.

♦ Educational websites and front of house campaigns have been hosted by some of the brands that are leading in the responsible business field (the Scandic 'Better World' campaign, for example, includes the company responsible business performance indicators and tips for integrating sustainability issues into personal behaviour on the hotel bill).

♦ Information provided through conference facilities. Hilton Worldwide, for example, offers Hilton Meetings coasters and name cards which include tips for more sustainable behaviours and a LightStay meeting calculator report provides an environmental footprint for the event and tips on how to tackle specific impacts.

♦ Information boards that support sustainable lifestyles (e.g. the Extreme Academy at Watergate Bay in Cornwall, UK).

♦ Campaigns to plant trees/restore biodiversity on behalf of customers (e.g. Marriott with the Amazon forest rescue programme).

♦ Involving local artists and artisans in providing products and decor for display in the business.

♦ Perhaps most innovative, the development of the Liveable Environmentally Sustainability Suite under development by LEED. This provides those guests in accommodation establishments that agree to use less water and energy over the course of their stay with a series of rewards.

Text box 42: The seven C's for selling sustainability

1. **Clarity** of the proposition: it is clear what you are asking people to do as a result of the communication.

2. **Compelling message**: your communication works at a rational and emotional level.

3. **Connection to the issues**: they are perceived to be relevant to people's everyday lives.

4. **Creativity**: you challenge perceptions by saying something new.

5. **Communications mix and shape**: your media planning is integrated, timely and effective.

6. **Consistency**: your message is reinforced through wider communication and policy activities.

7. **Confidence to act**: you use customer segmentation as an approximation of the marketplace. You act when the insight is good enough.

Source: NESTA (2008)

However, much remains to be done to truly engage customers in changing their behaviour when using hospitality products. This is especially the case for tackling the most significant impacts of hospitality (travel choices for hospitality experiences that are a part of leisure tourism and food choices for all businesses). There is a lot of excitement in industry in general about the potential of social marketing in this regard. In the words of Kotler (2002): 'Social marketing is the use of marketing principles and techniques to influence a target audience to voluntarily accept, reject, modify, or abandon a behaviour for the benefit of individuals, groups, or society as a whole.' To date, the concept of social marketing is both little known and little explored within industry in general and hospitality in particular. Its main uses have been to tackle health related issues such as the detection of disease, deterring alcohol or drug abuse and so on. However, it is attracting the attention of those involved in corporate philanthropy and responsible business and is likely to become a tool of choice when seeking to nudge consumers to adopt a wide range of sustainable behaviours.

4. Initiatives that seek to influence consumer choice to favour ethical or green options

In recent years, there has been an explosion of marketing initiatives and 'labels' that demonstrate the ethical credentials of everything from toilet cleaner to hotels. Within the hospitality sector alone, there are multiple initiatives that aim to 'help' customers select products that have a lower environmental and/or social impact. These range from labels that certify the characteristics of a building (LEED), through the management processes that reduce environmental impacts (ISO 14001), to the initiatives that a business is taking and the progress it is making across the range of responsible business initiatives. These labels – some of them credible – seek to enable consumers to make informed and sustainable choices. However, with a few exceptions,[25] the explosion of brands and the different criteria by which they are awarded has done little to inform and much to confuse consumers. Even the claims/labels that are credible (i.e. audited to reach minimum criteria across the responsible business agenda), rarely give great weight to the issues about which consumers are passionate when seeking a hospitality experience (for example, they often focus primarily on the issues of energy, waste and water management when customers really care about the integrity of communities in which hospitality experiences are based, local food, animal welfare standards and pesticide-related impacts of their choices). The reason for this is simple. The labels that have been developed to differentiate those businesses that are 'responsible' from those that are not, depend largely on membership fees from those that join them. The businesses that join them are eager to reap the rewards of resource efficiencies. There is an economic imperative, therefore, for these schemes to focus on cost-saving resource efficiency measures that are welcomed by businesses. It is to the credit of the companies that operate these schemes that many have gone beyond cost-efficiencies alone to address a wider range of issues, including in some instances ethical finance and biodiversity protection.

Those businesses that achieve 'green' awards are – without doubt – operating much more responsibly than the majority of those that don't. The labels that businesses choose either recognise good responsible business performance in mainstream businesses (e.g. the Green Tourism Business Scheme and Sustainable Restaurant Association in the UK, Travelife standard and Green Globe globally and Green Key in some parts of Europe) aor differentiate 'ethical' or green businesses from the mainstream (for example the certification offered by Ecotourism Australia).

To date, consumers barely recognise any of the logos that are in the marketplace. And even those who do recognise logos often confuse symbols of membership (such as the yellow daffodils that signify the Considerate Hoteliers Association in the UK)

---

25 For example, the Nordic Swan which is widely recognised by consumers in Nordic countries and associated with 'doing good' by around 80%, the ISO 14001 and LEED logos which are widely recognised by business buyers; the range of logos associated with fair trade.

with those that signify achievement (such as the green leaf of the audited Green Tourism Business Scheme standard).

Within the corporate marketplace, the evidence is slightly different. It is abundantly clear that corporate buyers are seeking to select hospitality businesses that can demonstrate good environmental, if not responsible business, credentials. Businesses seeking to sell into this marketplace and operating within the conference and meetings market have little choice but to accommodate the environmental preferences of buyers (see Text box 43). Those seeking to supply the London Olympics, for example, are required to comply with the sustainable event standard BS8901 as a condition of contract. Organisations such as CERES recognise the significance of this issue and have produced their own checklist from which to identify hotel businesses that have good environmental criteria.[26] Others rely on 'green' symbols.

The level of consumer confusion about the credentials of a responsible business programme is – at the current time – serving the interests of many hospitality businesses, and especially those that wish to gain the business benefits of being green without the cost or inconvenience of introducing a responsible business initiative. These business can choose to join a membership organisation that does not have audited criteria or to join one of the schemes that has a relatively low entry bar. In the long term, however, these cynical actions do a disservice to customers and clients. Those hospitality businesses that have sought to cynically gain a green advantage are likely to find themselves increasingly in the spotlight as consumers (and the media) become more adept at spotting – and communicating – the greenwash. The backlash is already evident to some extent on services such as TripAdvisor where a consistent theme is that of greenwash and in the media where publications such as the Guardian regularly query the responsible travel/food credentials of a number of major global brands.

Text box 43: The significance of responsible business criteria in the corporate hospitality marketplace

- 'Caterers unable to demonstrate a clear sustainability policy will not make it past the first stage' (Phil Roker, Vacherin).

- 'Potential clients are very keen on seeing prospective catering partners having sustainability high on their priority list, which is only good news for business success' (Caroline Fry, Charlton House).

- 'If we just comply with what expectations are, we will be fine but won't have any competitive advantage … if we go that extra mile, people notice and that gives us an advantage' (David James, Bartlett Mitchell).

Source: British Hospitality Association (2010)

---

26   CERES also provide a guest feedback card for hotel businesses, which can be accessed from http://www.ceres.org//Page.aspx?pid=761

Five indicators for business

☐ All employees are aware of their role in delivering responsible business objectives and have been provided with good quality training to adapt their behaviours at work and home.

☐ Employees recognise that responsible business outcomes match their personal values as well as those of the business.

☐ Appropriate processes are in place to collate progress by staff, celebrate success and monitor customer feedback at the unit level.

☐ The businesses communicates with consumers about its responsible business aspirations and achievement in an upbeat and positive manner.

☐ The business actively edits choices out of its product portfolio to progress its social and environmental ambitions.

The tools of the trade

Interestingly in some countries, regulation has played a hand in influencing this agenda. Decisions such as that by the UK Government to set standards for food procurement in some public sector settings (such as schools) and the New Zealand Government to include responsible business issues in the quality grading scheme have pushed the agenda forward.

A number of tools are available for those organisations seeking to engage employees in actions that support environmental, economic and social wellbeing. These include:

♦ Information on CDs, available from agencies such as the UN Ecotel concept to WWF, that seek to communicate the significance of sustainable or responsible business practices.

♦ Information made available from companies themselves, including Scandic's environmental training materials and those available from Accor. Strangely it seems that the sharing of experiences of this type is confined to the hotel sector, with few (actually we have been able to find no) restaurant, QSR and catering businesses making their training experiences available outside of the confines of the company.

♦ Information available from national tourism boards, such as the Green Edge programme provided by the Regional Tourist Board Partnership and VisitEngland (and written by the Responsible Hospitality Partnership).

♦ Interactive training programmes available from a range of organisations, from VisitEngland (www.better-tourism.org) to the innovation hotel concept of Inter-Continental Hotels Group.

♦ The training provided by the green certification schemes to help businesses meet or exceed their criteria.

♦ Training programmes provided specifically by businesses to all of their units. These include the training programmes of Aramark, Rezidor, Hilton and others.

There are also the range of so-called 'green' labels and logos. While these are not without their critics,[27] the materials that they produce are often useful training tools – specifying the steps required to operate more responsibly. Many provide promotional materials for the use of businesses that become their members.

Outside these tools, there are a number of indices of ethical business performance such as FTSE-4-Good and these are important indicators to the marketplace about the significance of responsible business within a company's strategy. The fact that many of the very large corporate hospitality businesses have joined these initiatives indicates the persuasive power of being seen to be green.

Altogether more limited are the tools for those businesses that seek to engage consumers in actions that support environmental, economic and social wellbeing. Those that are available tend to be in the form of information such as towel cards or visitor charters that can be downloaded from the internet. Those businesses that genuinely wish to engage consumers in the process of change need to utilise the more generic information that is available from organisations such as NESTA and the International Social Marketing Association.

Conclusion

Hospitality businesses have quickly realised the benefits of engaging employees in responsible business initiatives. Many have enabled responsible business initiatives to evolve to address not only the issues of resource efficiency but also to address local issues and match employee values. They have been justly rewarded for their efforts by better levels of staff morale and retention. But the picture is not quite so rosy as it could be. Motivated managers are crucial to employee engagement and many businesses (even those with excellent responsible business initiatives) have been unable to motivate their general managers to support responsible business ambitions uniformly across the business. Those managers that refuse to implement responsible business initiatives are only rarely challenged about their attitudes (this is in comparison to other areas of business management such as quality control or revenue management). Targets within management bonus structures have helped, but a failure to include responsible business commitments in job descriptions by some businesses or provide a code of ethics that supports these descriptions has hindered progress in some areas of the sector (combined with a poor coverage of the topic within many educational institutions).

---

27 See for example the work of Harold Goodwin and Xavier Font on these issues.

When it comes to consumers, hospitality businesses have recognised that there are a band of consumers who actively seek eco-experiences (in the case of leisure consumers) or responsible hospitality suppliers (in the case of the corporate market). A number of businesses have responded to this need by providing dedicated eco-suites or responsible business marketing materials (including green conference packages). When it comes to engaging with customers about other issues, however, the industry has been rather more timid. The industry has started down the route of choice editing with some high-profile products, but has not really progressed beyond a few fair trade and local alternatives. Customer engagement has – for the most part – not extended beyond offering customers the opportunity to offset the carbon associated with their journey/event or asking them to leave bath towels on a hook if they are prepared to use them for a second day or choosing a few high-profile fair trade products. For most hospitality businesses, actively changing the way in which customers behave remains strictly out of bounds.

References

Bendell, J. and Kleanthous, A. (2007), *Deeper Luxury*, Surrey: WWF

Bohdanowicz, P. and Zientara, P. (2008) 'Corporate social responsibility in hospitality: issues and implications. A case study of Scandic', *Scandinavian Journal of Hospitality and Tourism*, **8** (4), 271–293.

British Hospitality Association (2010) *Food Service and Management Survey*, London: BHA.

CERES (n.d.) *CERES' 21st century corporation vision: 20 key expectations*, available from www. ceres.org

Chan, E.S.W. and Hawkins, R. (2010) 'Attitudes towards EMS in an international hotel: an exploratory case study', *International Journal of Hospitality Management*, **29** (4), 641–651.

Chamorro, A. and Bañegil, T.M. (2006) 'Green marketing philosophy: a study of Spanish firms with ecolabels', *Corporate Social Responsibility and Envirnomental Management*, **13** (1), 11-24

Dimofte, C.V., Johansson, J.K. and Bagozzi, R.P. (2010) 'Global brands in the United States: how consumer ethnicity mediates the global brand effect', *Journal of International Marketing*, **18** (3), 81–105.

Food Service Footprint, http://www.foodservicefootprint.com/

Futerra (n.d.) *Sell the Sizzle*, available at http://www.futerra.co.uk/downloads/Sellthesizzle.pdf

Gordon, W. (2006) *Brand Green: Mainstream or Forever Niche*, London: Green Alliance

Grant, J. 2007, *The Green Marketing Manifesto*, Wiley.

Holbeche, L. (2009) *Aligning Human Resources and Business Strategy*, 2nd edn, Oxford: Butterworth-Heinemann.

ICC (2002) *Business in Society – Making a positive and responsible contribution*, ICC, Paris

Kanter, R.M. cited in Hollender, J. (2010) *The Responsibility Revolution*, San Francisco: Wiley.

Kasim, A. (2004) 'BESR in the hotel sector: a look at tourists' propensity towards environmentally and socially friendly hotel attributes in Pulau Pinang, Malaysia', *International Journal of Hospitality and Tourism Administration*, **5** (2), 61–85.

Kaur, H. (2011) "Impact of Human Resource Factors on Perceived Environmental Performance: an Empirical Analysis of a Sample of ISO 14001 EMS Companies in Malaysia", *Journal of Sustainable Development*, **4** (1), 211-224

Kingaby, H. (2011) *The Guardian* http://www.guardian.co.uk/sustainable-business/blog/ employee-engagement-job-satisfaction-motivation).

Kotler, P., Roberto, N. and Lee, N. (2002) *Social Marketing – Improving the Quality of Life*, Sage, California.

Miller, G., Rathouse, K., Scarles, C., Holmes, K. and Tribe, J. (2007). *Public understanding of sustainable leisure and tourism: A report to the Department for Environment, Food and Rural Affairs*. University of Surrey. Defra, London.

Mulgan, G. (2009) 'After capitalism', *Prospect*, April.

Nattras, B. and Altoman, M. (1999), *The Natural Step for Business: Wealth, Ecology & the Evolutionary Corporation*, New Society Publishers.

NESTA (2008) *Selling Sustainability – Seven Lessons from Advertising and Marketing to Sell Low Carbon Living*, London: NESTA.

Polonsky, M.J. and P.J. Rosenberger III (2001). "Re-evaluating to green marketing - An integrated approach", *Business Horizons*, **44**(5): 21-30

Rose, B. (2002) in *Brand Green – Mainstream or Forever Niche*, London: Green Alliance.

Sustainable Development Commission (2006), *I will if you will, Towards sustainable consumption*, available from http://www.sd-commission.org.uk/publications.php?id=367

Tapscott, D. and Ticoll, D. (2003) *The Naked Corporation*, New York: Free Press.

UNEP Finance Initiative (2011) *If You Ask Us – Making Environmental Employee Engagement Happen*, Paris: UNEP DTI.

USLF (1990) in *Education or Sustainable Development – A Review of the Literature*, Scottish Government, available at http://www.scotland.gov.uk/Publications/2006/05/23091323/11.

World Business Council for Sustainable Development (2008) *Sustainable Consumption – Facts and Trends*, Geneva: WBCSD.

Wu, H.C. (2010) 'The impact of environmental management practices on hotel operating costs', PhD thesis, Oxford Brookes University.

Principle 7: Contribute to the development of public policy that promotes environmental, social and economic wellbeing

It is now recognised that poverty reduction and sustainable development will not be achieved through government action alone. Policy makers are paying increasing attention to the potential contribution of the private sector to such policy objectives. The concept of corporate social responsibility (CSR) is sometimes used as shorthand for businesses' contribution to sustainable development.

Mumo Kivuitu (2006)

Most governments have concluded that the regulatory, financial and market based tools that they have access to have a role to play in reducing emissions associated with the production of goods and services. They are, however, poorly adapted to changing patterns of consumption or tackling social equity issues. The challenges of sustainable development cannot be met unless both of these aspects are tackled and to do so will require engagement with businesses among others. Those governments and intergovernmental agencies that are serious about achieving more sustainable forms of development have, thus, almost unanimously come to the conclusion that there is a need to harness the creative power of companies. Organisations such as the United Nations have actively nurtured dialogue with businesses and industry through processes such as the Marrakech Process and the World Economic Forum. These processes have been emulated within national policy dialogues, where businesses have increasingly been given a voice when it comes to formulating policy responses to sustainable development issues. Figure 40 demonstrates the range of policy tools that are within the scope of these dialogues.

Some view the inclusion of businesses – and especially multinational companies – in dialogue with governments as something of a betrayal. They view companies as seeking only to weaken the rules regarding advertising, biotechnology, emission control and so on through the policy debate. There is some justification for this point of view. In the words of Jeffrey Hollender 'for too long, despite business's supposed embrace of corporate responsibility, the vast majority of companies have deemed it entirely acceptable for their activities to diminish society and impair the environment' (p. xvii). Yet to exclude companies from the policy dialogue is to ignore the roles that these behemoths can play in, among other things, changing the behaviour of millions of individuals, challenging the traditional notion of businesses, developing accounting procedures that recognise the value of environmental and social and community resources and benefiting from the eco-efficiencies that accompany effective environmental management.

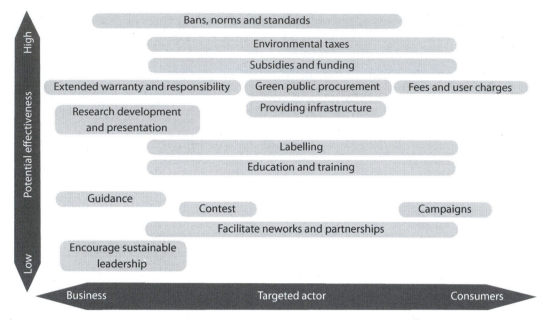

Figure 39: Policy Instruments for sustainable consumption

Source: UNEP/Wuppertal Institute/Centre on Sustainable Consumption and Production *et al.* (2010)

Text box 44: The issue of corruption

It is implicit within Principle 7 that businesses do not engage in corrupt practices. This is a simple statement to make, but not always easy to enforce. Any global company will be aware that when operating in some countries the line between normal business practices and corruption can become blurred. Openly corrupt demands for permission to build or gain the management contract to operate in a property may be easy to spot, if not to refuse. More difficult to manage are the smaller instances of corruption. These are relatively common in some countries when seeking to renew contracts to supply water to an existing hotel spa or gain the opportunity to bid to provide hospitality services to an oil rig and so on. It is when dealing with the issues of corruption at this level that businesses often overstep the mark. Companies that are serious about beating corruption actively ensure that dialogue with policy makers takes place to fight against corruption. Marriott, for example, addresses this issue through its Business Conduct Guide which is supported by a legal and ethical conduct survey to ensure compliance.

Source (http://www.marriott.com/corporate-social-responsibility/corporate-values).

Many businesses have long since recognised the benefits of policy dialogue – not least to ensure that policy interventions support responsible business initiatives and the regulatory bar is sufficiently high to target those businesses that 'do bad' – thus preventing the name of big business in general from being tarnished (www.edelman.com/trust/2011). The last decade, has, therefore seen extensive voluntary initiatives from businesses working in partnership with governments to tackle issues from corruption to obesity and poverty to carbon reduction.

Text box 45: The framework conditions for sustainable development

Many international organisations such as the OECD, World Business Council for Sustainable Development, Wuppertal Institute, IIED and so on, recognise that a number of conditions must be established by policy makers in consultation with stakeholders to enable the delivery of sustainable development objectives by businesses (they are usually called framework conditions). There is no unilateral agreement on what these 'framework conditions' include, but common themes are:

- The need to agree the scope of sustainable development initiatives;

- A base of progressive regulation that sets the minimum standard with which all operations must comply;

- Procedures are in place to tackle businesses that seek to bend the rules (by corruption or other means);

- A need for coherence within and between policy tools to ensure that they work together to support the achievement of sustainable development objectives; *

- The use of an effective blend of policy tools, that include regulation but also market mechanisms to encourage voluntary action;

- The establishment of policies and programmes that incentivise investments in 'clean' technologies;

- Support for research and development to help technologies and techniques that deliver change reach the market;

- The need to engage business not only in the process of emission control but also in delivering change through resource reduction, supply chain management and strategies to influence consumer behaviour;

- The need for stable strategies and policies that provide markets with the security that the conditions that stimulate investment in sustainable development now will remain stable in the medium to long term;

- The need to support developing countries in developing the capacity to deliver the framework conditions for sustainable development.

* Those who are engaged in the policy debate are only too aware of the complexities of establishing a coherent framework of policies that seek to deliver sustainable development. A complex web of historical precedents – including many that pre-date the sustainable development agenda and that favour economic growth at environmental cost – often result in perverse incentives for practices that are not sustainable. Some agencies are now seeking to review the policy framework. For example, the EU is funding a programme (known as EPISIS) to look at the policy framework to promote innovation for sustainable tourism.

For many businesses, the engagement with the policy debate starts from a desire to provide a stimulus for programmes that deliver tangible short-term benefits (usually in terms of cost savings). These initiatives include voluntary programmes to reduce carbon emissions across a sector in return for financial incentives or technical support in delivering those carbon savings. Initiatives to engage with policy makers that do not move beyond this ambition are, however, limited in the extreme and are unlikely to deliver the scale of transformational change that is required over the coming decades. Businesses (and the representative trade associations) that have really engaged in the policy agenda have come to realise that they can work in partnership with other stakeholders to move beyond regulation by setting voluntary emission targets or ensuring that the framework conditions for sustainable operations are in place (see Text box 45). To date, the hospitality and tourism sector has made some progress on setting voluntary targets. The World Travel & Tourism Council, for example, called on travel and tourism businesses to halve carbon emissions by 2035 over 2005 levels, the UK Food and Drink Federation launched its Five Fold Environmental Ambition in 2007 with the aim of helping members make a significant reduction in water use by 2020, the New Zealand tourism sector make commitments to a range of environmental improvements in the Tourism Strategy 2015.

For hospitality businesses, the aim of working with policy makers (either as individual companies or the umbrella associations that represent the sector) is to ensure that these framework conditions are established and regularly reviewed as knowledge develops.

What the responsible business guidelines say

It is a common misconception that many business organisations that seek to engage in the policy dialogue aim to undermine regulation and promote voluntary initiatives. In fact, many of the institutions that represent business interests acknowledge that regulation has an important role to play. Each of the sets of responsible business guidelines referenced in this book do not seek to replace, but to complement, policy tools and inform policy makers. Thus all of the responsible business guidelines are a mechanism for engaging with policy makers to explicitly move business initiatives above and beyond the requirements of regulation.

Since 1992 (the United Nations Conference on Environment and Development), when international inter-governmental institutions first formally invited representatives of major companies to the policy table, business has enthusiastically made input to the policy debate (although even ardent supporters of voluntary initiatives would acknowledge that the rhetoric has not always matched the action). As a result many of the world's largest businesses now have individuals whose sole job is to engage in the policy debate and to work with policy makers. A number of bespoke organisations have now been formed to represent the views of business and industry at the policy table. These include general organisations such as the World Business Council for Sustainable Development and those that represent the hospitality sector in its broadest context (e.g. the International Tourism Partnership and the International Hotel & Restaurant Association, the Caribbean Alliance for Sustainable Tourism and so on). Nationally there are also a number of associations that have as one of their core functions engagement with policy makers (albeit often in a lobbying capacity) and many of these have embraced the sustainable development agenda within their scope of responsibility or have links with organisations that do the same job (e.g. the Green Hotels Association in the USA).

Text box 46: The origins of the voluntary industry initiative

In Agenda 21, business and industry is encouraged to 'increase self-regulation, guided by appropriate codes, charters and initiatives integrated into all elements of business planning and decision-making and fostering openness and dialogue with employees and the public'. Such self-regulatory (or voluntary) approaches are said to represent a more effective and desirable alternative to achieving sustainability goals than the 'command and control' approach of government regulations and enforcement programmes. 'They provide flexibility', says the World Business Council on Sustainable Development, 'which allows business to achieve the desired goals in the most economically effective manner possible'. http://isforum.org/tobi/voluntary/mgreview/actionorpr.aspx

Voluntary initiatives are now a significant tool within the international policy agenda. They are defined as 'private or public efforts to improve corporate environmental behaviour beyond existing legal requirements, but they can become enshrined in law' (Schiavi and Solomon, 2007). These voluntary initiatives – so the argument goes – can provide an architecture through which businesses can collectively strive for more sustainable forms of development. So successful is the concept, that there are now quite literally hundreds of codes of conduct, compacts and so on that guide how businesses can contribute towards environmental protection or social equity (many of which are referred to throughout this text).

The fundamentals

Engagement with policy makers within the hospitality sector most commonly occurs:

♦ At an international level;

♦ Nationally, at the level of the associations that broadly represent the views of the sector;

♦ Between individual businesses and policy makers at national and international level.

International engagement in the policy debate

At an international level, the associations that represent the tourism and hospitality sectors have been vocal and have been effective at establishing a number of voluntary initiatives (see Chapter 4). As a result, many international policy organisations now view hospitality and the wider tourism sector as one that can play a leading role in the delivery of sustainable development objectives. Organisations including the International Hotels & Restaurants Association, the International Tourism Partnership, the World Travel & Tourism Council and Caribbean Alliance for Sustainable Tourism (CAST) have played an important role in raising the profile of the sector and of the enabling framework that is necessary to support its development in a sustainable manner. As a result, tourism (and by association hospitality) have specific streams in many of the major policy fora. These provide an important voice in which to raise the issues that are of concern to the sector and to promote the ways in which it can support the achievement of more sustainable forms of development.

Text box 47: The rise of industry-based initiatives

'The rise of industry-based initiatives in responsible business is one of the major transformations in the landscape of corporate social responsibility. Over the past three years, initiatives have grown in number and their membership has continued to expand, as has their reach.

Momentum is growing in developing countries around sustainability issues, and industry-based initiatives provide an architecture that allows for consultation between developed and developing countries and between the private and public sectors. Even within sectors, many of these coalitions allow for consultation between producers, buyers and retailers, consumers, NGOs and others. The organisations that host these initiatives are usually intermediaries, bringing stakeholders to a table that is growing to address myriad issues, from environmental, to social, financial, ethical and anti-trust matters.

Initiatives offer the possibility to create blueprints for change, allocating responsibilities among key actors, including governments, civil society and the private sector. Initiatives provide an interesting view into the field of CSR writ large; they are microcosms of CSR, where new trends and ideas are incubated and take root.'

Source: Ethical Corporation Institute (2009)

Many of the initiatives that have been achieved at an international level for the hospitality and/or tourism sector aim to deliver those blueprints. They effectively set out what tourism and/or hospitality can deliver to the sustainable development debate and on occasion set the framework conditions for sustainable development. Whether or not they actually deliver change is debated. Some commentators such as Harold Goodwin view these initiatives as weak because of the 'dominance of neo-liberal thinking [that] has resulted in a series of policy responses which have favoured voluntary and market solutions like carbon trading and carbon offsets' (Goodwin and Walmsley, 2010). Goodwin argues that these voluntary approaches permit, and even encourage, business as usual, permitting companies to purchase the right to pollute.

Engagement between national policy makers and trade associations

At a national level, the picture is rather more sketchy. Not all trade associations that represent the hospitality sector engage in the policy debate about responsible business or sustainable development. For some, their raison d'être revolves around promoting economic growth and ensuring that the conditions for business growth are maintained. [28] With the exception of a handful of international organisations, those that have engaged have largely been reactive and responded to policy rather than sought to initiate it. The focus for most is supporting the development of voluntary initiatives as the preferred mechanism through which to deliver sustainable development objectives in partnership with policy makers. As a result, codes of conduct, manuals, voluntary agreements on carbon reduction and water reduction, certification schemes, etc. have abounded.

The role of trade associations

Trade associations – and the major companies that support them – have effectively mobilised members around a small number of hot topics in western economies. These include nutritional standards and the associated issue of obesity, the use of alcohol, increasingly carbon and waste and issues of animal welfare standards. Outcomes include the Responsibility Deal in the UK for nutritional standards, the Australian Quick Service Restaurant Industry Initiative for Responsible Advertising and Marketing to Children and the UK Voluntary Waste Agreement. They demonstrate how industry can focus around common topics and agree principles that exceed regulatory standards and appease consumers.

On occasion, trade and professional associations have supported the establishment of organisations dedicated to promoting good responsible business practices. Examples include the Caribbean Alliance for Sustainable Tourism (CAST), an organisation that developed within the Caribbean Hotel Association and later became independent. CAST seeks to deliver the principles of Agenda 21 and provide a range of guidance to hotels and national programmes. More often than not, trade and professional associations integrate responsible business initiatives within their own remit. Thus the American Hotel & Lodging Association has a Green Task Force and set of environmental guidelines, and the UK-based Institute of Hospitality managed

---

28 Economic development is one fundamental condition for the achievement of sustainable development. However, the pursuit of economic growth objectives without consideration for environmental and social/community objectives will fail to deliver the conditions for either responsible business or sustainable development.

a carbon management programme in partnership with the Carbon Trust.[29]

Sometimes the associations that represent the sector have got their voluntary initiatives badly wrong. This is not necessarily because the initiatives have been voluntary, but because they have not addressed the core sustainable development impacts of an operation, they have chosen solutions that tackle the symptoms rather than the cause of the problem, as we noted when looking at the policy debate, or – more often – they do not have robust verification mechanisms in place to record achievement and/or they fail to engage with a sufficient range of stakeholders. See, for example, some of the early attempts by trade associations to promote voluntary 'green tourism certification schemes' within the leisure tourism sector and some of the early initiatives to offset carbon emissions from the sector that invested in carbon offset schemes that had limited potential to actually reduce carbon emissions.

Even for those associations that are convinced of the need for sustainable development it is not always easy to promote responsible business and sustainable development. Barriers to effective engagement include:

- The relative low priority afforded to hospitality and tourism sectors by many governments;

- The need to balance the role of lobbyist and responsible business advocate. Often trade associations need to choose between lobbying against the introduction of mechanisms such as carbon taxes that are intended to provide market mechanisms to stimulate responsible business practices and actively promoting sustainable development initiatives;

- Member demands when a small but vocal minority can position responsible business issues as an 'expensive luxury', regardless of the long-term vision of the trade association;

- The difficulties in communicating the long-term nature of sustainable development against the short-term ambitions of many business members;

- The difficulties in engaging policy makers in understanding the many dimensions of a large and complex industry like the hospitality sector;

- Within the hospitality sector specifically, a general lack of data about impacts from which to develop comprehensive policy dialogue and a general low level of awareness of the significance of the issues among many businesses;

- On occasion, the conflict between sustainable development and growth of the sector. See for example, the conflict in some islands like Bali where severe water shortages are leading some to call for a moratorium on hotel development – something that is broadly opposed by some of the trade associations (see the *Green Hotelier*, autumn 2011).

---

29 The agency that delivers reductions in carbon emissions on behalf of the UK Government. This programme has now ceased to function and is delivered under the auspices of the Carbon Trust alone.

Over recent years, however, many policy makers have recognised that partnerships are an effective tool for achieving responsible business ends, and as a result we have seen the emergence of policy tools such as voluntary energy efficiency and voluntary waste management agreements with industry sectors including hospitality. This is a trend that is likely to expand and gain increased recognition by consumers.

To date, it would be an over-statement to claim that the initiatives between trade and policy associations have created the 'blueprint for change' talked about by the ethical corporation. Some trade associations are, however, now starting to provide an important focus points in which businesses can identify new trends, incubate ideas, identify perverse policy incentives and exchange information in a safe environment. More effective engagement between trade associations and policy makers will, however, be essential to ensuring that the external environment can support those ideas that can make a difference to deliver tangible benefits in the long term.

Individual businesses

It may be the pervading view that businesses need to be coerced to meet sustainable development objectives, but it is not the case for all businesses. A handful of business leaders (and increasingly the major companies in the hospitality sector) have concluded that they need to work with policy makers not just to formulate the framework conditions for sustainable development, but also to drive the policy agenda further forward to address the sustainable development issues. These businesses are often global in scope and many have well-developed responsible business initiatives. Often working collaboratively, it is those businesses that are convinced of the need for more sustainable patterns of development that are seeking to develop policy still further. Global businesses that are leading the engaging with policy makers to take the dialogue further include:

♦ General Electric Energy, Unilever, Google, Danone, Nestlé and Otto Group among others all of which are seeking to encourage the EU to support – through a carbon emissions tax – an unconditional 30% carbon reduction target by 2020, compared to 1990;

♦ The World Business Council for Sustainable Development in its work on innovation and honing investment community to drive green growth;

♦ The work by Unilever and the World Wildlife Fund in 1997 to establish the Marine Stewardship Council (MSC), to address the problem of over-fishing and ensure the long-term sustainability of fish stocks.

These organisations may be from different industry sectors, but they are collectively engaged in thinking about sustainable development as something that is bigger than just their organisation. For them, responsible business is about playing a leadership role and engaging policy makers and others in going further. These businesses have gone beyond commenting on policy papers and proposals, to reframing the debate and looking at the core conditions for their own long-term success. It is these businesses that are seeking to establish an enabling framework for sustainable development and that recognise that this is essential for their own long-term viability as well as that of their competitors. Within the hospitality sector, a very small number of companies are starting to engage at this level. These include:

♦ Sodexo, which has a dedicated Government Relations Director. In its own words, the company is 'determined to play a leading role in transforming public service outcomes. To do so, it is essential that the company actively engages in the debate and builds strong relationships with senior civil servants and government ministers to better understand the scope and ambitions of policies with a view to providing expertise on the development of these policies. The company recognises that this cooperation will contribute to an outstanding delivery of public services to the benefits of citizens.'

♦ The hotel members of the International Tourism Partnership, including Rezidor, Marriott, Wyndham, Fairmont and InterContinental Hotels all of which have tried to inform the policy agenda through collective action.

Five key indicators for business

☐ The business does not condone or engage in corrupt practices.

☐ Input into policy extends beyond lobbying government to repeal regulations and includes actively advising the government on the sector and formulating possible new approaches to engage the sector in sustainable practices.

☐ The business actively shares examples of outstanding practice with policy makers and others.

☐ The business participates in stakeholder dialogues with policy makers (including policy consultations) to inform them of the industry's specific needs.

☐ The business works in partnership with other companies and trade associations in the sector to identify the framework conditions for sustainable development.

The tools of the trade

The many codes of conduct and trade associations that abound within the industry help to guide the policy dialogue between industry and policy makers. In many countries, industry associations will provide guidance on engaging with policy makers or will do so on the behalf of their members. The tools to help businesses engage directly with policy makers are rather more limited and are largely available from organisations such as the UN and Wuppertal Institute.

When it comes to the topic of corruption, organisations such as Transparency International provide a range of tools and advice.

Fora such as the World Business Council for Sustainable Development and the International Tourism Partnership provide mechanisms through which hospitality businesses can engage in dialogue about how to use responsible business initiatives to advance progress on the sustainable development agenda.

Conclusion

At an international level, the tourism industry (if not hospitality sector per se) has been relatively effective at engaging in the policy debate. International companies are often members of the organisations that engage in this international policy debate. These international companies usually have mature responsible business programmes and are well aware of the role these can play in supporting the achievement of international sustainable development outcomes.

At a national and regional level and within specific companies, the picture is rather different. A handful of companies have actively engaged in the policy debate – especially around the issues of alcohol, nutritional standards and health. Organisations have been much less willing at these levels to play a positive role on the development of the policy agenda preferring instead to play a more traditional lobbying role. Strategies of lobbying in the short term may seem effective (and in the case of trade and professional associations attract support from a small and vocal minority of businesses). What they do not do is engage policy makers in a debate about the frameworks that are important for the sector to help it genuinely make progress towards sustainability. Those organisations such as CAST that have played this role have found that they can be positive agents of change and have an important function not just in responding to regulation but also in forming it.

References

Ethical Corporation Institute (2009) *Guide to industry initiatives in corporate social responsibility*, Ethical Corporation.

Goodwin, H. and Walmsley, A. (2010) 'Indulging indulgence – tourism, carbon offsetting and climate change', ICRT Occasional Paper 20.

Hollender, J. and Breen, B. (2010) *The Responsibility Revolution – How the Next Generation of Businesses will Win*, San Francisco: Jossey-Bass.

Kivuitu, M. (2005), 'How can Social Responsibility deliver in Africa, *Perspectives*, 2005 **3** July, IIED, available from http://www.csr-weltweit.de/uploads/tx_jpdownloads/Mumo_Kivuitu_How_can_Social_Responsibility_deliver_in_Africa.pdf

Schiavi, P. and Solomon, F. (2007) 'Voluntary initiatives in the mining industry – do they work', *Greener Management International*, Issue 53, 28.

UNEP/Wuppertal Institute/Centre on Sustainable Consumption and Production *et al.* (2010) 'What public policy framework is required to encourage sustainable consumption business strategies', available from www.encourage-sustainable-lifestyles.net

Part 4: Fairness and transparency

It may seem strange to some readers that these two principles do not feature until near the end of this text. This especially the case for Principle 8: 'Define responsible business values and communicate good practice'. Many who advise on the development of responsible business programmes will recommend that organisations develop a mission statement, signed by the board of directors, as one of the very first steps on their journey. Most businesses with advanced responsible business programmes, however, have come to realise that early mission statements often fail to embrace the essence of responsible business initiatives, do not provide sufficient information about what the business will actually do and have little connectivity with the brand. It is often only when responsible business programmes reach maturity that businesses can genuinely define what responsible business means to the company and the brand, and to express this in a way that gives stakeholders confidence and delivers customer trust.

Principle 9, 'Building trust through transparency' is directly related to Principle 8. Many businesses interpret this as a diktat to issue a corporate environmental or responsibility report. But it is about much more than simply producing a report accompanied by a careful scoping statement that provides quantitative results about all (or more typically a small proportion) of the company's achievements and impacts.

In practice, these principles are among the most difficult of the ten to implement successfully, which is why they usually evolve as responsible business initiatives reach maturity. If implemented properly, they can be richly rewarding and provide ample evidence that a business is serious about its responsible business commitments. They can also generate the market advantage and other benefits that are often associated with responsible business practices (for example, being voted as one of the best companies to work for). Once a business engages with the principles, it is difficult to draw back from responsible business commitments (the benefits are such that many would not wish to).

Those businesses that are making progress with these principles, are those that have concluded that responsible business is about far more than positive public relations and short term eco-efficiency (although eco-efficiency is still important). They are those that have embedded the responsible business ethos throughout the organisation, that have worked with suppliers and trained their employees. They use their responsible business initiatives to build trust in the brand, insure against short-term price shocks, secure the long-term future of the brand and guard against accusations of greenwash. These companies recognise that responsible business is a journey that has changed – and will continue to change – the very nature of the business.

Principle 8: Define responsible business values and communicate good practice

…simply improving operational effectiveness does not provide a competitive advantage. Companies only gain advantages if they are able to achieve and sustain higher levels of operational effectiveness than (their) competitors. That is an exceedingly difficult proposition even in the best of circumstances. Once a company establishes a new best practice, its rivals tend to copy it quickly. Best practice competition eventually leads to competitive convergence, with many companies doing the same things in the same ways. Customers end up making decisions based on price, undermining industry profitability.

Michael E. Porter (2008: **<<page no>>**)

Typically, a company will express its attitude towards responsible business issues within a publically available statement signed by the CEO and board members. Such a statement is increasingly presented under the title 'Our Values', but may also take the form of a mission statement, an environmental or responsible business policy statement or a vision statement. Board statements about attitudes towards responsible business range from those adopted by mainstream businesses in traditional industries (see for example, BP's commitment to 'help the world meet its growing need for heat, light and mobility… [in a way that is] … affordable, secure and doesn't damage the environment' (www.bp.com) to those of businesses that have focused their entire operational model around ethical principles. See for example the Cooperative Bank's aim to 'deliver value to its stakeholders in an ecologically sustainable and socially responsible manner' (www.co-operative.coop/corporate/Sustainability09). For all businesses that have adopted the mantle of responsibility, the purpose of such statements is clear. It is to demonstrate that this is a businesses that has fully engaged with its responsibilities to operate not only as a profitable business, but also as one that is 'doing its bit' to protect the environment and society upon which it depends to operate.

The boards of many global companies agree to engage in the development of mission statements not just because they expect to gain short-term cost savings, but to protect corporate reputations, to minimise risks or in a few cases to change the positioning of the brand.[1] Mission statements can be an essential step in this process because they demonstrate why responsible business is important to the company and how it relates to overall brand values. What many businesses forget, however,

---

1   This is in sharp contrast to the way in which responsible business has been 'sold' into the hospitality sector specifically where cost savings are a major – and often only – strand of the argument.

is that while a good mission statement can be a useful expression of values and corporate culture vis-à-vis responsible business, 'in and of themselves, [mission statements] are not important — creating a management team with a sense of mission is crucial' (Campbell, 1992). To create this management team with a sense of mission, the statement has to: provide a clear definition of what responsible business means operationally for managers, be supported by training programmes, be reflected in the career development process, be demonstrated through good practice examples within the business and integrate with core business and brand values. Within a complex industry like hospitality that has multiple units across cultures, woolly statements of business values that lack definition and fail to be interpreted into managers day-to-day activities are a hostage to fortune. As many companies have found, a failure to define the mission statement in a way that is meaningful to managers (and that adds value to the brand) as well as to develop the procedures such as environmental management systems that underpin it, can be costly to corporate reputations. Some companies are now at pains to define what responsible business means to them. Sodexo, for example, in all of its corporate literature very clearly defines its responsible business ambitions and provides a road map for their achievement (see Figure 41).

Text box 48: Greenwash – An inconvenient truth

It is a sobering fact that the term 'greenwash' was first coined way back in 1986 by New York environmentalist Jay Westerveld after discovering some disingenuous hotel cost-cutting methods that were disguised as environmentally responsible. Mission or value statements that sound good in theory but cannot be substantiated in fact still regularly attract accusations of greenwash within the sector. GreenTraveller.co.uk, for example report that Tourism Concern has campaigned for the last 15 years against some of the worst offenders [of greenwash], such as the eviction of the Maasai and Samburu people from their lands in east Africa in order to establish what the developers called 'conservation and safari tourism' …

But ecotourism – and greenwashing – are no longer confined to the central American rainforest or the African bush. Just as the green agenda has gone mainstream, from city breaks to summer holidays in the Med, so we start hearing about so-called eco-friendly spas that do little more than sell fair trade bananas in the bistro. This undermines the genuine article' (http://www.greentraveller.co.uk/node/154). Even in the mainstream press, there are frequent comments on the propensity of the tourism (and by implication hospitality) industry to greenwash. See for example the article by Tom Robbins in the *Observer* that claimed 'From B&Bs to Boeing, everyone is jumping on the environmental bandwagon, but how can we be sure that what they promise is what they deliver?'

(*Observer*, 6 July 2008).

> ### The Better Tomorrow Plan
>
> A commitment to Corporate Citizenship is central to Sodexo's "Ambition 2015" strategy . Today, Sodexo is the recognized global sustainability leader in its market sector and, to take our credentials to the next level of performance, we have devised a new worldwide sustainability roadmap for the Sodexo Group - The Better Tomorrow Plan - covering 80 countries, 33,900 sites and engaging our 380,000 employees.
>
>
> Damien Verdier
> Group Executive Vice President and Chief Marketing Officer
> Offer Marketing, Supply Chain & Sustainable Development

Figure 40: Responsible business ambitions need to link to tangible actions with reach across the company

Businesses like Dow Chemicals, Vodafone, Shell, Sodexo and BP have invested significantly in the development and definition of their responsible business values (as well as in getting the engagement of the management team and employees). This expenditure is justified against a myriad of reasons and these inevitably include the anticipation that they will support positive value associations for the business, that they will help to generate the competitive edge described by Michael Porter and that they will help the business sustain in the long term. In the words of SAM, it is because these companies believe that by adjusting their strategies and 'adapt[ing] in good time, [they] will be the winners in the long run' (PWC, 2010).

What the responsible business guidelines say

All of the responsible business guidelines highlight the importance of the development of a mission statement and of the need to support these by creating a management team with a sense of mission. Some also engage businesses in identifying the connectivity with the main brand.

Good practice lies at the foundation of most of the guidelines. Of themselves, they are a definition of what constitutes 'good practice'[2] across the span of the responsible business agenda. All of the guidelines engage with a broadly similar range of issues, but the ambition for what businesses should seek to achieve within each issue is very varied. The guidelines promoted by organisations such as the International Chamber of Commerce do not extend beyond promoting good practice where those

---

2   Or in the case of some, they are the expression of acceptable practice. Many of these guidelines are developed by committee and this results in relatively conservative ambitions.

of organisation such as CERES – and to a certain extent the publications of leadership organisations like the World Business Council on Sustainable Development and the International Tourism Partnership – actively promote a visionary leadership role for members as expressed in their vision or mission statements.

Without exception, the guidelines acknowledge the importance for businesses to at least seek to operate according to good practice criteria. For example, the International Chamber of Commerce in its *Business in Society* booklet states that:

'ICC strongly encourages voluntary corporate responsibility initiatives by companies. Various studies have shown that companies practice good corporate citizenship by spreading best practice among customers and employees, suppliers and business associates – in areas such as labour, the environment and human rights – in countries where they operate. Responsible, long-term entrepreneurship is the driving force for sustainable economic development and for providing the managerial, technical and financial resources needed to meet social and environmental challenges' (p. 3).

They also acknowledge the importance of defining what 'responsible business' means within the context of the company.

The fundamentals: defining responsible business values

Most, but by no means all, global hospitality businesses have developed a mission or value statement. Of the 24 companies in our sample, 14 have a responsible business vision or mission statement. Mission statements are most prevalent among the hotel, QSR and contract catering businesses and least among the restaurant operators.

There are almost as many different types of mission statements as there are companies. These can be categorised as:

1 *Those that use the responsible business mission statement to set the company aside from its competitors and to define its role as transformational.* These are the exception rather than the rule. For them, responsible business is a core part of who they are and what they do. They seek to influence the practices of others and change the whole business landscape. Businesses with this type of mission statement include Interface, the carpet manufacturer, that aims to 'be the first company that, by its deeds, shows the entire industrial world what sustainability is in all its dimensions: people, process, product, place and profits – by 2020 – and in doing so we will become restorative through the power of influence.'

There are a handful of hospitality businesses among this group. Most but not all of them are small. Among the better known are:

- The **Scarlet Hotel** in Cornwall (part of the Red Hotels Group) that '… reflects our boldness, perhaps madness, in trying to build a hotel that might change perceptions of what [is] possible. The hotel owners wanted this hotel to be warm, deeply comfortable and welcoming, very different to the slick but elitist hotels that pass as luxury. We love the contrast of a rich red colour with our green ethos'.

- **Pret-a-Manger** with its commitment to 'Creating handmade natural food avoiding the obscure chemicals, additives and preservatives common to so much of the "prepared" and "fast" food on the market today.'

2 *Mainstream businesses that use their responsible business values as a part of the main brand, although it is not of itself their reason for being.* Many of the global international companies that are leading the policy debate fall into this category. For these businesses, responsible business is one of their core business values and is reflected in the main brand. Details about responsible business programmes, aims and targets are on a dedicated area of the company's website. The thing that differentiates these companies from those at point 3 below is the very clear link to responsible business values within the main brand and marketing materials.[3]

Companies in this category, include:

- **Unilever** who have clearly associated their whole brand with the responsible business ethos through the strap line 'Creating a better future every day',

- **Marks and Spence**r, which is 'Doing the Right Thing' via their *Plan A* campaign

- **Nestlé** have the 'Good Food, Good Life' strap line.

- Relatively few hospitality businesses fall into this category, but they include organisations like Sweden's oldest hamburger chain MAX Hamburgerrestauranger AB with its claim that 'We are part of the problem and therefore want to be part of the solution. Max has a long history of working to reduce its environmental impacts. Now we want to take the next step.' The company also promotes healthy eating, going so far as to discourage customers from certain menu options by publishing full life-cycle carbon footprints of each item on their menu).

3 *Those that clearly identify responsible business as a priority area, but where it is separate to the main product/service identity.* For these businesses, it is very clear that people and planet matter to the business (and in many cases are seen as a core part of corporate identity), but are not integrated within the main brand. Many of the hospitality businesses that lead the responsible business agenda and have excellent and far-reaching responsible business programmes fall within this category. Sodexo, for example, have the 'Better Tomorrow Plan', Whitbread the 'Good together' initiative, Starbucks aim to 'make sure everything we do honours that

---

3   i.e. there is no need to find a dedicated area of the website to become aware that this company has a commitment to responsible business values in principle at least.

connection [with each customer] – from our commitment to the highest quality coffee in the world, to the way we engage with our customers and communities to do business responsibly', Mitchells and Butlers have their in the heart of the community strap line and Yum! Have the How we win Together programme.

Without exception, these businesses, define what their statement of values means within a dedicated area of their website and use good practice to illustrate progress. Some use the Business in the Community Pillar concept to support these statements. In the case of Aramark, for example, four pillars are defined: health and wellbeing, employee welfare, environment and community. For each pillar, very specific information is included, for example on the topic of community, Aramark specifies that it will work in the following areas:

Charity support

♦ Identify nominated charities and media-led campaigns to support across the business, giving Aramark's people a choice of great causes to assist.

♦ Develop marketing programmes integrated with Aramark's retail initiatives to support these charities throughout the year.

♦ Work with client charities at a local level to support and enhance their activities.

Volunteering

♦ Develop a Star Teams network across all regions and identify key projects for them to support;

♦ To create a range of volunteering programmes that are accessible to all Aramark employees across the UK.

♦ To focus on support in schools during British Food Fortnight promoting the use of British products and healthy eating.

Growing Industry Talent

♦ Work with industry bodies to enable the unemployed and disadvantaged to gain access to work experience and permanent placement.

♦ Develop Aramark's own teams and provide guidance and support to maximise their opportunities.

4 *Those businesses that have responsible initiatives but do not make reference to them within customer facing materials.* There remain a number of hospitality businesses – including some of the major national and international players – that are engaged in initiatives that do good – and that refrain from publicising their activities. The reasons that companies do not publicise their green credentials are relatively under-explored.

It is clear that companies in some sectors have begun to clearly link their brand with their responsible business values. There are many benefits from this approach, but it is not without its risks. No matter how well motivated the board of a company, a failure to define and act on responsible business commitments (even within a single business unit that is isolated from the head office operation) can leave the company open to critics. For international brands, misdemeanours in this field can be used by those who are hostile to globalisation to demonstrate the ills of the modern multinational business. With the exception of those hospitality businesses that have grown from a sustainable ethos, few have as yet put their heads above the PR parapet and intricately linked their brand and their responsible business practices.

The fundamentals: communicating good practice

When it comes to developing and communicating good practice, a wide range of mechanisms have been used. When analysing these, it is surprising that the terms 'best' and 'good' practice are often used interchangeably. However, they refer to different things. There are remarkably few articles in the academic or trade press that comment on the growth of good and best practice in the sector or how it is defined within individual business contexts. There is also little independent verification of the extent to which the many publications and competitions set up to recognise good practice in this arena really reflect good as opposed to routine practices, or that have looked at the ways in which the definition of good practice in the sector has moved on in the light of the competitive advantage described by Porter.

When one looks across the range of good practice examples it would be easy to conclude that hospitality businesses are operating at and adept at communicating good (if not best) responsible business practice through a range of mechanisms. This is, however, a fallacy. It is true that there are many generic examples of energy, waste and water management in the sector. Many of these are, however, banal and cleansed of the information that makes them of value to those that seek to replicate them (e.g. few of the examples provide instances of the pitfalls they experienced as well as the successes, or of the true costs of installing equipment rather than simple payback calculations). This is especially the case in those parts of the sector where responsible business practices are known to provide competitive edge.

To date, within the hospitality sector, good practice examples tend to fall into one of four categories:

1 Information released into the public domain to gain positive PR

The very existence of this category of 'good practice' is an irony. The fact that some hospitality organisations seek to bathe in the glow of being seen to be a responsible business by making questionable claims demonstrates the appeal of the concept (and the inertia within many even mainstream businesses to change their practices). A number of major companies have fallen foul of making claims that quite simply cannot be substantiated in fact. They include car manufacturers, oil companies, airlines and many others. There are hospitality businesses that fall into this category.

A report by TerraChoice Environmental Marketing, for example, found that 99% of all products and hotel services in the USA that were being labelled as green by companies do not meet their own claims (TerraChoice, 2010).

There can be little doubt that a growth in the market for so-called responsible tourism has driven a number of companies, including hospitality businesses, to seek to cynically gain benefits from promoting their own 'good practice' without substantiating these in fact (or ensuring that they are in any way ahead of the norm). Canny businesses have, however, come to realise that as the public and NGO community become more knowledgeable about 'greenwash' hollow and unsubstantiated statements of good practice have more potential to undermine than support the brand. These businesses have increasingly sought external verification and also invested in internal mechanisms to ensure that they meet or exceed their green claims.

2 Information about single issues or from technology providers

Perhaps more common than false claims about good practice is the preponderance of information that is developed and distributed by well meaning companies or third parties. Typically, this data will not be put about by a company itself but by one of the agencies that is seeking to promote good practice throughout the sector. Such examples will include data about the benefits of using solar panels from a specific supplier within specific types of hotel business, the benefits of electric vs. gas cooking equipment and so on. Reports of this nature are generally well meaning (and are often seized on with interest by companies that are keen to improve their performance), but the lack of independent verification is an issue. It can and does lead to businesses selecting technologies that are inappropriate to their needs. Classic examples include energy efficient light bulbs (many businesses have invested in these without first checking that they are using the appropriate lamp for their specific needs). Verification by a third party organisation (such as the Carbon Trust in the UK and the Environmental Protection Agency in the USA) is now helping to rectify this issue. When this verification is accompanied by performance criteria that includes a comparison with industry standards and provides sufficient context information to assess whether or not the technology is appropriate to their specific circumstances, the good practice becomes much more useful.

Single issue approaches to good practice

To date, there has been a propensity to focus good practice examples around single issues and particularly around the cost-saving issues of energy, water and waste management. The focus on these issues and exclusion of wider responsible business practices have perpetuated the myth that eco-efficiency = responsible business.

When sharing examples of good practice between businesses, there is also a propensity to promote what has gone well whilst ignoring what has not. Those seeking to emulate the best practice often stand to learn as much from failures and pitfalls as from success, but a reluctance of corporate PR teams to allow failure to be reported renders this learning impossible. Thus, when best practice is released without a full and honest account of the context of that best practice and an appraisal of the real costs of implementing the practice and its overall success in other than purely financial terms, it can do more harm than good.

3 Award schemes

Within the hospitality sector, many award schemes are credible and independently verified. These schemes have very carefully defined criteria that are transparent and easily available in the public domain. Before awards are made and case studies publicised, these schemes openly identify the number of entrants they have in each award category, typically reward performance across the responsible business spectrum rather than for single issues, judging meetings are carefully recorded and checks are made to ensure that those businesses that are awarded the accolade of being best in class are implementing the practices that they claim.

Not all schemes are, however, credible. Some award good practice against single issues whilst ignoring poor practice elsewhere (for example, recognising a company that has a relatively poor responsible business programme but has done an excellent job of marketing its green credentials). Others insist upon making an award even when only one substandard entrant is received into a category. Award schemes that engage in such practice perpetuate and reward greenwash within the sector.

Text box 50: Award schemes – credibility can be an issue

One would expect the hundreds of award schemes that have been launched to recognise responsible practices in the hospitality sector in recent years to have provided credible examples of good practice. This is, however, a false premise. Winning an award for responsible business is a huge accolade for many companies and can bring considerable business benefits. However even credible organisations have to walk a fine line when promoting such awards as the very best in practice. As the commentary from Fred Pearce of *The Guardian* (9th July 2009) about the highly successful Business in the Community Awards indicates, successful award schemes cannot be seen to be too dependent on the businesses that they seek to reward (see below)!

'Well meaning it may be, but it seems to have tipped over from being a promoter of ethical business practice to an apologist for greenwash. But this week its 850 members were giving prizes to each other at a canapes-and-strawberries bash in the garden at Clarence House. The prize-giving seems to be financially sustainable, at least, with past winners saying thank you for the free publicity by forking out to pay for the marquees and sponsor the awards. But the chutzpah that lies behind it defies belief.'

---

4 Accreditation by an external agency

A dizzying array of external accreditations now exist to help consumers and client groups identify those organisations that are operating at good practice responsible business standards from those that are not. They include among their number the highly successful Green Tourism Business Scheme, the Green Key, Green Globe, the Sustainable Restaurant Association and Travelife among others. These are not without their critics and all verification schemes are not equal. However, those that have credible processes and are transparent about their criteria do provide independent verification that a business is meetings its own (and the certification agency's) minimum standards. Many of these agencies, including the Ecotourism Association of Australia, the Green Tourism Business Scheme in the UK and the Sustainable Restaurant Association in the UK provide case studies of good practice.

Tools of the trade

Developing and defining the responsible business mission

Good quality guidance on the issue of defining what responsible business means at corporate level and developing this into something that is meaningful for management teams is relatively difficult to find in the generic literature. Most of what is available is accessible via consultancies or organisations like Business in the Community and the Natural Step that actively support businesses through the process of implementing responsible business practices.

Communicating good practice

A number of credible publications now exist to communicate good practice. Some of these such as *Green Hotelier* are hosted by trade associations. Others are developed and supported by agencies such as the Carbon Trust in the UK and the US Environmental Protection Agency.

Award schemes for the sector are of variable quality. Those that publicise their criteria and the number of entrants into each category, include independent judges, request some form of verification of performance and that cross the range of responsible business issues are generally better than those that are run by associations for their own membership. Some of these are now well established, including the Virgin Responsible Travel Awards (see Text box 51) and Cateys.

Some award schemes are rather less rigorous in their approach. Their criteria are far from transparent, the judging panel includes sponsors of the award, the number of entries in each category are not disclosed (and sometimes only one entry is received and duly awarded) and often they often provide awards for single issues rather than across the responsible business agenda. Thus a company that has a very high carbon footprint because of poor energy management practices may be able to win an award and the associated publicity for a relatively minor achievement such as the best green advertising campaign.

Text box 51: The importance of credibility – The case of the Virgin Responsible Tourism Awards

The Responsible Tourism Awards were founded in 2004 to celebrate and inspire change in the tourism industry. The Awards rest on a simple principle – that all types of tourism, from niche to mainstream, can and should be organised in a way that preserves, respects and benefits destinations and local people. The award founders recognised that by providing a public accolade and case studies they could inspire others in the industry to recognise the benefits of responsible practices and understand the steps involved in implementing them.

From beginning to end, the judging process is among the most rigorous for all hospitality and tourism awards. Rather than handpick businesses to enter the awards or accept entries from any business, all entrants to the Responsible Travel Awards are nominated (by travellers and the industry). It takes only one nomination to enter the awards (thus smaller businesses are not discriminated against) and nominees are entered into one of 13 categories (e.g. best in a mountain environment, best hotel). Once nominations are received, businesses are asked to fill in an application form documenting their activities across the responsible business agenda. Application forms are then entered into the judging process and this has several stages designed with independent advice from the International Centre for Responsible Tourism at Leeds Metropolitan University. At each judging stage the list gets shorter, until the expert panel of judges meet to debate the winners on an annual Judging Day. References for winners are chased and referees are asked to answer questions about inconsistencies in the application before the final award is conferred.

The Virgin Holidays Responsible Tourism Awards are sponsored, but those with a direct commercial interest in providing services, technologies or products that can help the sector improve responsible business performance are excluded from any association.

As a result, the awards are trusted and have received over 10,000 nominations from members of the public, leading to awards to 201 unique organisations from 51 countries around the world over a period of seven years. For more information, see www.responsibletourismawards.com

---

Sustainable tourism certification schemes

The evolution of sustainable tourism certification schemes that require companies to take actions across a range of responsible business issues is now starting to drive the development of good practice examples that cut across the range of independent businesses and that can be proven to exceed industry benchmarks. Some of these schemes provide examples of businesses that have been audited to achieve a minimum benchmark level and across a range of responsible business issues. There has been criticism that some of these certification schemes focus on the issues that matter to business rather more than those that matter to consumers and this is an ongoing concern. Nevertheless the fact that they communicate good practice from audited sites and across multiple responsible business issues is a positive step forward.

Five indicators for business

☐ The business has a responsible business mission or vision statement that has coherence with the brand and its broader values.

☐ The business clearly defines the meaning of these responsible business values or mission.

☐ The responsible business values motivate managers and staff.

☐ The business vets the awards it enters on the basis of their credibility rather than the ease with which they will win an accolade.

☐ When the company promotes best practice it is willing to discuss pitfalls rather than just achievements.

Conclusion

Hospitality businesses have come a long way in recent years – developing their environmental policy statement into more broad-reaching responsible business statements. For the most part, those companies that have developed these mission statements have started the process of integrating them with brand values. When it comes to making that mission into something that is meaningful to managers and staff and gives them a sense of mission, businesses have made more variable progress. Some have developed mission statements without engaging managers and other staff or without ensuring that they have broader coherence with the brand. History has demonstrated that such approaches are dangerous and can lead to accusations of greenwash.

There can be few who argue that good or best practice has been one of the major drivers of change within the international hospitality sector. Given the enthusiasm for good practice, it is surprising that neither the academic or practitioner community have really examined the quality of examples that are used. There has been some criticism of the award schemes that recognise business, but little examination of the actual examples that have emerged to assess the extent to which they really emulate best or exceptional practice and the extent to which they are implementing measures that should be expected in any business context.

Good practice examples in the hospitality sector have been dogged by the focus on what has gone well (as opposed by the pitfalls that need to be avoided), a lack of external verification that the practices being demonstrated are indeed 'good', a preoccupation with demonstrating short-term paybacks of specific technologies rather than wider and longer-term benefits and a focus on the technologies that have delivered change as opposed to the management processes necessary to support and sustain that change. The result is the preponderance of focus on energy waste and water management and a relative dearth of information about social and economic impacts.

Moreover, the tendency to focus on a single aspect of (typically environmental) performance often ignores the fact that while the practice reported may provide good results in one area (for example the amount of waste sent to landfill in the case of businesses installing macerators to send food waste to the drain) it may also provide poor results in another (the biological oxygen demand of waste water and overall contribution towards poorer waste water quality). All too often unexpected consequences or 'lessons learned' in implementing the best practice are not reported and those organisations that seek to emulate the practices reported are unable to replicate the result.

As for those companies that chose to follow best practice that goes beyond eco-efficiency, it is likely that they will be rewarded as socially responsible investing has evolved from being a 'boutique' issue, to growing at a faster pace than the universe of all investment assets under professional management. As the next chapter demonstrates those businesses that can demonstrate their progress in achieving their responsible business objectives in reports stand to gain the benefits in the long term.

References

Campbell, A. (1992) 'The power of missions – aligning strategy and culture', *Strategy and Leadership*, **20** (5), 10.

Futerra (n.d.) *The Greenwash Guide*, London: Futerra, available from http://www.futerra.co.uk/downloads/Greenwash_Guide.pdf

Pearce, F. (2009) 'Greenwash: The Responsible Business Awards defy parody', *The Guardian*, 9 July, available at http://www.guardian.co.uk/environment/cif-green/2009/jul/09/greenwash-responsible-business

ICC (2002) *Business in society - Making a positive and responsible contribution A voluntary commitment by business to manage its activities responsibly*, ICC Paris.

Porter, M.E. (2008) *On Competition*, Cambridge, MA: Harvard Business School Pubishing.

PWC (2010) *The Sustainability Yearbook 2010*, download from http://www.sam-group.com/en/sustainability-insight/the-sustainability-yearbook.jsp

Terra Choice (2010) *Greenwashing Report*, available at http://sinsofgreenwashing.org/findings/greenwashing-report-2010/

Principle 9: Build trust through transparency

> *Generating commercial advantage from accountability requires a significant shift in thinking to understand value opportunities. An increasing number of companies are moving beyond seeing accountability as a block to doing business, or even as a worthy sideshow, and are beginning to derive real commercial value from a more accountable way of doing business.*

Engen and DiPiazza (2005)

As we have seen in earlier chapters, a series of corporate mishaps have put trust in global corporations at an all time low.[4] Information technology has revolutionised the potential for the discontented, abused or politically motivated to get their voice heard. Regulators are pushing companies to reveal ever more about previously confidential practices from executive pay to corporate governance and disgruntled suppliers.[5] Winning brands recognise that trust is the main ingredient in building customer engagement.[6] As Edelman has recently reported, however, trust is an ingredient that is in short supply when it comes to global businesses. In the words of Dave Balter (founder and CEO of Bzzagent and frequent contributor to the *Harvard Business Review*), 'the prevalent mindset is that companies are guilty until proven innocent'.

In the face of this mistrust, companies face a choice. They can choose to ignore the increased scrutiny that is being placed upon their every move or they can embrace the challenge and seek to win the trust of those they employ, work with and who buy their products. The former strategy may be effective for some (see Text box 52), but for those that are found out or screw up, it can be catastrophic.

The evidence for doing good?

> *The hard data on 'doing well by doing good' may not be there yet, but there is clear evidence that companies can do very badly by being bad. (Tapscott and Ticoll, 2003).*

---

4   See the Edelman barometer at www.edelman.com/trust

5   The fallout of corporate scandals such as the collapse of Enron and Worldcom has meant that some of the principles of transparent disclosure have become enshrined in law in some countries. For example, the Sarbanes Oxley Act (2002) in the USA covers issues including corporate governance, internal control assessment, and enhanced financial disclosure. European Directive 2003/51/EC requires large companies in Europe to report as follows 'to the extent necessary for an understanding of the company's development, performance or position, the analysis [in the annual review] shall include both financial and, where appropriate, non-financial key performance indicators relevant to the particular business, including information relating to environmental and employee matters'.

6   See, for example, blogs like (http://blog.peoplemetrics.com/the-two-routes-of-building-customer-trust/)

The corporate response to growing distrust has taken various forms. For a handful of global players – of which Google are probably the most frequently quoted – it has taken the form of building the whole business model around the concept of transparent operational practices.[7] For most it has – in part at least – taken the form of responsible business reports.[8] From Sainsburys to Eurostar and BP to Nestle responsible business reports (and increasingly web sites) seek to persuade critics and supporters alike that the business is operated with management procedures in place that support a fair and functioning society, promote responsible stewardship of the environment and respect and protect human dignity. In the very best cases, these reports demonstrate that these values are core to the company and permeate all aspects of the operation. In these organisations, responsible business reports provide a genuine review of what has been achieved and report on aspects of the programme that could be improved as well as successes. In the worst cases, they provide little more than a few good practice examples and statistics about a small portion of the overall business operations, cloaked in weasel words that seek to convince readers that the commitment to responsible business is more than a side line.

Hospitality businesses are relative newcomers to the practice of formal responsible business reporting.[9] Although the first environmental report from the sector was issued relatively early on (in 1996 by what was then InterContinental Hotels and Resorts), it was some years before any other organisation in the sector issued a report on environmental or social issues. There is a considerable difference between the early report of InterContinental Hotels & Resorts and the generation of reports that have appeared post 2005. These have emerged from across all aspects of the sector, including contract caterers such as Compass, restaurant groups such as McDonald's, pub chains such as Mitchells and Butlers, hotel groups such as Rezidor and IHG (the first hotel company to issue a report using the GRI G3 reporting guidelines).

The purpose of reporting

The Global Reporting Initiative defines sustainability reporting[10] as 'the practice of measuring, disclosing, and being accountable to internal and external stakeholders for organizational performance towards the goal of sustainable development. "Sustainability reporting" is a broad term considered synonymous with others used

---

7   It is not the purpose of this text to provide detailed information on the fascinating subject of transparency in a business context. Those with an interest, however, may wish to read *The Naked Corporation* by Don Tapscott and David Tickell, which provides compelling reading on the topic.

8   Companies call these by a wide variety of names, in some cases omitting any reference to the word responsible from the title. For example, M&S title their report 'How we do business – Doing the Right Thing'. Many businesses refer to these reports as 'sustainability' reports.

9   The history of measurement of environmental impacts in the sector is, however, not new and has been around for decades if not longer. Comprehensive measurement (to guide energy efficiency processes, for example) exist from at least the 1970s if not earlier.

10 The GRI talk about sustainability rather than responsible business reporting

to describe reporting on economic, environmental, and social impacts (e.g., triple bottom line, corporate responsibility reporting, etc.). A sustainability report should provide a balanced and reasonable representation of the sustainability performance of a reporting organization – including both positive and negative contributions.' UNGRI (version 3.0) *Sustainability Reporting Guidelines*

What the responsible business guidelines say

The issue of reporting on responsible business performance – and its relationship to trust and transparency – receives scant coverage in most of the responsible business guidelines.

The ICC in its *Business in Society* publication, recommends that 'A key way for companies to create confidence and trust in their commitment to responsible business conduct is to provide timely and reliable information on their financial, environmental and social performance and to communicate this to their stakeholders. Markets all over the world provide examples of companies who enjoy sustained public goodwill and respect by doing this successfully.'

The Caux Round Table principles make no reference at all to reporting progress or to the significance of such activities to building public trust in a company. The more visionary CERES principles (which seek to incorporate environmental and social principles into corporate DNA), are much more specific. Their vision for sustainability reporting is:

'Companies will report reguarly on their sustainability strategy and performance. Disclosure will include credible, standardized, independently verified metrics encompassing all material stakeholder concerns, and detail goals and plans for future action.'

The fundamentals of responsible business reporting

The responsible business, sustainable development or at the very least, social and environmental report has become almost ubiquitous to global corporations and is becoming increasingly prevalent among hospitality businesses. Figure 42 demonstrates the number of companies out of a selection of 24 of the largest businesses in the UK that have published environmental, social, corporate social or responsible business reports.

The data in Figure 41 looks impressive, but it is important to bear in mind that if one were to look across the hospitality sector as a whole, responsible business reporting would be undertaken only by a tiny proportion of all companies (it is easy to be critical of those who have reported, but perhaps attention should focus on the multitude of companies that have not).

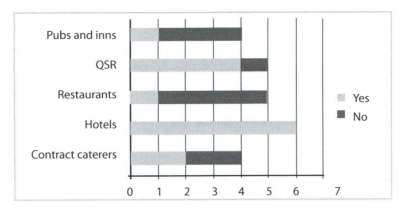

Figure 41: The prevalence of reporting among hospitality companies

Notes: Data compiled from published data on websites or in corporate reports from 24 large hospitality businesses (see Appendix 1 for a list of companies included).

Some companies have interests that cut across sectors – for example some businesses that are primarily pub operators (and are included in the pub category) also operate a small number of hotels.

Of course large companies are obliged to report on their environmental and social performance. Perhaps more remarkable is the range of smaller companies such as Apetito in the contract catering sector, Leon in the restaurant sector and Sanga Saby and Scandic in the hotel sector that provide reports and data on their websites because they perceive it to be a fundamental part of their identity that helps customers to trust and become loyal to the brand. These companies are in many ways putting their heads above the parapet because they perceive the benefits of reporting to significantly outweigh the costs.

The range of issues reported on is illustrated in Figure 42.

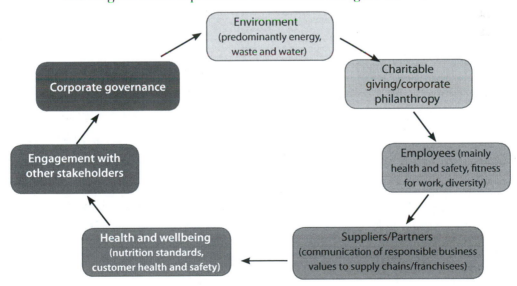

Figure 42: The range of issues covered in responsible business reports published by 14 hospitality businesses

Notes: Includes responsible retailing of alcohol for licensed premises. Some of the reports reviewed were for one country of operation only (mainly UK or USA); others had a global focus.

The range of issues included within reports for the most part reflects the relative maturity of the responsible business initiative. With the exception of the QSR and contract catering businesses, most hospitality business reports that we have reviewed focus primarily on environmental issues, employee welfare and in most cases local community or charitable giving. QSR and contract catering business reports have more of a focus on health and well-being and sustainable sourcing. These issues reflect the relative interest of different stakeholder groups and areas in which pressure groups and the media may have a particular interest. In all instances, the scope of reporting is difficult to ascertain with most reports representing head office aims and few reflecting progress across all outlets.

Measurement and reporting – a difficult craft to perfect

A recent UN Global Compact study led by Accenture, the consultancy, found that while 85 per cent of chief executives believe companies should integrate the measurement of sustainability into their businesses, only 64% thought their company did so effectively (Financial Times, 5 Dec 2010)

http://www.ft.com/cms/s/0/dec50c2e-cceb-11df-9bf0-00144feab49a.html#ixzz1Cw2vQdRL

Readers should not assume that responsible business reporting will, by its virtue, earn a business the reputation and trust of stakeholders. A large number of individuals and organisations point to the reports of companies like Enron (yes they had a corporate social responsibility report that received acclaim in some circles) and some of the major banks that have so recently been in the news to add credibility to their claim that these reports pay little more than lip service. Responsible business reports have a huge diversity of scope and content and numerous factors influence the credibility of that report. Responsible business reports can be sub-divided into four broad categories as follows:[11]

1 Good reports from bad companies

Matthew Ammiratio asks 'Is it enough to be green without being good?'. (http://www.mediapost.com/publications/?fa=Articles.showArticle&art_aid=129782). Some companies think so and the reports of many of these are captured under this heading. In the words of think tank Sustainability, good reports from bad companies are published by businesses that operate in suspect markets or fail to address the most material sustainability issues associated with the product. Examples of such reports may include organisations documenting significant environmental and social achievements from companies that manufacture products that are known to be hazardous to human health and/or the environment. Such reports will often make limited reference to the impacts of the product when in use, but provide ample evidence of the ways in which, for example, manufacturing processes have reduced

---

11   These categories are adapted from work by Sustainability, AccountAbility and others. They are not mutually exclusive.

carbon emissions or a philanthropic fund has supported specific (often under-privileged) groups of society.

That is not to say that companies in this category cannot publish very good responsible business reports that demonstrate considerable progress. Nor is it to say that they don't care about the issues that they report on. The essence of the product they manufacture is what damns companies to this category.

ASH would in all likelihood place the report of British American Tobacco into this category. But the report from this company – albeit the (Malaysia) Berhad operation – won the ACCA award for Best Social Report in 2008 despite the views of some that the product it produces is a net social ill (http://www.accaglobal.com/allnews/national/malaysia/mesra06_030507).

The nature of the hospitality industry means that most business from the sector are not included within this category. However, they are not wholly excluded from it. Historically, some critics have placed some fast food outlets into this category on account of their global pay and conditions and the potential health implications of their food. Other commentators, for example, Duncan Green, Head of Research for Oxfam, think that food and the food industry is likely to become the next oil industry and to run a greater risk of being placed in this category (http://www.oxfamblogs.org/fp2p/?p=3418).

2 Good news reports

Reports of this nature will often present the achievements of a company, whilst skimming over or failing to mention poor performance or an environmental or human rights mishap. When making their first report, many companies have slipped into this trap, but the practice of having reports externally audited has reduced this tendency.

Good news statements often proclaim what a business seeks rather than what it has achieved. *The Guardian* has picked up on a number of businesses that have fallen into this trap. ASDA, it notes, made a promise two years ago to ban products containing unsustainable palm oil from rainforest areas. (http://www.guardian.co.uk/business/2007/jul/22/supermarkets.corporatesocialresponsibility). When *The Guardian* went to press, it had not even updated consumers on its progress towards that target (http://www.guardian.co.uk/environment/cif-green/2009/jul/09/greenwash-responsible-business).

Futerra's greenwash guide ranks holiday and travel businesses as third in its list of 'worst sinners' for unsubstantiated green claims (admittedly in a range of literature and not just responsible business reports) commenting on the rapid growth in green claims about this sector (Futerra, n.d.). With NGOs such as GreenPeace and CorporateWatch increasingly on the lookout, the backlash from being caught telling only the good news can be severe.

Comparing hospitality performance

Even among those hospitality businesses that issue responsible business reports, the wide variety of measurement systems in place make comparisons between companies difficult to make. As a recent report for Cornell by Eric Ricaurte states, there is: 'a broader need for addressing non-financial performance data collectively and uniformly within the hotel industry. In response to requests from guests, investors, and other stakeholders regarding sustainability, most hotel companies have developed platforms to address these needs. Despite this promising development, the individual chains' reports, assumptions, and measures are not always communicated uniformly – although it's clear that stakeholders seek to use the data to make comparisons

(Ricaurte, 2011).

3 Good reports of limited scope

Within this category, are those reports that focus on either social or environmental performance or reports that focus on part of the business operation. These reports are prevalent among the vast majority of businesses and perpetuate throughout the hospitality sector.

Most of the hospitality businesses that fall into this category do seek to report across environmental and social issues. That being said, environmental issues dominate the agenda with social issues being confined largely to philanthropy.

Issues covered in responsible business reports

Among hospitality businesses, limited scope of reports arises from:

♦ The number of business units for which results are reported is generally small. Most hospitality businesses include in their reports data only for those units that they wholly own and/or manage. IHG, for example, include performance reports for its 648 owned and managed hotels within their report and this accounts for less than 15% of its portfolio of 4438 hotels. There are of course good reasons for this not least the difficulties of passing responsible business criteria onto franchised and leased units. While ownership patterns may be of relevance to the hospitality businesses that write the reports, they are not significant to consumers and other groups that use those reports to make judgements across what they perceive as the brand.

♦ The range of issues reported against is generally limited. With the possible exception of QSR businesses and contract caterers (where much of the focus is on supply chain issues), most hospitality businesses report performance on those issues that have a direct impact on the business and that result in cost savings. Other sectors have a much broader scope: Marks and Spencer, for example, report on: climate change, sustainable raw materials, fair partner performance, health performance as well as managing how they do business, in addition to the standard issues included in many hospitality business reports.

According to reporting think tank AccountAbility, there is a danger that for businesses in this category 'reporting on social and environmental performance will become an exercise in compliance, which contributes little to learning or innovation, with sustainability reports becoming bloated data-dumps (AccountAbility, 2006: 11).

4 Integrated reports

In the words of Sustainability, integrated reporting has become the Holy Grail in corporate public disclosure. Integrated reporting refers to a holistic and integrated representation of the company's performance in terms of both its finance and its sustainability. It is thought that businesses that adopt an integrated approach to reporting 'better understand how emerging sustainable development issues could be integrated into specific business practices' (AccountAbility, 2006 5).

Relatively few organisations produce integrated reports (none of them hospitality businesses as far as we can ascertain), but companies that are held up as seeking to take an integrated approach to reporting include: Heineken, Vodafone, SAB Miller, Unilever, Nike, and Coca Cola. In the case of Nike, 'Integrating sustainability [reporting] is not just a good opportunity for business. It is essential for success in a world of constrained resources. Right now every business has a choice to make. We choose to move fast, using sustainability as a force for innovation. We choose to embrace transparency, collaboration and advocacy as tools to unlock opportunity and enable us to thrive in a clean and green economy' (Mark Parker, CEO and President, Nike).

Many leading commentators believe that integrated reporting will become mainstream in the future and that those businesses that cannot produce credible triple bottom line reports will find it increasingly difficult to find a voice in the ethical marketplace. It is likely that those global companies that are leading responsible business initiatives in the hospitality sector will increasingly adopt this type of report.

Integrated reporting

It now seems inevitable to me that the notion of integrated reporting will gain increasing credence in business' … 'I think it's quite a way off, perhaps five years, before we see it done really well, or beginning to be.

Toby Webb, Founder Ethical Corporation www.ethicalcorp.com

In many ways the category that a company report falls into is an indicator of the sophistication and maturity of the responsible business programme and their attitudes towards transparency (an issue that has increasingly come to dominate the reporting agenda – see Toby Webb's comment, above). Businesses that are seeking to produce integrated reports tend to have reached the point at which sustainable development considerations are at the core of the company ethos and operations.

Failing to report

The companies that do report on performance remain in the minority of international hospitality businesses. Most fail to report at all on progress in a truly transparent way. This does a significant disservice to their stakeholders and to the image of the industry as a whole (having the potential to undermine its reputation as a clean industry, especially when those companies have a specified commitment to responsible business practices in the form of a mission or vision statement). A key priority for the future has got to be to increase both the number of companies reporting on their progress and the depth of reporting across all business units.

Transparency – a prerequisite for success

'The urgency and magnitude of the risks and threats to our collective sustainability, alongside increasing choice and opportunities, will make transparency about economic, environmental, and social impacts a fundamental component in effective stakeholder relations, investment decisions, and other market relations'.

(UNGRI (version 3.0) Sustainability Reporting Guidelines)

In the last few years, the concept of transparency has become a buzz word when it comes to reporting on responsible business performance. Greater transparency is generally seen as a way of guarding against accusations of greenwash, especially in the light of a greater blurring of the lines of corporate responsibility reporting and corporate company information in general. Greater transparency is also seen as a route to build trust in the brand.

And a handful of global businesses are recognising that greater transparency can be a business asset delivering, among other things, a greater level of trust and reducing corporate risks. This realisation has been driven by the combination of the revolution in information technology, the growth in public interest in the values of the businesses and the increase in the number of third sector organisations and policy makers on the lookout for corporate wrongdoing. These businesses recognise that the boundaries of traditional reporting are blurring and that corporate performance reporting is increasingly being seen as embracing all aspects of a company's communication rather than the physical report alone.

This development may change the current perception of many businesses that the risks associated with a failure to be transparent are seen as small. It will certainly bring into focus for many hospitality businesses the risks of the currently limited scope of corporate reports.

> **Text box 52: Pay differentials – an issue to watch**
>
> One of the issues that is currently focusing minds is the relative rates of pay at different levels within an organisation and the perceived fairness (or otherwise) of the differential between the highest and lowest paid. The underlying issue is a concern that very high levels of executive pay contributed to the market crisis in western economies and perpetuates business growth strategies that carry a high level of risk and are contrary to effective governance*.
>
> Politicians in a number of countries have examined this issue. For example, the UK has had a Fair Pay Commission and US House of Representatives voted in 2009 on control of executive pay.
>
> Institutional investors are starting to demand access to information about pay differentials (and executive pay) and it is likely that this will increasingly be embraced in responsible business reports. Few hospitality businesses have taken this step as yet. The gauntlet, however, has been thrown down and the processes of meeting these demands will without doubt be challenging with few commentators able to define what is a fair differential between the highest and lowest paid in society – especially within companies that have a global operating base and a high level of international employees.
>
> *Tangentially – but interestingly – Oliver James in his best seller *Affluenza* reported that 'happiness' was apparently greater in societies with less of a differential between the best and poorest paid employees

Five indicators for business

- ☐ The responsible business report is a tool to guide internal decisions and not just a piece of PR collateral.

- ☐ Responsible business reporting is not the sole function of the corporate responsibility team.

- ☐ The responsible business report includes as many business outlets as possible within its scope – including those that are franchised, tenanted and on management contract.

- ☐ The company reports and learns from responsible business initiatives that have been unsuccessful as well as those that have been successful.

- ☐ The company report and website provides information across the whole range of impacts and does not confine itself solely or mostly to energy (carbon), waste and water consumption issues.

The tools of the trade

A small number of tools have been developed to help businesses assess and report on their performance. These have been stimulated to some extent by regulation, but most have been driven by those companies that report as they seek to improve the practice of reporting itself.

Within the hospitality sector specifically, there is the SPOT (Sustainability Performance Operational Tool developed by ITP), which provides guidance on 15 sustainability indicators within five categories:

♦ Environmental management; energy use; water use.

♦ Waste control; pollution protection; habitat protection.

♦ Purchasing and sales; local community; education/training.

♦ Culture and heritage; health and safety; business ethics.

♦ Monitoring and assessment; supply chain; work and employment.

While not a reporting tool in its own right, SPOT provides a mechanism through which hotel businesses can collect data from individual hotel units. This data can then be integrated into corporate reports (once appropriate verification mechanisms have been used).

Probably the best known of the generic tools is the United Nations Standard for reporting, known as the Global Reporting Initiative.

The GRI seeks to support businesses through the process of:

♦ Identifying which issues they should report on.

♦ Assessing the quality, credibility and transparency of the data they choose to report.

♦ Specifying the extent of business activities that are embraced by the report.

♦ Assessing the nature of the narrative that is used to explain the report.

The GRI has sector specific guidance and this has been used to guide a number of reports, including that of IHG (the first hotel group to report against the framework) and Rezidor.

Contrary to popular belief the use of the GRI index does not specify a precise range of actions on which a business should report. Instead, it provides a reporting framework and businesses may chose what they will report against. This framework covers both management processes and performance measures.

The GRI of course is not the only reporting framework that exists. There are the rather less known guidelines, including:

♦ The social accountability standard known as SA 8000. This provides a management and reporting standard for human working conditions and is widely used by textile manufacturers and other sectors recruiting in a high degree of labour in developing countries. It is not much used by hospitality businesses (the authors are not aware of any that have sought to meet its requirements).

♦ The accountability standard known as AA 1000 – developed to help organisations become more **accountable**, **responsible** and **sustainable**. It addresses issues affecting governance, business models and organizational strategy, as well as providing operational guidance on sustainability assurance and stakeholder engagement. Despite its reliance on the stakeholder concept (something often talked about by hospitality businesses), the authors are not aware of any hospitality businesses that have sought to meet its requirements.

And then there are the guidelines that are externally verified and that have the purpose of helping to guide investment decisions, including the FTSE-4-Good, Dow Jones Sustainability Index and Business in the Community programme. These schemes each have a range of criteria against which they judge companies (with specific criteria for some sectors).

Collectively, these latter criteria have become hugely influential and are probably the 'gold standard' for any large company claiming to operate according to responsible business criteria. This is despite the fact that to your average environmentalist the criteria are not exactly likely to deliver the radical change in business practices required to face the challenges posed by the 'perfect storm' spoken of in the Introduction. A number of hospitality businesses have already achieved recognition within these schemes. For example, Compass – the largest food service company in the world – works with Business in the Community and has achieved FTSE-4-Good status. What they have achieved is significant – but it is clear, that more needs to be achieved.

Reporting of the nature described above is a significant step forward in the responsible business agenda. However, reporting is and will continue to be blighted by:

♦ Most reporting frameworks are oriented at large businesses and the vast majority of hospitality businesses are small or very small.

♦ Most reporting frameworks allow businesses to identify the boundaries of their report. Thus hospitality businesses may choose to report only on the facilities that they own. As we have seen, there is an increasing trend within hospitality businesses to operate premises owned by third parties and these can, therefore be excluded from the scope of reporting (despite the fact that they may account for the majority of the estate).

♦ Most reporting frameworks prioritise reporting on management processes and direct business activities, rather than impacts arising and activities through the supply chain. As we have seen in Principle 5, within the hospitality sector the impacts arising from the supply chain can (and often do) exceed those of the business itself.

- There is a patchwork of different arrangements for verifying the information contained within reports – but these are recognised by very few customers and so it is difficult to differentiate between the credible and incredible.

- Many reports fail to acknowledge the scale of the challenge that lies ahead. The ethos of reporting is to adopt a 'warts and all' approach, but to admit to poor practice is alien to many large businesses and thus reports tend to emphasise the good and ensure that the bad or poor practice is excluded by a carefully written scoping statement.

These shortcomings aside, it is clear that many large hospitality businesses have begun the process of reporting practice.

Conclusion

The fact that hospitality businesses have begun the process of reporting on responsible business performance is to be applauded. The inclusion of many small businesses (that have no external pressure to report) in reporting processes is positive and demonstrates the value businesses attribute to the reporting process and its links to brand image.

To date, only a few businesses in this sector have recognised the real value of this reporting – as a means of driving innovation, managing risks in the supply chain and building trust. This is disappointing. The drive for transparent reporting in this sector, however, is likely to grow. This drive will come from – among others – investors (including crucially the investment banks in developing countries), clients (especially the businesses and governments with a commitment to sustainable development), NGOs who are on the lookout for corporate wrongdoing and interestingly the sector itself especially when taking on long-term leases on properties. The question one has to ask is whether this drive for better and more transparent reporting will engage businesses in further documentation about their eco-efficiency and charitable giving programme (which some argue allows them to be a little less bad) or will drive innovation to play a key role in delivering a hospitality sector that meets the needs of a society in which energy and other resources are scarce, population pressures are significant, human rights need protection and the climate is changing (which will enable them to 'do good').

References

Accountability, BT Group and LRQA {2006) *The Materiality Report – Aligning strategy, performance and reporting*, available from www.accountability.org

Engen, T.A. and DiPiazza, S. (2005) *Beyond Reporting: Creating Business Value and Accountability*, Geneva: WBCSD.

Futerra (n.d.) *The Greenwash Guide*, London: Futerra, available from http://www.futerra.co.uk/downloads/Greenwash_Guide.pdf

Global Reporting Initiative (n.d.) *Sustainability Reporting Guidelines (v. 3.0)*, available at http://www.globalreporting.org/NR/rdonlyres/ED9E9B36-AB54-4DE1-BFF2-5F735235CA44/0/G3_GuidelinesENU.pdf

James, O. (2007) *Affluenza* , Vermillion

Ricaurte, E. (2011) 'Developing a sustainability measurement framework for hotels: towards an industry wide reporting structure', *Cornell Hospitality Reports*, **11** (13)

Tapscott, D. and Tiscoll, D. (2003)) *The Naked Corporation – How the Age of Transparency will Revolutionize Business*, New York: Free Press.

Part 5: Leadership and Future Directions

Within this concluding section, readers will find the final principle. This is rather an unconventional approach. After long and hard debate, however, it has been agreed that this final principle is the point at which responsible business is as central to the mainstream business operations as quality management, health and safety, research and development and so on. Readers will by now be familiar with the fact that the responsible business journey does not have an end point. So this last principle is not an end, but it is the point at which a business can be described as having transformed into one that genuinely seeks to operate responsibly.

The conclusions follow from this final principle.

Principle 10 : Take responsible business to the heart of the company

… for too long our definition of what constitutes 'responsible' corporate behaviour has been dangerously timid and blinkered. To confront the economy's and society's daunting challenges, companies must do more than monitor factories, donate to charities, and trumpet efforts to be a little less bad.

Jeffrey Hollender, author of the *Responsibility Revolution*

As we have seen, in 2011 few global organisations operate without some form of acknowledgement of their responsibilities towards the environment and society. The purpose of this acknowledgement is to demonstrate that they are capable of moving beyond the profit motive at all costs to pursue a more generous form of capitalism. Some organisations have now invested many millions of dollars in seeking to demonstrate that they are responsible and – by association – can be trusted to be a part of the solution to the many issues that are pressing on environment and society. Many have learned to their cost that investment alone cannot buy the reputation of being a responsible business. To be credible and trustworthy, responsible business initiatives have to be a core business value that is clearly defined, that permeates all decisions and departmental functions and that has coherence with the core product as well as playing a role in influencing new product development decisions. There is no point pretending that the transition to becoming a responsible business is easy or that we yet understand all of the steps in the process. It is tough, especially for a business that has traditionally operated upon more conventional principles. Those businesses that have got it wrong have on occasion lost more than a little investment.

Text box 53: Adopting responsible business values – the experiences of BP

BP, rebranded in 2000 as Beyond Petroleum, an attempt to take its image from one of an oil company to that of an energy company (the strap line was 'energy that doesn't damage the environment'). The logo adopted was that of Helios – the symbol of the Greek sun god. The rebranding reputedly cost in excess of US$600 million (Beder, 2002). Even before BP's current troubles off the coast of Louisiana, the result was questioned by many within the NGO community and especially those organisations with an aversion to the petrochemical sector. Other companies that have historically sought to make green claims via board or mission statements and have found themselves exposed to the derision of either mainstream or niche groups (notably CorporateWatch) include ExxonMobil, Monsanto, Rio Tinto and Nestlé. (www.corpwatch.org/article.php?id=3648). These niche groups, of course, are just that – niche. Their views may not be shared by the majority of consumers or investors, but as we have seen in previous chapters, they are verbal, media savvy and able to cause reputational damage that can take many years to reverse.

Those businesses that have got it right frequently end up on the lists not just of the most responsible businesses, but also the best businesses to work or and often to invest in. It is difficult to identify whether this is as a result of a responsible business ethos or because these businesses have better management processes in place that are a result of other factors.

The fundamentals: putting responsible business at the heart of the company

A small number of companies have managed to integrate responsible business considerations throughout their organisations. In some instances, this has meant wholly rethinking the product while in others it has meant an evolutionary process over many years. For all, it has completely transformed the operations of the business. Businesses that have gone through this process include, among others:

♦ **Interface** – the carpet manufacturing company whose boss underwent an epiphany as a result of reading Paul Hawken's *The Ecology of Commerce*. The company's mission is uncompromising on the quality of product and environmental impact with an aim to eliminate any negative impact on the environment by 2020.

♦ **Triodos** – the bank that believes profit doesn't need to be at the expense of the world's most pressing environmental problems. The company finances organisations that match its own ethical beliefs – from organic food and farming businesses and pioneering renewable energy enterprises, to recycling companies and nature conservation projects.

♦ **Unilever** – the corporate giant that has reoriented its corporate strategy around three big environmental commitments as a result of the realisation by Paul Polman (CEO) that if the company wanted to be in business for the long term it had to start doing business differently.

♦ **Rezidor** – the hotel company that recently made it onto the Ethisphere Institute's list of the most ethical companies. Kurt Ritter, the Chief Executive of the group has a passion for responsible business issues and has ensured that they are reflected throughout the company's operations.

♦ **Accor** – one of the largest hotel companies in the world that took on the environmental agenda in the early 1990s and has subsequently made a huge raft of its materials available to the public domain. As early as 1974, the group management team classified the environment as one of its core business attributes and since then the group has been working to reduce negative impacts throughout all brands as well as playing a leadership role within the sector.

♦ **Sodexo** – one of the relative latecomers to the responsible business agenda that makes it onto Two Tomorrow's list of one of the most ethical food service businesses. The group fundamentals that underpin the Better Tomorrow Plan are central to the core businesses and the time that has been taken to embed this ethos throughout the company is fundamental to its success. Rather than proclaiming its commitment to responsible business in the early days of the movement (when significant PR benefits could be gained), Sodexo took time to understand the implications of responsible business and get the commitment of all senior managers. This time investment has paid off. The senior management team is embedding responsible business principles not just within Sodexo, but playing a leadership role within the sector as a whole.

♦ **Scandic** – the hotel business that under the guidance of J.P. Bergkvist used the Natural Step to develop and deliver its ethos that is summed up in the Omtanke philosophy. The success of the company is such that – despite many changes in ownership – it remains broadly synonymous with environmental responsibility for many in the industry.

Responsible business – the role of committed leaders

Kurt Ritter of Rezidor believes that responsibility must be a core part of company strategy:

'Rezidor has a long history of being a responsible company, with our Scandinavian roots and environmental and safety & security programmes dating back more than 20 years. These programmes have been – and will continue to be – constantly developed, improved and expanded. Rezidor is one of the fastest growing hotel companies worldwide. We openly acknowledge that our increasing size which may give us greater visibility and influence in the marketplace also gives us an increased opportunity to take on an even bigger share of that responsibility.'

So what is the difference between those businesses that integrate responsible business issues at the heart of the business and those that don't? The answer is complex, but at its centre lies the attitude of the chief executive and Board and particularly the former. In short, the extent to which the leaders of the business have bought into their own statement of values.

Integrating responsibility?

One of the risks if you have people with sustainability job titles is that everybody else just defers – it's a huge mistake. Where sustainability works best is where an organisation's leadership gets it and wants it to happen and enables it to happen – so everyone from the person who sweeps the floor to the finance director feels part of that conversation.

Will Day, Chairman, Sustainable Development Commission (2010)

Some chief executives fundamentally believe that 'the time is ripe for a true paradigm shift to a more sustainable economy' (Volans, n.d.). Companies that effectively make the transition to place responsible business practices at their core always have a chief executive and a board who are personally committed to this belief. The difference is tangible between the small band of businesses for which this is the case and those where responsible business initiatives have been adopted because of a 'rational' business motive[1] or the need to be seen to do the right thing.

The advice that is available through the codes of conduct that seek to act as a guide to responsible business initiatives, generally specifies that the 'route' to placing these issues at the heart of a company is by:

♦ Ensuring that the board and/or CEO 'treat responsible business conduct as a core priority';

♦ Stating the company's purpose and agreeing on its values.

(adapted from ICC Charter for Responsible Business)

These steps are of course important, but they overlook the importance of a committed leader or leadership team. Responsible business programmes in companies that lack this leadership often become little more than a departmental function treated in the same way as financial management, customer services, or quality control rather than a core 'value' that informs all other aspects of the business. So a third bullet point is added to the list:

♦ Having a leader and/or board that is genuinely engaged in and committed to the responsible business agenda.

Visionary leadership required

Visionary business leaders who have placed responsible business at the very core of their company ethos are well known. They include Anita Roddick of the Body Shop, Paul Polman of Unilever, Ray Anderson of Interface. Among large hospitality companies, they include Jan Peter Bergkvist (formerly of Scandic and Hilton and now of SleepWell.nu), Kurt Ritter of Rezidor, John Forte (of Forte Hotels), Jean-Marc Espalioux, Chairman of Management Board & CEO of Accor and the Carlson sisters of Carlson-Wagonlit. Within smaller businesses, such leaders are more common and frequently are able to associate the entire business with their responsible ethos.

The challenge of leadership

Without dramatic leadership from chairmen, many companies will wander into 2009 focused more on survival than revitalization, hoping that their past view of the world will be restored. As a result, they will find themselves struggling to withstand tough conditions and badly positioned in the new environment. By shaking up the natural rhythms of the board and challenging corporate directors to re-examine their thinking, chairmen can ensure that their companies are ready to meet the challenges of the coming year.

Mckinsey Quarterly, February 2009

---

1   That is not to say that responsible businesses should sacrifice their economic value. Responsible business decisions have to fit within a business framework of which profit is core. It is often the timescale for profit that changes. See the quote from Paul Polman on page 125.

Despite the rhetoric and PR, however, it is likely that responsible business remains a departmental function rather than a core business value for many hospitality businesses. This is not because CEOs or board members are in any way disingenuous in developing responsible business initiatives. It is instead the fact that a comprehensive responsible business initiative requires a cultural change across the organisation and this needs to be led by a committed leader. In any organisation, this is a process that requires time and commitment. Many senior executives in the industry are aware that this culture change will need to be facilitated. For example, a recent survey (undertaken Oxford Brookes University) of 75 senior executives and policy makers in this field found that 41 respondents considered that adapting to the demands of the Green Economy would be important or very important to the future of their business. Twenty respondents to the same survey considered training and the facilitation of leadership development on this agenda to be lacking.

Text box 54: New leaders – new rules

The dependence on great leaders to imbibe the responsibility culture combines with the relative lack of focus on this issue in higher and further education institutions to represent a considerable threat to the future development of responsible business initiatives. Those leaders with a commitment to responsible business have often taken it upon themselves to learn the 'tools of the trade', because they have been lacking in their formal education. When these leaders move on, too many companies have discovered that they can take the enthusiasm for responsible business with them. Those companies that have lost leaders with a commitment to responsible business practices are often left with pockets of good practice and a heritage of programmes that reduce costs. However, the lack the innovation, drive and enthusiasm means that momentum is lost and the programme stagnates. Within such a framework, it is difficult for global companies to make consistent progress. Conversely, consistency of leadership is one of the reasons that small and (usually) family-owned businesses are able to excel and maintain the momentum of their responsible business initiatives and to use them as a source of innovation and competitive edge.

Board commitment essential

In global companies, even the most visionary of leaders in large companies cannot achieve responsible business objectives without board level support (and preferably active engagement). The International Chamber of Commerce in its *Business in Society* booklet states that 'Rather than reacting to outside pressures, a company's adoption of its own business principles should be motivated by the desire to express the values that guide its approach to doing business'. This point is well made. There is a world of difference between a board that signs a commitment to responsible business practices because it believes in the principles and can see a clear match between them and its core business values, and one that either:

♦ Has been convinced that it is in the business' interests to be seen to be responsible (for example because it will reduce operating costs, minimise reputational risk or enhance brand reputation) , or

♦ Has been caught in the act of unethical behaviour and needs to make amends (usually within the context of a PR exercise to restore brand value).

Businesses that take the latter two routes, for example, rarely examine the implications of their product development decisions in the light of the responsible business commitment. It is businesses in these categories that prioritise conventional modes of doing business and departmentalise responsible business issues. Businesses that take the former route almost always frame new product developments in the light of their responsible business values. In a hospitality context, this may involve reviewing the entire supply chain to ensure that products that do not match the business' 'responsible values' are replaced with alternatives. As a result it is the businesses in the former category that inevitably become more 'responsible' over time.

The process of recruiting and maintaining the interest of board members towards responsible business issues should not be underestimated. Responsible business initiatives are just one of a range of issues for which the Board is responsible. And boards are generally conservative in their nature. Campbell and Sinclair (2009) found, for example, that even when reacting to a crisis – such as reputational risk from an environmental incident 'most corporate directors are likely to assume that radical change is unnecessary and that "normal service" will soon resume'. In these instances, the role of an influential leader is particularly important.

How responsible business is integral to business strategy

> IHG's business strategy now encompasses two key aspects: where we choose to compete and how we will win when we compete. Our 'Where' strategy is that IHG will grow a portfolio of differentiated hospitality brands in select strategic countries and global key cities to maximise our scale advantage. The 'How' aspect of our strategy flows from our core purpose and from our research at the hotel level, as to what really makes a difference. Based on our hotel level research we are focused on the four things that really make a difference to our guests. Responsible business is one of IHG's four key strategic priorities, one of the 'how we win' aspects.

> *IHG Corporate Responsibility Report 2008*

Within hospitality businesses, many boards nominate a member with specific responsibility for the Responsible Business issues. Figure 43 demonstrates the typical 'structure' used by many hospitality businesses when dealing with responsible business issues. In reality of course, the extent to which responsible business values are woven throughout this structure will depend upon the level of genuine commitment of the board. That genuine commitment is generally demonstrated not just through the nomination of a board member to oversee responsible business issues, but also through the development of detailed long-term plans for that issue, the allocation of a budget to the implementation of those plans and the dedication of human resources towards its implementation.

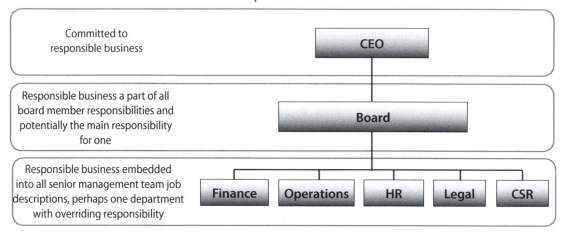

Figure 43: Sample board structure for dealing with responsible business issues

Note: Many businesses do not have a CSR or Responsible Business Executive. For these businesses, integration of responsible business values into core job descriptions is essential.

With a genuinely committed CEO and board, many of the other conditions for delivering on responsible business initiatives can be put in place. These include finance to support longer-term investments in sustainable technologies, appropriate processes for monitoring progress and rewarding success, guidelines to ensure that new development decisions are taken with a view to responsible business priorities, a strategy for dealing with longer-term risks such as climate change adaptation, mechanisms to engage stakeholders in dialogue about the business, ensuring ethical or responsible business criteria are included in all job descriptions, appropriate procedures to define and review responsible business values and mechanisms to measure and report on success (and respond to failure).

The role of trade and professional associations

The trade and professional associations have been surprising reticent about engaging in the debate about responsible business. With a few notable exceptions (including the World Travel & Tourism Council in its earlier years, the International Tourism Partnership, the Caribbean Hotels Association, the Costa Rican Hotels Association, ABTA through its Travellife programme), these organisations have addressed the eco-efficiency agenda but provided little or no leadership on the broader responsible business agenda. Without clear leadership from the trade and professional associations, individual businesses have been left to define their own responsible business approaches and strategies. International companies that have the resources for the development of comprehensive responsible business programmes have invested in and developed their own initiatives. For the many smaller businesses, however, there is a dearth of information from which to learn and develop and a lack of strategic direction for the sector as a whole. These businesses have had little choice but to educate themselves about these issues or to turn to one of the certification agencies or consultancies for support.

Five indicators for business

☐ The chief executive is committed to embedding responsible business principles throughout the company.

☐ Responsible business issues are intertwined within the company's mission statement and core brand values.

☐ Responsible business criteria are a core part of everybody's job description and annual performance reviews.

☐ Responsible business issues are allocated a budget that is not justified only on short-term payback periods.

☐ Shareholders are fully engaged in working with the company to support responsible business initiatives in the interests of long-term profitability.

The responsible business toolbox

The relative lack of leadership from the trade and professional associations on responsible business issues for the hospitality sector is mirrored by the small number of tools available to support business leaders in the transition to becoming a responsible business. Those that are available include:

♦ The services of consultancies – from the global giants like PWC to universities, associations like the International Tourism Partnership and smaller organisations that seek to help businesses review strategy, define objectives and develop comprehensive responsible business plans. Many large hospitality businesses have used the services of such consultants to support them through the process of responsible business strategy development. These arrangements work best when consultancies work in partnership with a member of the senior management team and other stakeholders in the business. Responsible business advice that is commissioned wholly from an outside consultancy without significant time and resource commitment from the senior management team is unlikely to succeed. However, a number of organisations do now provide excellent bespoke responsible business consulting services.

♦ The generic tools that are widely used by hospitality businesses. These include many of the advice services such as Business in the Community and the Natural Step (used to guide the Scandic and Max Hamburger programme). These tools have much in common with consultancies and have the added advantage that they usually help businesses network with other like-minded organisations.

A number of hospitality businesses have worked with this type of organisation. Some of these businesses belong to more than one such organisation.

At a smaller scale there are a small number of governmental services that help businesses place responsible business issues at the heart of the operation. These include tools like Business Link's Ethical Trading tool (www.businesslink.gov.uk). These tools are used on a self-help basis so it is difficult to assess usage among hospitality businesses.

Conclusions

It is perhaps a reflection of the real value that is placed upon responsible business that many of the routine fora for hospitality businesses do not integrate responsible business as anything other than a side show, and that trade associations rarely incorporate learning or other materials on their websites or genuinely work to engage managers in the agenda.[2] Industry leaders seeking information in this field are often unsupported and find themselves taking general qualifications in environmental management as they are unable to access learning resources through the mainstream mechanisms of the industry.

There is genuine engagement and commitment to delivering on responsible business priorities among some hospitality businesses. The large global companies that are vulnerable to criticism by external stakeholders have been particularly proactive on the agenda and the large food service businesses have responded with the most comprehensive and far-reaching initiatives at a head office level. Some companies are now emerging with coherent responsible business strategies that can deliver cost savings, build business resilience and achieve social and environmental objectives and have the genuine commitment of the board. As to whether or not they really permeate throughout the company is for anyone to guess. Those individuals who hold CSR roles and have had to justify their existence during hard economic times will probably be well aware that for their business 'doing well by doing good' is a mantra that works well in times of prosperity but is less popular in times of economic hardship. Those businesses who lay off CSR staff at these times are perhaps less committed to responsible business practices than those who continue to invest in the belief that responsible business initiatives are a core element of the business strategy for today and lie at the heart of business resilience in the future.

---

2   The exceptions of course are the World Travel Market that has hosted a Responsible Tourism Day for a number of years and Hotelympia (the major UK trade show) that has increasingly had a focus on sustainability issues in recent years (including gaining certification to BS8901 – the sustainable event standard).

References

Campbell, A. and Sinclair, S. (2009) 'The crisis: mobilizing boards for change', *McKinsey Quarterly*, February.

Day, Will (2010) in an interview with SD Scene, download from *sd.defra.gov.uk*

Hollender J and Breen B (2010) *The Responsibility Revolution – How the next generation of businesses will win* Jossey Bas, San Francisco

Hawken, P. (1994) *The Ecology of Commerce*, Harper Business

IHG (2008) *Corporate Responsibility Report*, available at http://www.ihgplc.com/index.asp?pageid=718

Sharon Beder, 'bp: Beyond Petroleum?' in *Battling Big Business: Countering greenwash, infiltration and other forms of corporate bullying*, edited by Eveline Lubbers, Green Books, Devon, UK, 2002, pp. 26-32)

Jeffries, S. and Moss, S. (2008) 'Who wants a recession', *The Guardian*, Friday, 8 February.

Volans, (n.d.) *The Phoenix Economy – 50 Pioneers in the Business of Social Innovation*, Volans Ventures Ltd, London.

5 | A Faustian bargain?

The past 20 years have been decisively swept away. Capitalism is not in meltdown but it is at a critical juncture, as William Davies argues in this significant contribution to the debate about the future of the firm and its relationship with society. For many years it has been the received wisdom that the pursuit of 'shareholder value' was the best way to motivate management and maximise value for shareholders. The crisis has exposed the weaknesses of the drive for short-term maximum gain.

Charlie Mayfield, Chairman of the John Lewis Partnership, in Davies (2009)

When it first emerged, there were many who predicted that the new-found concern among businesses about their environmental impacts would be nothing short of a flash in the pan. Some 20 years later it is to the credit of the business community, the trade associations that represent them, the NGO community and other stakeholders that have supported (and occasionally criticised) them that the concept of environmental responsibility within major global businesses has not only survived, but evolved. The concept has moved beyond environmental responsibility to include social and economic dimensions. Of course, there remain many businesses that do not acknowledge their environmental (let alone social) responsibilities – almost certainly the majority of businesses worldwide. There are also some that lay claim to achievements that cannot be substantiated in fact. These factors, however, should not undermine the scale of the responsibility revolution that has swept through the global business community. Nor should it diminish the fact that the responsible business programmes of some global companies are far more ambitious in scope and scale now than those that were evident at the start of the mainstream responsible business movement.

Those businesses that have made the greatest progress in this agenda are not simply seeking to put a green veneer over their activities. They are instead those businesses that have recognised that a failure to embrace responsible business practices now may critically increase the costs and diminish the opportunities for doing business in the long term.

The hospitality sector was a latecomer to the responsible business debate and with the exception of a few companies, still lags behind many other sectors in its achievements. Nevertheless – supported and occasionally harangued by their stakeholders – many (but by no means all) major international companies in the sector are now responding to the agenda. Some of these businesses have come a long way from the days when responsible hospitality meant little more than taking a few cost saving environmental management initiatives and engaging in corporate philanthropy. Over the years, some outstanding examples of good practice have emerged to illustrate the powerful role the sector can play. Some of these examples have emerged from unexpected places such as large integrated resorts or fast food outlets. In doing so, they have brought into question the conventional wisdom that specific types of business are bad. There is, as a result, an emerging realisation that it is not the nature of a business that counts, but the extent to which it does good or causes harm. It is the extent to which a business believes in and is able to implement responsible business values that dictates the level of impact and harm or good.

Text box 55: The good, the bad and the ugly

There is incontrovertible evidence that while many hospitality business do good, some do cause harm: undermining the societies in which they are based, degrading the environment, failing to respect human dignity and actively exploiting others with whom they do business. On occasion, hospitality businesses that do harm, act out of ignorance. This is especially the case for the millions of small and medium hospitality businesses. Perhaps most damaging among businesses that do harm are those companies that lay claim to responsible business attributes that they do not possess or that cynically position themselves in the marketplace by dint of utilising a few products that are of ethical origin to gain favourable (and eminently newsworthy) reviews while ignoring the main impacts of their operation. Increased public awareness combines with the growth in media-savvy NGOs and certification schemes to make this latter path risky. Nevertheless the appeal of being seen to be responsible will without a doubt mean that some hospitality businesses will continue to pursue this route. Whether or not they succeed will ultimately depend upon the extent to which customers, clients, investors, policy makers and suppliers can recognise and care about responsible business programmes.

Canny businesses have long since recognised that cost savings can accrue from many aspects of the responsible hospitality agenda. Those companies that have pursued initiatives to reduce energy, water and waste costs have already saved millions of pounds not to mention the tonnes of carbon, etc. that would otherwise have been emitted into the atmosphere. There is no shame in using responsible business programmes to deliver cost savings – in fact to fail to do so would be to ignore the economic and environmental aspects of the responsible business agenda and to deprive shareholders and investors of their due rewards. The businesses that engage *only* in responsible business initiatives that deliver these cost savings, however, are playing by the 'old rules' of business. For these businesses, initiatives that cannot meet the following criteria are rarely prioritised or implemented: pay back on the initial investment within a defined and short-term timeline (generally five years or less); an immediate and compelling market advantage; easy introduction of initiatives. Moreover, in these businesses responsible considerations are rarely at the forefront (or even rear guard) when opportunities for business expansion arise, when supply chain discussions are taking place or when discussions are in train with policy makers. This 'old rules of business' mentality is understandable and has, in some instances, been endorsed by the third sector community through a perpetuation of the myth that 'responsible business makes cents'[3]. The hospitality businesses that adopt this 'old rules' approach will inevitably gain short-term benefits, but miss the opportunities to adapt now for operating in a world that is warmer, more crowded and less resource rich.

The challenge of operating in a world that is Hot, Flat and Crowded

> In a world that is getting hot, flat, and crowded, the task of creating the tools, systems, energy sources, and ethics that will allow the planet to grow in cleaner, more sustainable ways is going to be the biggest challenge of our lifetime.

> Tom Friedman – Hot Flat and Crowded

Hospitality businesses that are rising to the future challenges are those that have moved beyond these old rules of business to: build partnerships with stakeholders; ensure their responsible business values support and enhance their reputation; future proof the business against the challenges of climate change, water scarcity and so on and embed responsible business principles throughout the organisation. In so doing, these companies are transforming their business model to genuinely embed responsible criteria with the company DNA (see Figure 45) as well as maximising cost savings.[4] Harsh while it may sound, within the global hospitality sector, these businesses are few and far between. Even among the hospitality businesses that make it onto the lists of the world's most 'sustainable' companies, most would acknowledge that their responsible business initiatives still have a considerable way to go to catch up with the major players in some other sectors.[5] What is encouraging is the fact that there are global hospitality businesses that make it onto these lists. More encouraging still is the fact that many of these businesses are determined to progress their own initiatives and play a leadership role in the sector. According to the ranking agencies,[6] the global companies that are seeking to play this role include some surprising candidates. As at 2011, those businesses that rank in these lists (or that are on more than one) include (in no particular order): McDonald's, Starbucks, Marriott

---

3   This was the message that was used to see the responsible business ethos into many hospitality businesses in the early days of the movement.

4   Many companies claim that responsible business is within their DNA. Depressingly, this is true only for the handful of businesses that have reached the transformation stage in the evolution of their programme.

5   There are many examples of small businesses that have already engaged with the full range of principles of responsible hospitality.

6   These organisations provide the corporate sustainability ratings that rank companies according to a range of responsible business criteria. Company data publicised in the following sources is included in this analysis: CR Magazine 100 Best Corporate Citizens, CSR Hub, Ethisphere Institute, Global 100 most sustainable institutions in the World, Newsweek Green Rankings and Two Tomorrow's. Other lists exist such as FTSE4Good but could not be accessed at the time of going to print. Some of these lists do not include any hospitality business representation and others have specific geographical boundaries. Most include only companies that are listed on the stock exchanges.

International, IHG, Accor, Yum!, Compass Group, Starwood Hotels and Restaurants, Wyndham Worldwide, Rezidor, Kimpton Hotels, Whitbread, Sodexo.[7]

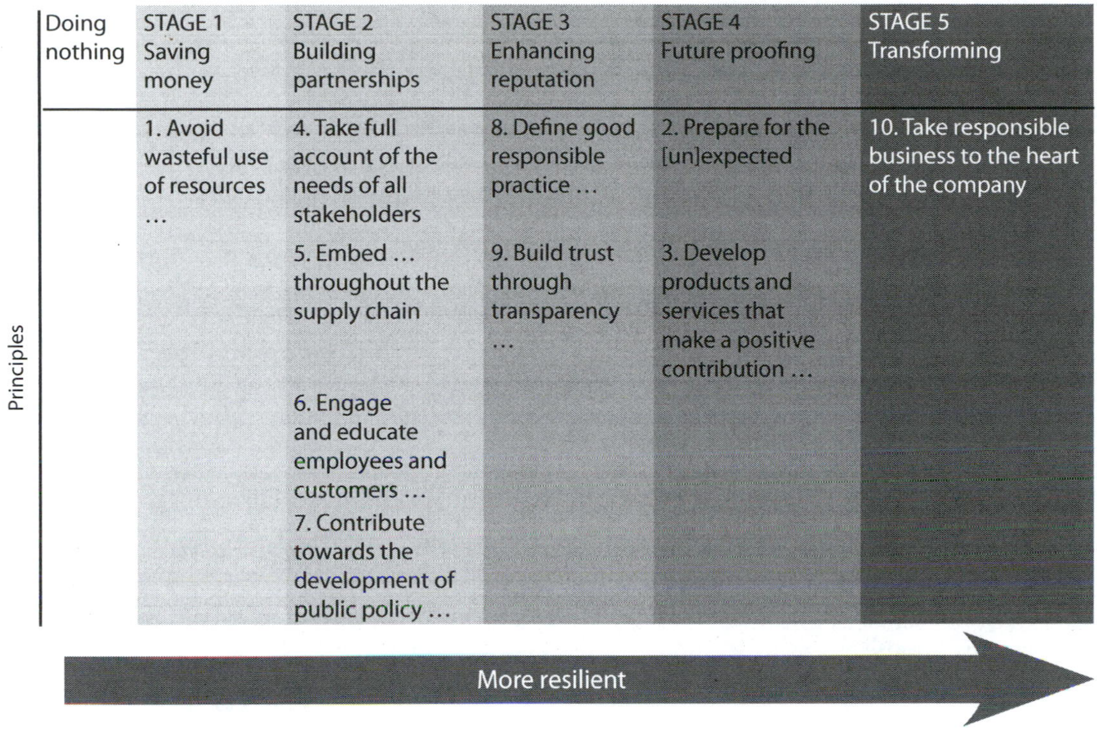

Doing nothing	STAGE 1 Saving money	STAGE 2 Building partnerships	STAGE 3 Enhancing reputation	STAGE 4 Future proofing	STAGE 5 Transforming
	1. Avoid wasteful use of resources …	4. Take full account of the needs of all stakeholders	8. Define good responsible practice …	2. Prepare for the [un]expected	10. Take responsible business to the heart of the company
		5. Embed … throughout the supply chain	9. Build trust through transparency …	3. Develop products and services that make a positive contribution …	
		6. Engage and educate employees and customers …			
		7. Contribute towards the development of public policy …			

Principles (vertical axis label)

More resilient →

Figure 45: The evolution of responsible hospitality initiatives

Even among the businesses on these lists and other companies that are smaller and, therefore not included in its scope, there are crucial gaps in responsible business programmes. Many of these have been explored in Parts 2–4. Perhaps most significant among them are:

♦ Slow progress on adapting to the challenges posed by climate change (and the associated issue of water scarcity), food security and resource scarcity.

♦ With the possible exception of some of the very large contract caterers and QSR businesses, a lack of engagement with stakeholders to address key impacts. This is especially the case with suppliers.

♦ The relative 'slowness' of embedding responsible design criteria into new facilities and especially those that are built/owned by third parties, but operated by hospitality companies.[8]

---

7   There may be companies excluded from this list who we have missed on our search or who are not listed on the stock exchange. They include companies like Scandic.

8   Admittedly there is reluctance by the investment/developer community. A unified approach to integrating responsible issues into brand standards would certainly focus minds and ensure that business operating costs (for energy and water at least) can be effectively managed.

♦ A failure to embrace 'Fairy Godmother' technologies that have a pay-back period of three years or more.

♦ With the exception of the corporate marketplace, a lack of understanding of customer perceptions and expectations of responsible hospitality initiatives. This has left the sector open to accusations of greenwash.

As well as gaps, there are challenges. Principal among these is the need to engage a wider range of corporate and small hospitality businesses in responsible practices. It is easy when reading books of this nature to conclude that responsible practice is the norm within an industry sector. This is not the case. Many global hospitality businesses – including some household names – have yet to even adopt an environmental policy statement that is available in the public domain or to pay any real attention to implementing eco-efficiency initiatives, let alone responsible business. There are some leading lights among small businesses (many with programmes that go way beyond those of the corporate sector). Overall, businesses with a commitment to responsibility remain a tiny minority of all businesses in the sector. Until responsible business becomes as natural a part of the hospitality agenda as service quality, it is unlikely that the sector will be able to play a true role in the green economy. Other challenges include:

♦ **Defining responsible hospitality!** The subject of this book but an issue on which there is no widespread agreement beyond eco-efficiency.

♦ **Finding mechanisms to embed responsible business initiatives** throughout entire complex global organisations. Even those businesses that are global leaders on the responsible hospitality agenda find it hard to integrate responsible principles in practice in all units (especially those that are not directly owned or managed by the head office operation or that are based in a culture where responsible business issues are not considered significant). Training initiatives are starting to make an impact and those businesses that integrate responsible hospitality within their core philosophy are having more success than others. Much more needs to be done, however, to ensure that head office claims can be substantiated in fact throughout all units.

♦ **Supporting chief executives** in understanding trends in the responsible hospitality agenda. To date, those chief executives that have been committed to the responsible hospitality agenda have achieved remarkable things. All too often, however, their departure from the company spells the start of a slow death for the responsible business programme. The major conferences that convene rarely include responsibility within their agendas (and some that do pay little more than lip service).

♦ **Finding new ways in which to define success**. As we explain, success in the hospitality sector is judged on growth and economic value. Economic growth data is, however, a poor indicator of the long-term viability or health of the sector or its future potential and will not secure its role in the green economy. Crucial are ways to decouple economic success, environmental impacts and physical growth.

♦ **Finding effective mechanisms for communicating success.** Many hospitality businesses have put their head over the parapet about success in their initiatives and find a hostile audience. Those businesses that greenwash or that do not build transparency into their procedures are deserving of criticism. Those that are dammed by dint of the business type are not (unless the business by its very nature does harm). It is a fact of life that global companies use standardised products and practices. It is not a fact of life that those companies are by definition 'bad'. Where they are progressing responsible hospitality procedures that are deserving of praise, it is essential that mechanisms are found to help businesses that do good communicate their success in a way that is meangful to customers and clients as well other audiences.

Green economy

The term 'green economy' is used by UNEP and other international and national agencies to describe economic growth that stimulates new jobs and eradicates poverty while minimising negative environmental impacts through the reshaping of policies and investments towards clean technologies, renewable energy, water, transportation, green buildings, sustainable agriculture or forests.. For more information, see UNEP's publication, *Towards a Green Economy*.

In many instances, the sector cannot address these challenges alone. It will require support from a range of stakeholders to make progress. Specifically, there is a need for support from:

♦ Those that invest in the sector to understand the benefits of responsible business initiatives. This is not just a priority for new facilities, but also for those that refurbish existing ones. We describe in Chapter 5 the evolution of Fairy Godmother technologies. As a sector that has always been at the heart of innovation (some of the first heating and hot water systems were installed into hotels and many modern cooking technologies emerged within commercial kitchens), we would hope that those that invest in the industry will champion these technologies and support their integration into new facilities to ensure that they can deliver resource and cost reductions in the long term.

♦ The professional and trade association that represent the sector. With a few notable exceptions[9] – these organisations have not supported the development of responsible business expertise within the industry. Most of the initiatives by

---

9   Including the Caribbean Hotels Association, which established CAST; the Costa Rican Hotels Association, the World Travel & Tourism Council, the International Tourism Partnership, a handful of new business such as Footprint Forum and those mentioned at other points throughout this text.

associations have focused their effort on providing cost-saving utility management initiatives (while these are important they are hardly visionary), circulating best practice examples (generally focused on utility management) or on lobbying government about the introduction of new environmental regulations/taxation. At an international and/or national scale, these organisations have largely failed to construct a definition of what responsible business means within a hospitality context, to identify possible futures for the sector in a world where oil and other resources may be scarce or to develop position papers on the role of hospitality businesses in delivering against climate change, green economy and other commitments.

♦ The formal training and education sector, which has for the most part not responded to the responsible hospitality imperative. Those who will become leaders of the sector in the future all too often leave their formal education with little or no sustainable development literacy, let alone an understanding of the principles of responsible hospitality, outside the need for eco-efficiency.

♦ Governments and other buyers of hospitality services to continue to support those businesses that have responsible business credentials, through, for example the conferment of preferred supplier status on hospitality businesses that can demonstrate progress against responsible hospitality priorities.

Hard economic times may make it seem unlikely that these challenges will be addressed. In all likelihood some of them won't. Hospitality, like other business sectors, however, now faces a critical juncture. It can perpetuate the model of doing business by the old rules or embrace the new. In the words of the OECD, to choose the former path 'would indeed be unwise and ultimately unsustainable, involving risks that could impose human costs and constraints on economic growth and development. It could result in increased water scarcity, resource bottlenecks, air and water pollution, climate change and biodiversity loss which would be irreversible' (OECD, 2011). The latter will help to ensure that 'the progress in living standards we have seen these past fifty years does not grind to a halt'.

In reality, there is no choice. In the long term all businesses will need to adapt their modus operandi to become a part of the solution to global environmental and economic problems. Those that don't adapt will no doubt face increasing costs of doing business and risk the role of being seen as a pariah. Some in the sector are already playing a leadership role. The time has now come to help others adapt by building a long-term vision of what responsibility means for the hospitality sector (using the principles in this book) and specifying the steps to achieve that vision. To do otherwise would be throw away the opportunities for greater economic and environmental stability in the interests of replicating the past.

A vision of the future?

> *Unless we are guided by a conscious vision of the kind of future we want, we will be guided by an unconscious vision of the kind of present we already have.*

(The Edge magazine 1995)

References

Mayfield, C. in Davies, W. (2009) *Reinventing the Firm*, London: Demos.

Friedman, T (2008) *Hot, Flat and Crowded – Why we need a green revolution and how it can renew America.* Farrar, Strauss and Giroux

OECD (2011) *Towards Green Growth,* available from www.oecd.org/greengrowth.

Afterword

When asked to write an 'Afterword' I must confess to being somewhat uncertain about how to reply. I'd never heard of the concept and it seemed rather like an *after-thought* in the book's lifecycle. One destined to produce the kind of vanilla result the stranger got when he asked Abraham Lincoln to write an inscription in a novel the man had written and the President hadn't read. So he wrote "for people who like this kind of book – this is the kind of book they will like".

But of course Rebecca is no stranger. I suspect there are few people in the world with as much practical experience in helping travel and tourism companies to embrace sustainable and responsible practices. She is a friend and talented colleague whose work I've respected, since the early 1990s when we were exploring early green tourism concepts inspired by the Rio Earth Summit and its Chairman Maurice Strong. Our work for WTTC in the 1990s on Agenda 21 for the Travel and Tourism Industry and Green Globe Certification, has withstood the test of time.

So I welcome the opportunity to strongly endorse the ideas, assessments and conclusions in this book; the need for industry engagement in the global sustainable development agenda and the keen analysis of strengths and weaknesses of hospitality practices; the deep insights into responsible business and best practice which are rightly identified as key elements in fast tracking the industry into the global sustainable development mainstream; and particularly the essential leadership which will not only improve bottom lines but will be the beacon that attracts and drives the industry towards a sustainable future.

I particularly welcome the chance to help position these realities in the context of the Green Growth paradigm – which is an important feature of the conclusions.

Green Growth will require a massive switch to clean energy, harnessing InfoTech to boost efficiency and manage change, technology and finance for poor countries and a strong conservation commitment for planetary and species well-being.

The complexity, scale and scope of this transformation required between now and 2050 in every production, consumption and investment activity on Earth is almost incomprehensible – given different socio-politico-economic realities and the multi-trillion dollar cost. The entire economy will need to adapt progressively.

Hospitality can and must play its part. We represent some 5% of overall global carbon output, with the pivotal air transport component at 2% of worldwide emissions, but we support directly and indirectly some 10% of the world economy. Like other sectors we must lower our impacts while expanding our socio-economic contribution, which is central to world commerce, employment, development and human interaction. Fortunately, the potential to mitigate and adapt is significant with new techniques, technologies, products and operational practices already in the pipeline.

We can not only make the change, but the hospitality industry can be a lead catalyst for change in other sectors.

The challenges are huge but so are the opportunities and there are no alternatives. This book helps chart the directions for change.

Geoffrey Lipman

Green Earth Travel

Appendix 1: Companies included in the data analysis

The reports and to a lesser extent web sites and other company documentation of the companies listed below have been used to develop the analytical tables of progress of hospitality businesses in implementing responsible business initiatives.

The companies that we have selected to report on include many of the leading companies in the sector. However, they have not been selected within a statistical sample frame. We have deliberately excluded large corporate organisations such as Tragus (operators of the Café Rouge, Bella Italia, Strada and brasserie brands including Amalfi, Potters and Huxleys) that do not have any form of environmental or responsible business reporting on their web sites from our analysis. Most – but not all – of the companies included are publically listed. Readers should note that many of the case studies of good practice are from companies that are not listed (e.g. Scandic, Red Hotels, Apetito).

The purpose of providing the analysis was to get a flavour of the nature and direction of reporting within the sector rather than to provide a statistical commentary on the standard or content of reporting. The company reports included within the analysis are as follows – all have been taken from the UK web site of the companies in question. Different results would have been achieved had this analysis been undertaken within a different country context.

The data included in the tables below is sourced from Caterlyst (www.caterlyst.com) and the British Hospitality Association (2010) *Trends and Developments 2010*, BHA, London.

Contract caterers

Company	Number of outlets
Compass	7,000
Sodexo	2,300
Elior	1,400
Aramark UK	1,200

Hotels

Owner	Est. no. of global outlets (and rooms)	Brands operating (mainly UK)
Whitbread	584 (42,500)	Premier Inn
Intercontinental Hotels Group (IHG)	4,500 (656,000+)	Intercontinental, Crowne Plaza, Hotel Indigo, Holiday Inn, Holiday Inn Express, Staybridge Suites
Accor Hotels	4,111 (492,545)	Sofitel, Novotel, Mercure, Ibis, All Seasons, Etap, Formule1
Hilton Worldwide	3,600+ (599,000)	Waldorf Astoria, Hilton Hotels, Doubletree by Hilton, Hampton by Hilton, Hilton Garden Inn, Hilton Grand Vacations
Marriott Hotels	3,489 (507,000)	J W Marriott, Renaissance, Marriott, Courtyard, Grand Residences

Restaurant Groups

Owner	Est. number of outlets (UK)	Brands operating in UK
Mitchells & Butlers	1,212	Harvester, Browns, Toby, Vintage Inns, All Bar One
Gondola	631	Pizza Express, Ask, Zizzi
Restaurant Group	375	Frankie & Benny's, Garfunkels, Chiquitos
Whitbread	373	Beefeater, Brewer's Fayre, Table Table
Nando's	293	Nando's, Gourmet Burger Kitchen, Real Greek

Quick Service Restaurant Groups

Owner	Est. number of outlets (UK)	Brands operating in UK
Yum	1,400	KFC, Pizza Hut
Subway	1,342	Subway
McDonald's	1,255	McDonald's
Burger King	633	Burger King
Domino's	501	Domino's

Pubs and Inns

Owner	Selected brands
Punch Taverns	
Marstons	Pitcher & Piano
Greene King	
J D Wetherspoon	
Mitchells & Butlers	Ember, Scream, O'Neills

Appendix 2: The Deming Cycle and environmental management systems

Environmental management systems have come increasingly to the fore when it comes to delivering resource savings. As a general rule, these management systems are loosely based on a cyclical process that includes the following elements (these are based on what is known as the Deming Cycle).

EMS Model

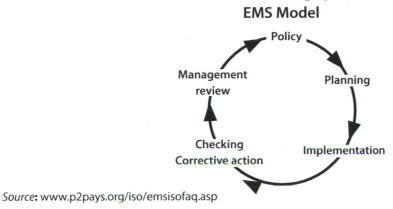

Source: www.p2pays.org/iso/emsisofaq.asp

The critical steps involved in the Deming Cycle in an environmental management context are as follows:

1. Environmental policy statement

Usually undertaken following a review of the major impacts of the business, the formation of an environmental policy is the first visible evidence that a business is serious about reducing its impacts.

The policy statement normally reflects the organisation's beliefs, mission and vision, environmental concerns, stakeholder requirements, guiding principles and risk analysis. It is a blend of practical and ethical concerns; not only stating what will be done, but also what has been achieved and why the organisation believes in doing it.

2. Planning (strategic)

Planning has relevance at both head office level for corporate businesses and at individual unit level. Generally, at corporate head office level the type of planning activity undertaken will be strategic, where at unit level it will be practical. Planning will embrace:

- Identifying the legal and other requirements of the firm vis-à-vis the environment and society;

- A set of clearly defined objectives and targets for environmental improvement (at head office and possibly also unit level);

- The means by which those objectives will be achieved and targets to measure progress towards their achievement.

Objectives and targets can generally be categorised as follows (Bird, 1997): (i) monitoring objectives - stating a commitment to monitoring or researching specific issues that are likely to bring about a change in circumstances, allowing improvement objectives to be set; (ii) management objectives - ensuring that all controls relating to a particular impact are systematically applied, and (iii) improvement objectives - demonstrate that environmental performance is being improved and will always be part of a system's commitment to continuous improvements.

3 – Implementation

The implementation process is usually the process of delivering change within a business. The nature and scale of change is usually specified within an implementation plan. Where action plans are developed at head office level there is often a need to refine the head office aspirations into a specific action plan that has resonance for a specific hospitality business, especially when working in a culture that is very different to that which predominates within the head office.

The implementation process usually involves: (i) getting the active support of the general management and senior management team, (ii) finding an enthusiastic and popular environmental champion for the cause, (iii) the recruitment of a Green Team to drive the programme, (iv) the implementation of staff training, (v) an assessment of the current situation from which to assess future achievements. This means regular meter readings and checking progress against process based objectives, (vii) on-going monitoring of performance including customer satisfaction (it is usual to test technologies and other interventions carefully before rolling out).

As a general rule, the issues considered within this chapter are those that are addressed within the implementation stage.

4. Checking and corrective action

Sometimes included within the management review phase, this is the stage at which the effectiveness of the implementation process is assessed. It often includes quantitative measurement (e.g. the amount of energy consumed this year compared with previous years), but also includes qualitative assessments (e.g. the nature of involvement in community projects; a review of stakeholder attitudes towards the project, and assessment of the impact of the environmental programme on staff attitudes towards their jobs).

5. Management review

This is the stage at which senior management team consider the results of the programme and use them to inform decisions about future investments which are in turn fed into the policy statement at individual unit and head office level and into the development of revised implementation plans.

A key feature of the Deming cycle is its cyclical nature and the implied feedback of information within the process to deliver continual improvement. This process – and in particular the concept of continual improvement – is central to many of the international environmental management standards such as the International Standard for Environmental Management Systems (ISO 14001), the EU's Eco-Management and Audit Scheme (with an additional step included from management review to include the responsibility of external reporting) and the new UK standard for sustainable event management BS 8901 which is pivotal to those companies that are seeking to contribute towards the London Olympic Games in 2012. It is also the core concept underpinning many of the 'green' or 'sustainable' certification schemes that have emerged in recent years to accredit those hospitality and (predominantly) tourism businesses that have good environmental management processes in place. These include the EU Flower for Hotels, the UK Green Tourism Business Scheme (the most successful such scheme if one considers membership numbers alone) and Green Globe.

.

Glossary of terms

Brundtland Report: The report that resulted from the meeting of the World Commission on Environment and Development in 1987. The meeting was chaired by then Prime Minister of Norway Gro Harlem Brundtland after whom it is named. Titled *Our Common Future*, the report proposes a global agenda for change and specifies how sustainable development can be achieved. It defined sustainable development as "development that meets the needs of the present without compromising the ability of future generations to meet their own needs". It contains within it two key concepts: (i) the concept of 'needs', in particular the essential needs of the world's poor, to which overriding priority should be given; and (ii) the idea of limitations imposed by the state of technology and social organization on the environment's ability to meet present and future needs.

Business and industry: Term used to describe the subdivision of the food service sector which caters for staff working in businesses and industrial sites (as opposed to staff catering in the retail sector or public sector). B & I is the leading sector in the contract catering market, accounting for more than half of all outlets and more than 40% of meals served.

Corporate social responsibility: Another more formal term to describe responsible business. In some countries, formal standards have been developed to recognise companies that operate according to prescribed CSR criteria.

Cost sector catering: The provision of a catering service within a facility occupied by another organisation. The catering service provided within such facilities is rarely the main purpose of the organisation and the catering service may not be operated with profit as the main aim.

Eco-efficiency: The concept of producing more, while using fewer resources and producing less waste.

Food service: The term which describes the provision, serving, or preparation of food; and the industry concerned with this. The food service sector includes all hospitality businesses (see below) where food is a core part of the offer, as well as catering throughout the public sector, retail and leisure.

Greenwash: A term that is commonly used to describe a business that lays claims to environmental practices or responsible business programmes that either do not materially address its key impacts or that it cannot substantiate in fact.

Greenhouse gases: A greenhouse gas (sometimes abbreviated GHG) is an atmospheric gas that absorbs and emits radiation in the infrared range. The main greenhouse gases are water vapour, carbon dioxide, methane, nitrous oxide, and ozone.

Hazard Analysis and Critical Control Points (HACCP): HACCP is a quality management system which identifies and evaluates points during production or preparation of food, in order to set up measures and control hazards to ensure product safety.

Hospitality sector: This includes catering businesses, hotels, restaurants, camp sites, caravan sites, guest houses and pubs within its scope. Businesses operate in the private or public sector.

Hotel: In this book we use the term 'hotel' to include all forms of serviced accommodation. Thus the term 'hotel' refers to any business that provides accommodation and meals as a part of its core offer.

ISO 14001: An internationally accepted standard that sets out how to go about putting in place an effective 'environmental management system' (EMS). The standard is designed to address the delicate balance between maintaining profitability and reducing environmental impact.

Leaseback : An arrangement whereby a hotel, restaurant or other hospitality business leases the physical property from which it operates. In some instances, these arrangements are utilised in properties that were once owned by the hospitality business that now holds the lease.

Managed [estate], [pub], [hotel], [restaurant]: A property portfolio where managers are employed by the property owners and where running of the establishment is under central control.

Management contract: An arrangement whereby operational control of a business is contracted to a company that does not own the physical property in which that business is based (see above).

Millennium Development Goals: A commitment by national governments to eliminate child poverty globally by 2015.

Peak oil: The point at which global oil production reaches its peak and from which it begins to decline.

Profit sector catering: The provision of a catering service where food service is the primary function of the organisation and profit the primary motive for offering it.

Quick service restaurant (QSR): Establishment selling food for immediate consumption, often off the premises. Properties included under this classification include fish and chip shops, sandwich bars, mobile catering vans, tea and coffee shops, burger bars and so on

Resource efficiency: The management and reduction of raw materials, energy and water in order to minimise waste of these, and thereby reduce cost.

Sustainable development: Development that meets the needs of the present without compromising the ability of future generations to meet their own needs (see Brundtland Report above).

Tenanted [pub], [hotel], [QSR], [restaurant]: A property portfolio comprising establishments where the corporate owner of the freehold of the properties offers a tenancy to individuals who wish to run the establishment. A common arrangement with breweries and hotels.

Triple bottom line: Also known as people, planet and profit or the three pillars of sustainable development. It reflects the dimensions that businesses must address to ensure development that meets the needs of the economy, society and the environment – today and in the future.

Wholesaler: In the context of this book, a company which buys and sells on goods in bulk to caterers and other foodservice operators. The large food wholesalers ('delivered wholesalers'), such as 3663, Brakes and DBC, run delivery fleets offering 'multi drop' services, whereby the efficiency of deliveries to foodservice outlets is maximised. These companies offer a range of goods from 'own brand' to products nominated by their customers. Suppliers often have to pay to have their products listed by these wholesalers.

List of acronyms

CAST   Caribbean Alliance for Sustainable Tourism
CSR   corporate social responsibility
GHG   greenhouse gases
GMOs   genetically modified organisms
HACCP   Hazard Analysis and Critical Control Point
IFC   International Finance Corporation
IH&RA   International Hotel & Restaurant Association
ITP   International Tourism Partnership
LEED   Leadership in Energy and Environmental Design
LOHAS   lifestyles of health and sustainability
QSR   quick service restaurant
TOI   Tour Operators Initiative
UNEP   United Nations Environment Programme
UNFCCC   United Nations Framework Convention on Climate Change

Index